The Politics of God

Christian Theologies and Social Justice

Kathryn Tanner

FORTRESS PRESS MINNEAPOLIS

THE POLITICS OF GOD
Christian Theologies and Social Justice

Cover design: Pollock Design Group

Library of Congress Cataloging-in-Publication Data

Tanner, Kathryn, 1957–
The politics of God : Christian theologies and social justice / Kathryn Tanner.
p. cm.
Includes bibliographical refereces and index.
ISBN 0-8006-2613-3 (alk. paper)
1. Sociology, Christian. 2. Christianity and justice. 3. Christianity and politics. 4. Social justice. I. Title.
BT738.T266 1992
261.8—dc20 92-19360
CIP

The paper used in this publication meets the minimum requirements of American National Standard for Information Sciences—Permanence of Paper for Printed Library Materials, ANSI Z329.48-1984. ™

Manufactured in the U.S.A. AF 1-2613

2 3 4 5 6 7 8 9 10

The Politics of God

"Kathryn Tanner's *The Politics of God* clearly and forcefully addresses Christian beliefs and practices about God and the world. Consistently applying the art of internal critique, Tanner offers a reconstruction of Christian tradition as a prophetic challenge to the political status quo."

—*Rebecca Chopp*
Candler School of Theology
Emory University

Contents

Preface

> Our theological discussion has . . . been divided into a conservative insistence on the dogmatic tradition, and a liberal repudiation of dogmatic content in exchange for an ethic of shared humanity. We are thus falling back into the worst tradition of the nineteenth century, in which conservative theologians were wont to be conservative in politics also, and the liberals believed themselves obliged to discard dogma in exchange for humanism. But this means tearing asunder things that belong together. Every article of the Confession of Faith has explosive and aggressive significance for the status quo of the old world, and an article that leaves our relationship . . . to society as it was, is not worthy to be an article of the Christian Faith.
>
> —*Helmut Gollwitzer*[1]

THIS BOOK concerns the political import of Christian beliefs about God and the world. These beliefs and the political practices of the Christians holding them have taken many different forms over the course of the last twenty centuries. This book tries to bring a little analytical clarity to the complex connections between them. Efforts at clarification are subordinate, however, to a normative concern. I hope to show how Christian beliefs about God and the world may be disentangled from a history of use in support of a status quo of injustice and reconstituted as a resource for commitment to progressive social change.

1. Helmut Gollwitzer, *The Rich Christians and Poor Lazarus*, trans. David Cairns (New York: Macmillan, 1970), 3.

The analytical task of the book is marked by an interdisciplinary focus. I combine philosophical and sociological approaches to the general question of how belief and comportment are related in an effort to make sense of the complex history of Christian action. In a fashion that might remind some readers of Max Weber, I break down the multifarious, ever-changing particulars of Christian history into types of beliefs and types of ethical stances in order to make clear how and why certain forms of beliefs and ethical stances might be found together.

The sophistication of this interdisciplinary perspective naturally informs my normative agenda, giving it an almost hyperconscious feel and, perhaps to some, an oddly distanced air. Direct exhortations to Christian social action come as a reward to patient readers in later chapters. Reflexive or self-conscious thinking about patterns of Christian thought and behavior is offered here in the hope that, having seen those patterns, Christians will no longer be able to say and do with a good conscience what they have so often said and done in the past.

Particularly in its attention to the history of Christian thought, the normative and constructive project of the book shares a concern of the early Reinhold Niebuhr. The constructive project revolves around the question whether Christian action might not combine "a more radical political orientation and more conservative religious convictions than are comprehended in the culture of our age."[2] Or, in the terms I use later in the book, one could say the constructive project of the book explores the possibility of an "internal" rather than "totalistic" critique of traditional Christian beliefs. Instead of being rejected outright, Christian traditions that lend support to a status quo of injustice are turned against themselves. The diverse and complex beliefs about God and the world that have been passed down as Christian traditions are not radically reconstructed to fit a particular political agenda but are at most sifted, shifted, or realigned to reveal their own progressive potential. Should Christians balk before that potential, one may simply counsel them to take the political import of their own beliefs more seriously. Should they accuse one of tampering with the faith for political ends, one can claim to be at least as conservative of that faith as they are.

2. Reinhold Niebuhr, *Reflections on the End of an Era* (New York: Charles Scribner's Sons, 1934), ix.

Internal critique is a tactic in a fight over the forms of action that Christians think it reasonable to display. The activity of describing what reality is like is always politically loaded since the limits of what one can think also set limits on what one can think of doing. This book shows that the activity of theological description is no exception to this general principle: one's understanding of God and the world influences one's understanding of the rights and responsibilities one has toward others. In the fight over the political import of beliefs about God and the world in which I am engaged here, I try to conserve as much as possible of mainstream Christian beliefs. I choose to engage these beliefs not because I view tradition as a good in itself—to be carefully guarded against dissenting voices and heretically innovative opinions—but because an effort of that sort allows one to charge opponents with hypocrisy and a failure of nerve while countering insinuations that political purposes are dragging one's own Christian convictions in tow.

Indeed, internal critique is more than simply a good tactic in a fight over the politics of belief in God. It is a way of resolving a conflict of personal loyalties that commonly afflicts Christians of good will today. One might not like the genuinely disturbing political associations of Christianity that history so amply exhibits. The beliefs at issue may nevertheless seem an essential part of one's Christian identity, their influence over one's daily life not easily shirked. The religious turns of one's personal history, one's formal intellectual training, and the Christian sensibilities of those people who have decisively shaped one's life may converge, as they do for me, to make rejection of these traditional beliefs and the search for creative alternatives to them seem shallow, loss-filled pursuits. One simply finds oneself believing as one does, despite the horrible history of actions perpetrated in the name of those beliefs, and one is pushed thereby to hope that such a history is not their necessary effect. In this book I attempt to show that such hope is well-founded and not an act of personal cowardice or deluded trust.

As Niebuhr's own shift from socialist to official establishment theologian demonstrates, the danger of a theological program like mine is its tendency to drift from a radical politics to a qualified affirmation of the status quo.[3] The common sense of established politics at any particular time fills in the implications for social action that theology itself leaves vague or undercuts by too exclusive a focus on the dispositions of individuals. I hope to prevent this sort of drift by deriving substantive principles for the evaluation of institutional life from clearly defined starting points in Christian belief. Application of these principles does not have cautious reformism as its end. Like other similar efforts in a North American or European context, the present theological project directs a prophetic challenge to the status quo. Unlike other such efforts of prophetic challenge, however, the present project avoids a disinterested stance of universal criticism that lapses into de facto support for the status quo by shunning particular judgments of fault and particular commitments to action for social change.

I would like to thank Yale University for a Morse Fellowship in 1988–89 which gave me a year's leave for research and writing. David Dawson, Charles Wood, David Burrell, Rowan Williams, and the members of the Graduate Theology Seminar at Yale in spring of 1990, read an early draft of the first few chapters and offered encouragement and intellectual stimulation for which I am very grateful. David Kelsey, Gene Outka, Margaret Farley, Cyril O'Regan, and Serene Jones gave generously of their time in reading and commenting on the first full draft. I thank Beryl Satter for her inspiration and confidence in me; without them, the book would probably never have been written. Michael West of Fortress Press has been an unfailing source of good advice and good-natured enthusiasm; David Lott expertly guided the production process.

I dedicate this book to Elaine Prassas Tanner (1924–1976) and Hans Frei (1922–1988), two good Christians, who would no doubt be uncomfortable so described. To the character of their life and witness I hope this book is loyal.

3. "Official establishment theologian" is the moniker Niebuhr gained after the March 8, 1948 cover story of him in *Time* magazine. Concerning the political shifts in Niebuhr's work, see, among recent treatments of the topic, Richard Fox, *Reinhold Niebuhr* (San Francisco: Harper & Row, 1985), chaps. 9–11; Cornel West, *The American Evasion of Philosophy* (Madison: Univ. of Wisconsin Press, 1989), 150–64; and Dennis McCann, *Christian Realism and Liberation Theology* (Maryknoll, N.Y.: Orbis, 1981), chap. 5.

ONE
Beliefs, Actions, Attitudes

THIS BOOK concerns how beliefs about God and the world that have figured prominently in Christian thought are connected with attitudes and actions that Christians have historically displayed in their relations with others. How are people who hold such beliefs about God and the world inclined to comport themselves? What are their attitudes and actions toward others likely to be? What judgments are Christians liable to make about proper human relations should their judgments be informed by beliefs about, for example, God's transcendence or God's relation to the world as its creator?[1]

The topic gains its urgency from what any student of Christianity knows. Probably more often than not over the course of Western history, Christians have used beliefs about God and the world to undergird attitudes and actions with a highly problematic political import. First, Christians have deployed beliefs about God and the world to shore up the social and political status quo and thereby dampen any thought of the possibility or need for social or political change. For example, a claim that political authority is granted by God, even when it is illegally gained or tyrannically exercised, has had that effect.

1. Questions of this kind could be extended to a whole host of other Christian beliefs that concern more than the general nature of God and God's relation to the world—for example, christological and trinitarian ones. The complexities involved in answering such questions demand restrictions on the number and type of beliefs considered, however. The ones I have chosen are fundamental or basic; one might argue that they are presupposed by most others. For example, certain general notions of the way in which God works in the world might be presupposed by claims that we are saved by Christ. This can be true even if such general notions of God's relation with the world are originally derived from christological claims.

Second, Christians have used beliefs about God and the world to prevent the inequitable character of social and political relations from being seen as such. According to many Christians God directly establishes or lays down the natural grounds for human orders of a rigidly hierarchical sort. How therefore could they possibly be deemed unjust? Finally, Christians have employed beliefs about God and the world to hamper development of the attitudes necessary for outrage against injustice and sustained efforts to remedy it. On the one hand, Christian beliefs have functioned to take away the dignity and sense of self that fuel resistance in situations of institutionalized ill-treatment. For example, Christians have hammered home the awfulness of the sins of theft, laziness, or ingratitude against the impoverished and the dispossessed. Disquiet or unrest on their part becomes a show of disrespect for the will of God manifest in their assignment to lowly social roles. On the other hand, Christians have used beliefs about God and the world to underline the self-righteous complacency of people who benefit disproportionately from sociopolitical relations of structural injustice. God wishes the best for God's creatures; the wealthy and the powerful should therefore simply praise God for benefits bestowed.

Conservative adherence to established political and social relations, willing complicity in social injustice, quiescence before conditions that cry out for change—these are only three types of attitude and behavior with which Christian beliefs about God and the world have historically been associated. The examples could be multiplied exponentially. Such a woeful display suggests that a disdainful judgment, suitable for an avowed enemy of Christianity like Voltaire, may be in order: the history of Christianity is a catalog of crimes against humanity.

The topic of this book takes on, consequently, a more than theoretical interest for all people of good will committed to Christianity or simply worried about the continued influence of Christianity in public life. A disinterested question concerning how Christian beliefs about God and the world may be connected with forms of attitude and action becomes the more pointed, even frantic, concern: Is there some way of uncoupling these Christian beliefs from the sort of attitudes and actions I have just described? Can the Christian theological tradition be wrenched free of a blind respect for the status quo, support for injustice, and apolitical passivity?

I argue that such an uncoupling is possible, at least for a certain strand of the Christian theological tradition that concerns God's nature and relation to the world. I address each of the types of attitude and behavior I have mentioned in turn, with an increasingly positive focus on identifying and developing an account of God and the world with a far more progressive sociopolitical punch.

Such an agenda—pulling apart Christian beliefs from their historical associations with certain sociopolitical uses and realigning them with others—is a problematic and complicated endeavor, however. It is not clear whether such a project is possible at all or, if possible, what steps might be taken to further it. Deciding these matters requires that one turn philosophical, sociocultural, and historical lenses upon the initial general question: the connection between attitudes and actions, and Christian beliefs about God and the world. This introductory chapter addresses the difficulties and complexities of this project. Showing the way in which they can be addressed by taking the perspectives just mentioned—philosophical, sociocultural, and historical—will establish the procedures for the rest of the book.

DOUBTS AND COMPLEXITIES

The whole project could be undercut at the start by doubts about whether it is possible to disentangle Christian beliefs about God and the world from the kinds of practices I have recounted. If it is not possible, the Christian theological tradition is likely to be vitiated for many people by the recorded history of its uses. If one is a Christian, the abhorrent character of that history will either force one to drop Christianity altogether, or incline one to start afresh as a Christian by tearing down and rebuilding from the bottom up an account of God and the world with different sociopolitical associations.

The unrelenting character of that history is indeed a primary reason for thinking Christian beliefs cannot be uncoupled from it. If Christian beliefs about God and the world have always been associated with the uses I have mentioned, why would anyone ever think they could be disentangled from them? The history of Christianity's political associations is more complex, however, than indicated. Dicta from Voltaire do not tell the whole story, although they may tell most of it.

Christian beliefs about God and the world have had, on occasion at least, the power to contest established political and social orders. Claims about God's mystery or transcendence, about God's free sovereignty, or about the ubiquity of sin have sometimes been used to argue that established political and social institutions fail to correspond to God's will; the legitimacy of those institutions is thereby threatened. Followers of a prophetic tradition in Christianity have made a point like that on occasion. Christian beliefs about God and the world have also had the effect sporadically of highlighting inequities in sociopolitical relations. Belief that God as the creator and redeemer of all is no respecter of persons can suggest that one must judge social relations according to a norm of equality. Levellers, Ranters, and Diggers in seventeenth-century England availed themselves of this sort of potential in Christian belief.[2] Finally, the historical record provides evidence that Christian beliefs about God and the world sometimes foster attitudes of resistance. Out of a belief in God's free offer of grace to all, a dignity can emerge to counter a slavish submissiveness. Some Christian slaves gained a measure of self-respect from such a belief.[3]

The complexity that these facts introduce eliminates the need for a blanket reconstruction, or total rejection, of Christian beliefs about God and the world. The history of Christianity's ethical and political associations is not the monolith that would be necessary to exclude the possibility of uncoupling the Christian beliefs at issue from their historical associations with the forces of reaction and inhumanity.[4] The history of Christianity shows that Christian beliefs about God and the

2. See Christopher Hill, *The World Turned Upside Down* (London: Penguin Books, 1975), chaps. 7–9; Norman Cohn, *The Pursuit of the Millennium* (Oxford: Oxford Univ. Press, 1970), 287-330.

3. See Albert Raboteau, *Slave Religion* (Oxford: Oxford Univ. Press, 1978), chap. 6; Donald Matthews, *Religion in the Old South* (Chicago: Univ. of Chicago Press, 1977), chaps. 5 and 6.

4. The need for blanket theological reconstruction, of course, does not have to have these grounds. It can be recommended, for example, purely for strategic reasons: given the fact that Christianity has so often been associated with the forces of reaction and inhumanity, it is best to try to overhaul it altogether if one is interested in blocking such associations in future. An assessment of the positive potentials and dangers of such a strategy is offered in the conclusion to chap. 7.

world have in fact been disengaged from those associations; therefore, they obviously *can* be.[5]

The complexity of the historical record suggests, moreover, an easy avenue for approaching the current project. The Christian beliefs about God and the world that have political and ethical associations are themselves various. A knowledge of Christian history points up not just the diverse *uses* of Christian beliefs but the diverse *beliefs* employed for those purposes. One might therefore hope that the historical record would allow one simply to isolate Christian beliefs with progressive associations from those without them. Instead of having to rework Christian theology from the bottom up, could not one simply highlight existing beliefs with less problematic associations? Christian theological traditions might be modified to emphasize such beliefs. Theological traditions that prominently display these beliefs could be promoted over others that do not. Perhaps not the whole of Christian belief but a good part of it might be salvaged in this way.

This is a helpful avenue of approach—and one that I follow in chapters to come—but it is insufficient for my purposes. Even if history helps one isolate promising versions of Christian beliefs about God and the world, a great deal of theological work still needs to be done to show that the beliefs one wishes to maintain can be logically disentangled from those one would like to downplay or ignore. Indeed, a suspicion that Christian beliefs with abhorrent consequences are essentially bound up with all the rest is probably behind a sense that a fundamental reworking of Christian theology is required to avoid them. The study of the history of Christianity cannot really help one to determine whether such a suspicion is well-founded.

One cannot presume, furthermore, that Christian beliefs that are progressive on one front will be equally so on others. For example, the inimitable majesty of God may deflate the pretensions of human rulers while encouraging the self-loathing and despair of those beaten down by poverty, prejudice, and humiliation before their social superiors. The historical record of Christian beliefs and practices does suggest this sort of inconsistency of consequences. Even if one can

5. Notice that the issue here is not affected by how often Christian beliefs have been so uncoupled. I do not think, on balance, that they *have* been all that often. My argument does not hinge, then, on any attempt to whitewash the history of Christianity's political and ethical associations.

isolate Christian beliefs associated with struggles for liberation, at the very least a careful balancing act may be necessary to retain the progressive potentials of such beliefs while staying their other, less progressive associations.

Much more importantly, however, the complex record of the history of Christianity belies the major presumption of any simple project of isolating Christian beliefs with progressive associations from those without them: different beliefs about God and the world simply do not correlate or line up neatly with different sorts of attitude and action. Close attention to the historical span of Christian practices and even to their intricacies at any one place and time shows that the very same beliefs have been associated with very different actions and attitudes. For example, a claim of equality before God has suggested to Christian slaves both the irrelevance of sociopolitical inequality and its insufferable unacceptability. A belief that God grants political authority has been used, on the one hand, to support the absolute authority of kings (e.g., by James I of England) and, on the other, to justify constitutional challenges to it (e.g., by French Huguenots).

This historical fact—that opposed attitudes and actions have appealed to the same Christian claims—does not merely work *against* efforts to specify Christian beliefs with a progressive potential. In a way, it opens up the possibilities *for* such a pursuit by expanding the range of Christian beliefs with a progressive potential. The historical record clearly demonstrates that beliefs connected with support for a status quo of injustice at one place and time are not so associated at other places and times. Therefore, contrary to those inclined to reenvision Christian belief from the bottom up, one should not be quick to assume that an association with injustice vitiates certain Christian beliefs altogether.

The same historical fact does, however, make the alignment of some Christian beliefs with progressive attitudes and actions a more difficult procedure. There still might be some point to singling out Christian beliefs with the greatest potential on this score. After all, some Christian beliefs might very rarely, if ever, serve to criticize established orders of injustice. That even the most promising Christian beliefs are still susceptible to reactionary uses does not disqualify efforts to draw distinctions among Christian beliefs on the grounds of their political and ethical associations. But it does mean that specifying the most promising Christian beliefs does not suffice for my purposes. One also has to offer some account of the factors behind variations in their use. Something besides the beliefs at issue must be influencing the political and ethical directions in which they are taken. When these additional factors vary, so do the attitudes and actions associated with them.

In this chapter I identify the types of factors involved. In later chapters I assign values to such variables in order to establish the conditions under which the Christian beliefs that I recommend demonstrate a clear connection with progressive attitudes and actions. That is, I specify the shape that the factors at issue must take if the progressive potential of certain Christian beliefs is to be realized.

It is not sufficient for my purposes, however, simply to determine the types of factors involved. These factors might finally decide the particular practical directions in which a Christian belief is taken independently of any influence exerted by that belief itself. In other words, the Christian beliefs at issue might have no say about the way such factors come into play. If Christian beliefs do not have that sort of say, it would not make sense to do what I did in beginning this chapter: blame (or praise) Christianity for the particular attitudes and actions with which it is associated. Praise or blame should be lodged elsewhere—with whatever it is that gives shape to the factors that finally determine Christianity's practical dimensions.

If Christian beliefs have no influence here, one would also not be able to say whether Christian beliefs are being used properly when they have such associations. It would be impossible to determine whether the particular attitudes and behaviors with which they are aligned are proper ones for people holding those Christian beliefs to display. As a Christian theologian I want to keep this normative dimension a part of the discussion. I want to be able to say in subsequent chapters not just that such-and-such a Christian belief under such-and-such conditions should have progressive effects but that, given that belief, it is proper for attitudes and actions of that sort to follow. In this introductory chapter I need to show, then, that Christian beliefs can set up guidelines for the way other factors are to influence the practical directions in which such beliefs are taken.

BELIEFS AS AN INFLUENCE ON ATTITUDES AND ACTIONS

My first concern is to establish that Christian beliefs have some influence over the directions of their practical use, to establish that Christian beliefs are at least one factor behind the variation in attitudes and behaviors that Christians display. Some ways of accounting for this variation undercut altogether the influence of Christian beliefs themselves. According to such accounts, Christian beliefs are like soft wax. They lend their support to actions and attitudes simply as particular interests or the general norms of the times direct. Whatever one's interests, whatever the mores of the day, Christian beliefs will accommodate themselves to them. Christian beliefs in this way drop out entirely as a factor influencing the attitudes and actions that Christians display.

Accounts like this of the variety of actions and attitudes exhibited by Christians—one might call some radically historicist, others "vulgar" Marxist—can be attacked on any number of fronts. I will rein in my own criticisms to ones that help make clear the project undertaken in subsequent chapters. I do not follow accounts like this for two major reasons that have a great deal to do with the two perspectives—philosophical and sociocultural—from which I view the general topic of the book: the connection between Christian beliefs, on the one hand, and attitudes and actions, on the other.

A Sociocultural Perspective

Connections of this sort are formed because Christian beliefs are lived beliefs. The bearers of such beliefs are not simply thinkers; they live the whole of their lives, including the sociopolitical and ethical practices in which they are engaged, as the bearers of such beliefs. Through the course of concrete existence, therefore, the beliefs at issue come together with the attitudes and actions structuring one's engagements with others. In such a process religious beliefs in particular are unlikely to be cordoned off, or segregated in their influence, from other aspects of human life (e.g., from judgments about proper human behaviors). To the contrary, in that they concern what is of highest or ultimate import for human life, religious beliefs are prone to supply an overarching interpretive framework for the whole of life; they are relevant for understanding all of life.[6] Religious beliefs tend to be already at work, therefore, when and wherever judgments of proper attitude and action are necessary. One makes such judgments as a religious believer, not just in the weak sense that the same human life brings together those beliefs and judgments, but in the strong sense that such beliefs and judgments share the same logical space—they have something to say to one another. In short, religious beliefs are a form of culture, inextricably implicated in the material practices of daily social living on the part of those who hold them. This is what I have in mind most generally by a sociocultural perspective on the connection between Christian beliefs, on the one hand, and attitudes and actions, on the other.

From such a perspective, accounts of variation in the attitudes and actions of Christians that emphasize the influence of prior interests and practical commitments so as to bypass any influence exerted by Christian beliefs can be convicted of an overly abstract analysis of the connections between beliefs, on the one hand, and actions, attitudes, and interests, on the other. Such accounts presume a situation in which actions, attitudes, and interests are fully formed independently of the beliefs one holds. Beliefs come in only after the fact to ratify the interests one already has or the actions and attitudes one already deems proper because of the times in which one lives and one's social allegiances. In the concrete circumstances in which beliefs are lived, however, actions, attitudes, and interests are likely to be as much infiltrated and informed by the beliefs one holds as beliefs are to be influenced by actions, attitudes, and interests. One is not a Christian and then an interested social agent, or a social agent and then a Christian, but a Christian inevitably engaged in social action from a particular social location. In the concrete circumstances of life, actions and interests do not exist per se isolated from the beliefs one holds; nor do beliefs exist per se isolated from one's actions and interests with reference to others.

6. The likelihood of such an interpretive dimension for religion is admittedly dampened in circumstances—like those in modern Western industrialized nations—where religion does not occupy central institutionalized social and cultural roles, for example, where religious leaders have no institutionalized lines of authority over political officials or control over public education, or where economic organizations abide by no overtly religious norms. But the point still stands that an overarching interpretive dimension for religion is fostered by the content of religious beliefs themselves. It is arguable, moreover, that even in the circumstances mentioned religion is enormously if less ostentatiously influential.

Instead, one finds actions and interests that are already interpreted: actions and interests that are inevitably understood in terms of what one already believes, and the beliefs of persons who are already implicated in the politico-ethical responses that are part and parcel of a life lived with others. The actions and interests of persons who also believe certain things, the beliefs of persons who also act and have interests—this is the same concrete circumstance of human life from different points of view. Making one aspect of this concrete situation come first, insisting on the real priority in time of attitudes, actions, or interests, is therefore wide of the mark. Such a procedure passes off an abstract analysis for reality; aspects of the same material social processes, which are separable in thought, are illicitly reified, that is, made into elements that can exist independently of one another, and that can therefore follow one after the other.[7]

From a perspective that views Christian belief as a lived culture, the appropriate question to ask is not which comes first independently of the others to establish some exclusive line of influence—the beliefs, or the actions, attitudes, and interests that fund them. Instead, if beliefs, attitudes, and actions are found together in some whole of mutual influence, it is appropriate to ask whether and to what extent they all hang together intelligibly as aspects of a Christian form of life. Beliefs, actions, and attitudes, if they are mutually informing, can influence one another by way of relations of intelligibility, of logical compatibility and incompatibility, of coherence and incoherence. One must ask how the intelligibility of the beliefs one holds depends on the actions and attitudes in which one is engaged, and vice versa. One must ask in what way one's beliefs are able to make sense of, or withhold sense from, one's attitudes and actions, and the reverse. Figuring out now the general form of these logical relations or relations of intelligibility will help specify the role that beliefs play in the attitudes

7. See Raymond Williams, *Marxism and Literature* (Oxford: Oxford Univ. Press, 1977), 75–100, for a classic statement of an argument like this against certain forms of Marxist interpretation of the relation between beliefs and socioeconomic practice.

Notice that I am not claiming here that Christian beliefs cannot come after the fact to justify independently attractive interests or forms of action. Christian beliefs obviously do work that way in some circumstances. Actions and interests are always already informed by beliefs, but that does not mean they are always informed from the start by Christian ones. I am contesting the claim that Christian beliefs *have* to function in an after-the-fact justificatory fashion because of the general way in which beliefs, actions, and interests are determined with reference to one another.

and actions to which one ascribes, and help determine that Christian beliefs are one factor influencing the shape of the attitudes and actions that Christians display.[8]

A Philosophical Analysis

An abstract philosophical perspective on lived belief is required here to establish the general way that beliefs, attitudes, and actions are logically connected. This sort of analysis will also be necessary in later chapters to specify the shape such connections take when particular beliefs, attitudes, and actions are at issue.

The very closeness or immediacy with which beliefs, attitudes, and actions are found together in concrete life obscures the nature of the logical connections or relations of intelligibility that hold among them. As I have suggested, actions and attitudes do not proceed apart from interpretation. Beliefs about what is the case—for example, about the nature of the circumstances to which one responds, or about the relation of the acts one takes to the goals one pursues—are part and parcel of acts and attitudes in so far as those are meaningful phenomena. Beliefs tend to infiltrate and inform, therefore, the very understanding and formulation of proposals of proper comportment. Highly ramified recommendations of attitude and action, recommendations of attitude and action that show on their face the influence of beliefs about what is the case, are the result. For example, "Side with the oppressed in the attempt to bring about the kingdom of God on earth by doing God's will in the fight for political justice" is a highly ramified recommendation in this sense. The very way in which it is formulated displays the influence of a number of Christian beliefs—beliefs about, among other things, the sinful state of present affairs, the religious

8. Concentrating on the connections among beliefs, attitudes, and actions as connections of intelligibility means that I am not addressing questions of their causal relations. I do not discuss in this book how one actually comes to believe or to act or to hold certain attitudes. For example, I do not ask whether one's actions are sufficient to bring one to believe or whether beliefs, when combined with the other factors I mention, are sufficient to bring one to act. Figuring out such matters would require much more, indeed, than a consideration of the additional factors I mention later as entering into the equation. A full-blown institutional and cultural analysis of the place of a religion in particular historical settings would be necessary. One would need such analyses in order to tell, for example, how seriously people take their Christian commitments and whether political or other circumstances might be working to dissuade them from acting as their Christian beliefs might direct.

character of insurrectionary action, the nature of God and of God's kingdom.

If one wants to make clear the logic of such an influence, one must consider less highly ramified recommendations. One must analyze the often highly ramified proposals of real life so as to separate out in thought the proposals for action that are being made from the beliefs that inform them. Thus one might substitute for a complex recommendation like the one above a much simpler one—say, "Rebel against injustice." In that way the lines of logical dependence between beliefs and proposals, which the fact of highly ramified proposals suggests, can be more precisely detailed.

The philosophical account of the general logic of relations among beliefs, attitudes, and actions proceeds with the understanding, then, that I am employing unusually abstract or thinly ramified characterizations of proposed actions and attitudes—proposals for action like "Rebel against injustice" or "Submit to the powers that be." I begin with logical relations between proposals for action and belief, and then gradually introduce attitudes into consideration.

First, logical connections are formed between proposals for action and beliefs about the nature of reality because certain types of action require certain existents and conditions of existence in order to be relevant. For rebellion against injustice to be meaningful, for example, a society of persons organized along lines of nonequitable distributions of wealth and power must exist. For action of that sort to be a practical possibility, suitable agents must also exist—namely, human beings with the independence of mind to form judgments running counter to those that are socially entrenched. If beliefs about such states of affairs are challenged, these beliefs may be backed up by other ones—by relevant evidence, perhaps by explicitly religious claims warranting assent to them. For example, the claim that human beings are empowered by God to be agents of God's will might provide backing for the practical presupposition of rebellion just mentioned.

Second, logical relations are established between proposals for action and beliefs because people usually have reasons for acting as they do. That a reason for an action can be given is a presumption for proposing it. If challenged, some reason or other—even if it is only the minimal "this is the way it has always been done"—is to be proffered. Reasons can take the form of beliefs about the nature of reality, and Christian beliefs about God and the world may supply them. Thus if a proposal to submit to the powers that be is challenged, one might respond with one of the following reasons for such action that take the form of a claim about what is the case: Submitting to the powers that be at least ensures one's survival. Submitting to the powers that be is necessary to keep the peace. Finally, a religious one: submitting to the powers that be is a way of glorifying God.

Reasons of the sort just mentioned—reasons that show how proposed actions contribute to certain ends or goals—can be challenged in turn. One might challenge the appropriateness of the proposed ends for the sort of action at issue. Beliefs about God and the world might enter again here to provide backing. Those who have power are granted it by God; submitting to human rulers is therefore an appropriate way to show respect for God. This world is a fallen place populated by the wicked, who are restrained from evil deeds only by unquestioned authority backed by force; submission to political authorities makes sense then as a requirement for keeping the peace.

One could also challenge such reasons, however, by simply questioning the value of the ends that are advocated: why bother to glorify God, save oneself, maintain the peace? Proposing an action usually presumes the value of its end; to question that value is also therefore to question the merit of the proposal. Once again, a description of what is the case can supply a kind of backing. If certain circumstances hold, it might make sense or be fitting to find a certain end valuable. Thus if life is the presupposition for attaining all other goods—health, happiness, wealth, acclaim—it makes sense to hold it dear. If the God who demands respect holds the key to one's election or damnation, a certain importance will naturally accrue to the attempt to glorify God in compliance with that demand.

This question of the value of the ends of action introduces the question of what motivates action. Meaningful human action presumes not only that reasons for an action can be given but that persons are sufficiently motivated so to act. Often such motivation is supplied by the perceived value of an action or its end; the one or the other seems a good thing. In such cases motivated action banks on an appropriate attitude, a positive evaluative stance, toward an action or its end. Attitudes toward the one proposing a form of action, attitudes in the form of affections or feelings toward him or her, can also motivate action irrespective of attitudes that involve evaluation of an act or its end. Thus gratitude or fear or love of God may prompt one to follow divine commands. In any case, one can see here a logical connection between actions and attitudes via the need for motivated action.

Attitudes can, however, have other, weaker connections with action. Affections or evaluative judgments may simply incline one toward outward conformity with a proposed course of action without supplying any direct motivation or special concern for its performance. Thus an attitude of respectful diffidence to those in authority might encourage inattentive obedience to whatever the laws of the land happen to be; an attitude of indifference to a spiritually irrelevant realm of power might have much the same effect. Attitudes may also supply the practical requirements for action's effectiveness. When action encounters resistance, courage is necessary; when action encounters setbacks, one must eschew confidence in the easy achievement of one's goals in order to continue.

The intelligibility of the attitudes one displays depends, however, on the beliefs one holds about the objects of those attitudes. The connections between attitudes and actions that I have just discussed bring along with them, therefore, another avenue for a logical relation between actions and beliefs. Beliefs not only provide conditions of relevance and reasons for proposed courses of action, and the backing for both; they also serve to make the attitudes necessary for motivated action seem appropriate.

Thus, when positive evaluation of the importance or significance of an action or its end motivates action, descriptions of that action or its end should show it to be desirable. Typically, religions demonstrate the desirability of the actions or ends of action they hope to motivate by way of beliefs about salvation—beliefs about its character and consequences and the means of access to it. By definition, salvation is desirable; action that is somehow bound up with it is therefore deemed important and thereby motivated. Thus motivation to pray and meditate might come by way of the belief that salvation is achieved in a contemplative union with God; motivation to act according to scriptural mandates might come by way of a belief that salvation involves a union of wills between God and the Christian. These claims about the character of salvation presuppose in turn certain beliefs about the character of God and human beings and the mode of their relations.

Finally, the importance or value of salvation itself and therefore one's interest in it can be bolstered by statements of what is the case—by descriptions of a sorry state of existence to match the particular remedy offered. Salvation is important because one needs to be saved from present conditions and because salvation provides a release from the specific ills under which one suffers.

Attitudes of feeling or affection that motivate action are also rendered intelligible by beliefs that show their appropriateness. On the one hand, the belief that God gives everything one has makes gratitude an appropriate attitude to have toward God. On the other hand, a belief in God's arbitrary power makes fear suitable. Beliefs about what is the case can also, of course, support affections that are less directly connected with motivations for action, affections that merely encourage passive conformity or that provide practical support in difficult or trying times for action in which one is already engaged. As an example of the former case, beliefs that bifurcate the spiritual and the material, the heavenly and the earthly, make indifference to the exercise of political power seem reasonable.

This is the usual logical relation between statements of fact and proposals of attitude—beliefs about the character of that to which one responds establish the fittingness of one's attitudes. Beliefs about God and the world can also provide, however, reasons for what might be called counterfactual attitudes—attitudes that do not seem fitting with respect to the actual nature of the objects toward which they are directed. Thus humility does not seem a fitting attitude with respect to exceptional achievements; but it is appropriate if one believes that the unmerited help of God is behind one's working. Self-respect in a circumstance of abject humiliation is appropriate, not in virtue of one's abasement before other people, but in recognition of one's status before God. Hope in the face of impossible odds and constant setbacks is reasonable only with reference to some helping power or agency beyond those of this world.

This whole account of the logical relations among beliefs, attitudes, and actions highlights the way beliefs about what is the case influence action, either directly or by way of the attitudes that motivate or favor such action. Beliefs have power over actions and attitudes to the extent that such beliefs are necessary in order for those actions and attitudes to make sense. Beliefs have power over actions since beliefs about what is the case are necessary in order for action to appear reasonable, meaningful, practically possible, and motivated. Because these relations of intelligibility hold, beliefs can promote certain forms of action and attitude—those that make sense given those beliefs. Or such beliefs can countermand certain forms of action and attitude, undercutting attitudes by making them appear out of place, bizarrely quixotic, or nonsensical, and undercutting forms of action by making them seem unreasonable, unmotivated, irrelevant, or pointless. In short, a philosophical perspective on the connection between Christian beliefs and comportment shows that it is wrong to account for variation in Christian actions and attitudes by bypassing the influence of Christian beliefs. Christian beliefs have the power to direct the attitudes and behaviors that Christians display.

This analysis shows, moreover, that beliefs about what is the case have a logical priority over attitudes and actions. They come first in that they are the logical presuppositions for meaningful action and attitude, for reasonable and motivated action. It will therefore make sense in later chapters to start from Christian beliefs in figuring out their attitudinal and behavioral associations.

Actions and attitudes are not in the same way presuppositions for the meaningfulness or relevance of beliefs. In other words, the dependence that actions and attitudes have on beliefs does not also hold in reverse. Contrary to the Marxist or historicist account of variation in Christian attitudes and actions discussed above, the influence of Christian beliefs has a logical precedence over that of actions and attitudes. Actions and attitudes require appropriate beliefs to a much greater degree than beliefs need appropriate actions and attitudes.

There is room for mutual influence here: beliefs imply the propriety of actions and attitudes, while actions and attitudes supply a psychosocial support for beliefs. If the attitudes and actions commonly displayed by members of one's social group are attitudes and actions that make sense in terms of one's beliefs about reality, those actions and attitudes will confirm these beliefs. Mores, valuations, and sentiments become an experiential confirmation of the beliefs one holds; one's beliefs are shored up by living in a social world where attitudes and actions reflect them.[9] It is still the case, however, that the one

9. See Clifford Geertz, *The Interpretation of Cultures* (New York: Harper Colophon Books, 1973), 90, 131, for an account of the way in which a society's ethos and worldview can be mutually supportive.

relation of dependence is much stronger than the other. Beliefs do not require this psychosocial confirmation by appropriate attitudes and actions the way attitudes and actions require the support of appropriate beliefs. One can maintain one's beliefs without psychosocial confirmation; attitudes and actions become simply nonsensical without appropriate beliefs to sustain them.

THE GAP BETWEEN BELIEFS AND PROPOSALS OF ATTITUDE AND ACTION

One must take care, however, in stressing the importance of belief's influence on action and attitude. My analysis of logical relations among beliefs, attitudes, and actions might suggest so strong a relation of dependence of attitudes and actions upon beliefs that beliefs cannot be uncoupled from them. If that were so, then the influence of beliefs would exclude the need for any other factors influencing attitudes and actions. I would thereby reintroduce a position on the variety of Christian attitudes and actions that I already rejected on historical grounds: different attitudes and actions would line up in one-to-one correspondence with different Christian beliefs.

Logical analysis would in this way confirm an impression that lived belief also gives. How actions might be uncoupled from the beliefs they presuppose is not at all clear when, as is so often the case in lived belief, the very terms in which action is understood are informed by those beliefs. If, for example, all one means by a king is the sole, divinely instituted, earthly authority, and all one means by a subject is someone whose salvation is bound up with simple conformity to God's will, then a subject's absolute obedience to a king will seem a necessary implication of those beliefs. Given those beliefs, one would have no meaningful or reasonable option but to obey. And obedience would not seem a viable and meaningful option without those beliefs.

Conclusions of a necessary connection between beliefs and actions are not, however, the proper ones to draw from my philosophical analysis. The abstract quality of that philosophical analysis indeed makes clear, once again, what lived belief obscures: There is a logical gap between beliefs, on the one hand, and the actions and attitudes with which they are conjoined, on the other. By a logical gap I mean the following: First, no specific course of action or attitude is entailed by beliefs about what is the case. One cannot deduce the propriety of any particular form of attitude or action from a particular belief about the way things are. Second, no single account of what is the case is a necessary presupposition for a particular attitude or action. One cannot deduce, therefore, any particular belief as a logical presupposition for a given form of action or attitude.

Specific beliefs will be able to rule out or preclude certain forms of attitude or action. For example, it makes no logical sense to recommend a happy-go-lucky optimism if one believes in a hostile, perpetually threatening world ruled by principles that take no account of human wants or needs. Similarly, it makes no sense to demand methodically disciplined action according to precise calculation of means and ends if one believes that the world is a chaotic and unpredictable whirl.[10] This is a hard logical relation of exclusion; certain attitudes and actions are simply incompatible with some beliefs.

The logical relation by which a belief suggests, positively, the propriety of certain attitudes and actions is not, however, of this strict sort. It is not one of logical necessity but one of mere consistency or compatibility. For example, some belief or beliefs must be able to show how a proposal for action is reasonable and motivated. But no one belief in particular is required to make the reasonable and motivated character of a proposed action clear. Different beliefs can show the meaningfulness of the same sort of action. Thus both a belief that it is impossible to discern who is elect and a belief that God elects no one can suggest the appropriateness of egalitarian forms of social relation. Similarly, a single belief can back up a whole range of forms of attitude and action. If one believes that the world is a blind run of atoms, both retreat from it and action to bend it to human purposes appear to be meaningful responses.

10. Of course, human beings have been known to make a virtue of the very quixotic character of certain recommendations for action. The unfeasibility of a practice can be worn as a badge of one's nobility in a world that makes a mockery of human efforts to make sense of life. But such a myth of Sisyphus courage, à la Camus, only concedes my point here about the irrationality of certain recommendations given certain beliefs.

Actions and attitudes that fail to make sense, given the way the world is believed to be, can also serve as psychological defenses against truths that are too hard to accept, as tactics to avoid what one does not want to admit. But once again this fact concedes the relation of exclusion I am talking about. Methodical discipline could not make sense as a psychological defense against admitting the absolute unpredictability of life, if that sort of belief did not logically exclude the propriety of such a form of living.

BRIDGING THE GAP

I am brought back then to the question of additional factors. What factors influence variation in action and attitude, what factors push action or attitude in a particular direction, if beliefs themselves are not sufficient to do it? The sociocultural perspective I have been taking on the question of connections among beliefs, attitudes, and actions will help here to identify what fills in the logical gap I have been talking about between beliefs, on the one hand, and attitudes and actions, on the other. It will help to specify all the relevant factors that account for variation in Christian attitudes and actions.

Changes in Meaning

A sociocultural perspective on Christian beliefs can clarify what might not be apparent from a mere logical analysis of the importance of belief for practice: the meaning of such beliefs changes with changes in the meaning of their central terms. The specific meaning of any particular Christian belief is therefore a variable influencing its practical import.

Considering Christian beliefs from a sociocultural perspective amounts here (as I have said) to considering them as inextricably intertwined with social relations. One considers them, like all beliefs, to be part of what is put into play in the back and forth of sociopolitical interactions. From such a perspective, it makes little sense to consider the meaning of these beliefs to be something lodged within them. Meaning is not something that a claim like "God is transcendent" holds all by itself. It is a product instead of what people make of such a claim in their interactions with one another; it is a product of what they do with it in those settings. Meaning, whether of religious beliefs or otherwise, is in sum a product of language use by real people in the course of historically specific and politically charged interactions.

One would therefore expect the meaning of such beliefs to be fluid. Meaning will vary, for example, with different traditions of use. Moreover, the meaning of any particular belief for any one such tradition is always a potentially temporary distillate of language use that is still in progress. Beliefs are likely to be polyvalent with time, therefore, and with differences in group affiliation among those holding them.

The sociopolitically charged nature of such ongoing processes and varying traditions of use is another reason to expect changes in the meaning of beliefs. Beliefs like those about God's nature and relation to the world—beliefs that say something about the character of the world and the people in it—are able to rule out or make plausible certain forms of social relations by defining the situations at issue and the nature of the actors in them. The general mechanism by which they do so should be clear from the philosophical analysis I have given of the importance of beliefs for meaningful and motivated action. For example, beliefs about the nature of womanhood obviously make a big difference in undercutting or supporting certain forms of social relation between men and women. Believing that one's circumstances are the result of one's free choices as an autonomous individual does quite a bit to limit the way in which distributions of wealth in a society can appear to be unjust. Processes that determine the meaning of socially circulating beliefs about such matters—for example, the meaning of "femininity" in the socially circulating belief "women should be feminine," or the meaning of the freedom that is commonly thought to characterize the lot of working men and women—are liable therefore to be sites of political struggle. The parties that effectively maintain their own vision of reality over competing ones have gone some distance in promoting their own idea of how society should operate. Thus tactical maneuvers among those fighting to maintain or rearrange social relations are prone to be part of the social processes by which the meaning of beliefs is established and reestablished, and to be part of what divides competing traditions or schools of thought on such matters. The ups and downs of such tactical struggles tend to produce changes in a belief's meaning.

Variation in meaning is at most a complicating factor, however, for the analysis I have already provided of the importance for practice of beliefs. If beliefs about God and the world influence Christian attitudes and behaviors, it stands to reason that variation in the meaning of such beliefs is one factor behind the direction that those attitudes and behaviors take. A sociocultural perspective on Christian belief just provides grounds for expecting such variation in fact. An expectation of that sort is an important addition to my philosophical analysis, but it does not help to bridge the logical gap that this philosophical analysis leaves—the logical gap between a Christian belief (with a definite meaning) and a particular form of practice. In other words, it is not yet clear how a sociocultural perspective on Christian belief helps specify the factors that point Christian attitudes and behaviors in one direction or another.

How Beliefs Are Combined

The grounds that lead one to expect variation in the meaning of Christian beliefs are also enough, however, to suggest at least one such factor. Consider what happens if the whole of Christian belief is subject to the constantly renewable processes of negotiation and periodically recurrent struggles over meaning that I have talked about. It is unlikely that the whole of Christian belief will exhibit any organic coherence as a cultural formation. Even at a single place and time it is unlikely that the different beliefs that constitute that whole will fit together neatly as a matter of course, for example, by way of some unbreakable logical interconnections. Instead, that whole will likely form an internally fissured and disjointed mass. The result is a freedom to select some beliefs and leave others behind, to highlight some and leave others in shadows. The particular combination of beliefs that one puts forward is therefore left open, as is the manner in which they might be brought together. For example, one is free to resolve logical conflicts in practical implications among the beliefs one maintains by weighting some more heavily than others. Thus, a new variable for consideration as a factor in determining a Christian belief's practical associations is the way that belief is combined with others.

Two Situation-Specific Factors

The historically specific character of the social interactions in which Christian beliefs are implicated suggests another general factor: the historically various life situations of those involved in such interactions, their experiential circumstances or interests. For example, even if the meaning of freedom is undisputed, a belief in freedom will clearly have a different meaning *for* one—it will be associated with different attitudes and actions—depending on whether one is a corporate executive officer or a migrant farm worker.

If circumstances of life are a first situation-specific factor, a second is the scope of a belief's application. Insofar as beliefs are part of social interactions, situations of various sorts of people—those advocating such beliefs, those addressed by them, and those talked about without being directly addressed—become relevant. Beliefs invoked in a particular situation may pertain to any, some, or all of such classes of persons. For example, a husband may propose for his wife's acceptance a belief in the value of submissiveness in a way that makes clear its pertinence to her alone. The relations that seem appropriate between them in that case are clearly different from those that would seem appropriate were the same belief to have a wider application and include the husband as well.

I have specified four general kinds of factor at work in setting the relationship of belief to action or attitude: (1) the meaning of the belief at issue; (2) the other beliefs with which it is combined; (3) the life situations of those to whom the belief applies; (4) the scope of the belief's application or reference. An example will clarify how such factors might work to specify the practical import of particular Christian beliefs.

AN EXAMPLE OF FACTORS AT WORK

My example is a belief in predestination—the belief that damnation and salvation (understood in the traditional terms of one's transformation and acceptance by God) are determined by God's will from all eternity without regard to merit and therefore not as a response to one's works.[11] The belief's practical connections as I develop them here are not all that relevant for the explicitly political topics treated in this book, but I choose this particular belief for discussion because its practical connections are not at all obvious and, perhaps for that reason, exhibit an enormous variation.

Attitudes and actions that might presuppose belief in predestination include the following (in listing them, I have tried to indicate the manner in which they might be suggested by a belief in predestination, but the reader should go through them slowly, if he or she has the patience, thinking about why one might feel or act in such a way if one so believed):

11. This is generally a Calvinist position, common in the sixteenth and seventeenth centuries, although one also finds Luther espousing it in some works (notably in *De Servo Arbitrio* [1525]).

(1) terror over the inefficacy of the works one had counted on to secure one's righteousness before God; *or*

(2) comfort in the assurance that one's failings may be remedied by God;

(3) rage against an arbitrary and potentially cruel fate; *or*

(4) thankfulness and love for God's free mercy;

(5) anxiety over whether one has really been saved in Christ; *or*

(6) trust that God's offer of salvation in Christ is reliable;

(7) arrogant and complacent confidence about one's standing before God; *or*

(8) healthy fear, compatible with simple confidence but ruling out any smug assurance, about one's own election;

(9) quietistic resignation in the face of a destiny one cannot influence;

(10) perhaps even unrestrained profligacy in keeping with the recognition that one's final end may bear no resemblance to the life one lived; *or*

(11) concern for good works as the appropriate consequence of one's election;

(12) humility rather than self-glorification for the good works one performs for others as a Christian; *or*

(13) prideful disdain for the "ungodly" lives of people whom God has not chosen;

(14) forgiving tolerance of the failings displayed by oneself and others, in recognition of the fact that moral achievements are not what distinguishes persons in the eyes of God; *or*

(15) rigid behavioral requirements for church membership as indications of election, and moral scrupulosity, therefore, about any failure to abide by such norms;

(16) courage to persevere as a Christian worker in the struggle to overcome sin and evil;

(17) confidence that people who stand in the way of the ends for which Christians work will not triumph since even they are finally under the sway of God's indefatigable predestinating will; *or*

(18) failure of nerve in the face of opposition from people who have as good a right to claim to be among the elect as one does oneself.

Some of this variation in attitudes and actions may result from differences in the way one understands a belief in predestination. Thus quietistic resignation (9) and unrestrained profligacy (10) may be distinguished from the other attitudes and actions on the list by presupposing a different understanding of predestination, one in which God's election and damnation exclude by definition any place for human working. (This question of how Christian beliefs portray the relation between God's working and human working will be of general relevance in the investigation of the role of Christian beliefs in revolutionary or reactionary politico-ethical postures.) Similarly, attitudes that involve pride (7 and 13) may be distinguished from others by supposing that election is somehow owed to one, or somehow one's possession, or something that reflects well on one, assumptions that alter the apparent meaning of predestination as a free and sovereign choice by God to do as God wills.

Some of these differences in attitude and action seem to be the result of the influence of additional beliefs. Thus, instead of assuming a different understanding of predestination, quietistic resignation and profligacy may simply leave out a belief that other attitudes and actions include: the belief that good works are the necessary concomitants (though not the conditions) of election.[12] Similarly, what seems to distinguish love and thankfulness (4) from rage (3), or comfort (2) from terror (1), or trust (6) from anxiety (5), is the addition of a belief about God's offer of salvation in Christ. Presumably, as Christians all holders of a belief in predestination maintain this belief about God's salvation in Christ as well. What matters is the weight one gives it vis-à-vis a belief in predestination. For example, does a belief in the salvation that Christ offers overcome any suggestion that God's predestinating will is arbitrary or utterly formless? If the logical implications of the two beliefs seem to conflict, will the implications of a belief that Christ saves take precedence over those of a belief in predestination? The universalistic implications of a belief in God's offer of salvation in Christ—that is, the belief that Christ comes to save everyone—may have taken precedence over a belief in predestination to damnation in cases where comfort and trust (rather than terror and anxiety) are the results of a belief in predestination.

12. Often only a gray line divides changes in meaning of a belief from the addition of others; such additions may alter the sense of the belief with which one starts.

Even where the same basic nexus of beliefs is presupposed, variation in attitudes and actions can result from the different situations and interests of those adhering to that nexus of beliefs. Suppose that prior to a belief in predestination one believed that God's favor depended on moral achievement; belief in predestination now ousts that belief. Whether belief in predestination makes intelligible an attitude of relief (2) in this process depends upon whether one had been confident or desperate about one's abilities to do what one thought was required. In the first case, one would have an interest in meriting salvation through good works, and this interest is now thrown to the ground by belief in predestination. Terror before a divine will one cannot influence replaces the confidence in one's own works that one now recognizes to have been horribly misplaced. In the second case, one would have had a desperate concern to attain salvation apart from works, and this concern is now met by the same belief. A belief in predestination turns one away from preoccupation with oneself and one's failings and turns one toward belief in what God works *for* one. Hence predestination is a word of comfort and hope.

A number of the attitudes and actions listed presuppose an interest in knowing whether one is saved. This interest is heightened by belief in predestination—particularly by the belief in God's freedom to damn. Attitudes differ, however, in the degree to which they suppose that such an interest can be satisfied. Additional beliefs are the crucial factor here. Some of these attitudes and actions (e.g., 2, 8, 16, and 17) seem to presume the existence of signs of one's election or damnation. Others (e.g., 5 and 18) seem to leave out any such beliefs; the result in that case is an anxiety without remedy. Presumably, the more limited the number of signs of election—say, they are limited to good works—the more interested one is in the signs that remain, and the more important the remaining ones loom. Witness therefore scrupulosity about works (15). Moreover, the various attitudes and behaviors listed seem to differ in their understanding of the reliability of any of these signs. Attitudes approaching arrogant confidence (7) seem to presume that such signs are quite reliable; attitudes that include an element of fear (8 and 18) obviously presuppose some doubts about them.

In either case, a difference in circumstance enters here again to differentiate further the attitudes that are appropriate. For example, if signs are quite reliable, a smug confidence will make sense only for persons whose lives exhibit them. If one's life does not, sheer terror makes much better sense. If signs are not that reliable, any tendency to complacency on the part of people whose lives exhibit them will be checked; people whose lives do not will find a tendency to despair checked for the same reason.

A belief in predestination forms all by itself, moreover, a complex of claims to which one can appeal in different situations for different practical effects. Like a number of the Christian beliefs I discuss in subsequent chapters, a belief in predestination (as I originally presented it) has two sides; it can be formulated in either a positive or a negative way. On the positive side, it means that nothing that happens on this earth can break God's will for one of God's elect. On the negative side, it means that one can never count on one's election, since God's will remains free and sovereign and therefore unconditioned by anything one does. When the negative side of this belief is used to address people confident of their election, it counters any tendency to arrogance or complacency concerning it. If the positive side is stressed in addressing the same people, these very dangers, instead of being countered, will be encouraged and confirmed: "I am saved and you are not and I can be sure of it whatever the circumstances" captures the attitude that is liable to seem appropriate. Similarly, if the positive side of the belief is stressed when addressing people inclined to lose confidence in their salvation out of disgust at the character of their own lives, such inclinations to distrust and despair may be checked: one realizes that one cannot lose one's standing before God if God chooses to stand by one. The negative side of a belief in predestination will, however, only confirm the validity of those feelings. The knowledge that one cannot count on one's election encourages worry: "Maybe God is not with me; I am a failure; maybe my defeats are simply as they seem—without a remedy."

These sorts of situation-specific effects are even more complicated. In what I have just said I have left out one complicating factor: the use of such beliefs in social interactions. I assumed therefore that the different formulations of a belief in predestination applied to people addressed by them without considering whether they might also apply to those addressing them, or apply to a third party instead of either. People prone to arrogant confidence concerning their election could address, say, the negative side of a belief in predestination against those already prone to distrust and despair, thereby reserving the positive side for a reference to themselves. "The morally frail members of a community may not be among the elect," they might say, suggesting thereby that their own election is secure. The appropriateness of arrogant presumption on their part would in this way be confirmed to a greater extent than would be the case were they simply to refer the positive side—God's unbreakable will for God's elect—to themselves. People prone to arrogant presumption can also talk in the same way among themselves about those prone to distrust and despair without directly addressing them. Arrogant presumption in that case gains social support from among the like-minded.

These last examples of variation in the scope of a belief's reference are somewhat artificial for the belief at hand, but they do help suggest the way in which the application of Christian beliefs can involve a power play. In the treatment of Christian beliefs offered in subsequent chapters these relations of power become much more explicit because the situation-specific variables upon which I will focus directly concern relative degrees of power over one's own life, degrees of privilege, degrees of acclimation to or disgruntlement with the status quo. I will not ask questions like how a belief that one is in sin (to change the example) affects a person despairing of her or his own abilities to merit salvation through good works. Instead I will ask how a belief in sin affects one's sense of one's own ability to effect social change when one is humiliated by the daily indignities one suffers as a member of an underclass. Variations in the application of a belief will concern the same groups of people. If, in the example I am using, a member of an underclass holds out the belief that humanity exists in a state of sin, to whom does such a belief pertain—to himself or herself? to the privileged of society whom one thereby addresses in a challenging way, or talks about in forming bonds of solidarity with other oppressed members of society? to everyone without exception? The forms of social relation and political action that might be appropriate in each of these cases are obviously quite different. Similarly, if a person of privilege and power proclaims that humanity is depraved, is this a statement criticizing his or her own social position? a statement attacking the rights of the poor or calling for the privileged to close ranks against people of different social standing? Again, what matters is the scope of a belief's reference in the social interactions of which it is a part.

PROPER AND IMPROPER ATTITUDES AND ACTIONS

So far I have determined the factors behind variation in the attitudes and actions that seem appropriate on the basis of a given belief. When these factors take a particular shape and form, those attitudes and actions do also. Subsequent chapters specify the shape and form that these factors must take if an active resistance to a status quo of injustice is to seem appropriate on the basis of certain Christian beliefs about God and the world. The arguments will have the general form: given such-and-such a belief, with this particular meaning, combined in this particular way with these other beliefs and applied in this particular fashion to these particular groups of people, active resistance to a status quo of injustice makes sense. Contrary political programs appealing to these beliefs alter those specifications: some sort of slippage occurs in the meaning of the belief; it is not weighted the same way vis-à-vis others; or the scope and situation of the people it pertains to are different.

I argue more than this, however, in subsequent chapters, more than "these are the proper political consequences of such beliefs given the particular specifications of the relevant factors." As I mentioned before, I want to be able to say that these are simply the proper effects *of those beliefs*. In other words, active resistance to a status quo of injustice is the sort of effect that these beliefs themselves demand. Conservative, oppressive, and passive effects are ruled out as appropriate effects of such beliefs by those very beliefs themselves. To make such a claim, I have to show that the beliefs I recommend have the power to direct the particular shape taken by the factors I have talked about. I have to show that these beliefs are able to set up guidelines, in other words, for specifying the shape such factors take.

With respect to the first two factors—a belief's meaning and combination with others—I do not claim that the beliefs I recommend can mean only what I say they mean or be combined with other beliefs only in the ways I propose. The extremely diverse and fluid nature of Christian beliefs, which is apparent from the historical and sociocultural perspectives on Christian belief and which is essential to the whole project of this book, discourages me from those tactics. Instead, I propose, without a great deal of argument, that the meanings and combinations of beliefs that I specify have as good a claim as any to be of the kind Christians can hold. Readers with a knowledge of the history of Christian thought will not, I presume, find my own understandings of, say, God's transcendence and God's relation to the world as its creator, especially odd or bizarre ones for a Christian to maintain.[13]

I also do not claim that my way of specifying the third factor—the power differences in the situations of those people to whom a belief pertains—is demanded by the Christian beliefs with which I work. My own interests are the primary reason why my treatment of the factor of situation is limited to matters having to do with socioeconomic or political power. That kind of account of circumstance is simply the most pertinent to the sort of practical associations of Christian belief that I have chosen to explore here—political ones of resistance to and condemnation of injustice.

By focusing on this aspect of situations, I am assuming, however, that nothing about the import or function of Christian beliefs themselves renders this influence of power differences on the practical associations of Christian belief suspect per se. In other words, power differences do not always produce ideological distortions of the practical associations of Christian belief. Only an idealist understanding of the import and function of Christian beliefs would maintain that such a result is inevitable. The content of Christian beliefs about God and the world as I develop them, and the sociocultural perspective on Christian belief that I take here, block that kind of idealist understanding of Christian belief. I must wait to develop the content of Christian beliefs that suggests the pertinence of figuring in questions of social power when determining the practical associations of those beliefs. But on the basis of what I have said so far in this chapter it is at least clear that Christian beliefs do not fall into human history from a purely theoretical and apolitical realm to suffer inevitably thereby an unfortunate warping. From my point of view, Christian beliefs do not have any specific practical effects apart from the situations of those to whom they pertain, and power relations are simply part of them. Christian

13. I provide evidence for the claim that these understandings are commonly found in Christian theology in *God and Creation in Christian Theology: Tyranny or Empowerment?* (Oxford: Basil Blackwell, 1988). The accounts of God's nature and relation to the world offered here are developed in that book.

beliefs are always already implicated in social interactions in which power relations are established and contested; they have no standing therefore apart from social interactions in which power figures.

What matters is the *way* in which power differences influence the practical associations of Christian beliefs. Here I come to a point where Christian beliefs themselves clearly pose guidelines. Given the beliefs at issue, some ways in which power differences influence the practical associations of those beliefs are proper and some improper.

Chapters 4 through 7 illustrate that the Christian beliefs about God's relation to the world whose meaning and combinations I will have specified by then have a *general* practical import. This general practical import has to be respected by any differences in particular practical associations influenced by shifting situational factors. Only on such a condition are such differences in practical association proper.

These differences may still be major. The practices that are appropriate from a position of power may be the exact opposite of those appropriate from a situation of relative powerlessness. Their ultimate import, however, will have to be much the same, if both are to be proper. Different means, in keeping with radically different situations, should bring all to the same general sort of end. If, for example, what I call nonidolatrous self-esteem is the appropriate attitude for a creature of God to have, the pretensions of the mighty may have to be lowered and the feeble self-regard of the lowly may have to be raised to effect the same outcome. In this manner the general practical import of Christian beliefs directs the way these beliefs should pertain to the situations of those who are either rich or poor, privileged or powerless. Certain ways of applying them to people in these different circumstances are ruled out. It is improper, for example, to use a belief that creatures are only creatures to beat down those convinced of their worthlessness by situations of oppression, or to use a belief in the value of human beings as God's creation to confirm the overbearing sense of their own entitlement so often expressed by the privileged. Both these ways of bringing a belief that human beings are creatures of God to bear in specific socioeconomic circumstances are improper because their practical outcomes violate the general practical import of the belief. The influence of power differences in only these cases are suspect of being ideological; here differences in power are genuinely warping.

The content of the beliefs I develop will establish, moreover, a guideline for the scope of their application. These beliefs include a demand for a universal reference that excludes restrictions on the scope of their application. For example, everyone is a creature of God; therefore both the powerful and the powerless should feel the general practical import of that claim. The privileged of society cannot turn the general practical import of that belief against the underclasses without also directing it against themselves. Were they to do so, the influence of power differences on the practical associations of Christian belief could be convicted of being ideological, of being merely a power play.

A LOOK AHEAD

I have anticipated myself quite a bit here. As I mentioned, I do not begin to discuss these matters until chapter 4. The next two chapters are solely concerned with the following, more descriptive tasks: the need to recommend for their practical potential certain Christian beliefs about God and the world from among those in historical circulation, and to establish the way in which they might be combined for the sort of progressive practical effects that are my focus.[14] The primary beliefs I recommend are, first, a belief in God's transcendence and, second, what I call a belief in God's universal providential agency. These are the Christian beliefs that I select for their progressive political potentials from among those that concern either God's nature or God's relation to the world.

The first belief has the greater logical weight when combined with the second, and with a number of other beliefs (like a belief in

14. I make no exclusive claim of Christian authenticity for the beliefs I pick. In other words, I do not claim that these beliefs are the only authentically Christian ones among the beliefs about God and the world in historical circulation. The authenticity of these beliefs is not therefore the operative criterion by which I picked them over others—their practical potential is. Nor do I have any interest then in using the practical consequences of a belief as a standard for deciding whether a belief is Christian. I am simply choosing from among the sorts of beliefs about God and the world that have been in historical circulation among Christians and banking on the fact that the beliefs I choose will not seem unusual ones for Christians to hold. (In the same way, I am banking on the fact that the meaning I give to those beliefs will not seem unusual.) This is a weak claim of authenticity but it holds an important strategic value, which I develop in chapter 7: the practical consequences of these beliefs are not the only reason for Christians to hold them; these beliefs are already circulating, already believed by at least some Christians.

sin) that I bring in to develop by the end of chapter 3 a full account of God's nature and relation to the world. In other words, belief in God's universal providential agency is partly the effect of making the belief that Christians commonly hold about God's intimate involvement with the world as its creator, provential guide, and redeemer compatible with a belief that God's nature is not ours. A belief in the transcendence of God has this logical priority because it is the belief, I argue in chapter 2, with the greatest potential to make criticism of established sociopolitical arrangements a meaningful course of action. That belief establishes that a sociocultural status quo is the sort of thing that one *can* criticize, and is therefore the logical presupposition for questions about what such a status quo is to be criticized for—injustice (chapters 4 through 6)—and about the attitudes necessary if one is to offer actual resistance to the status quo (chapter 7). A knowledge on Christian grounds that a society is unjust—the topic that I address beginning with chapter 4—does not itself amount to a criticism of it if that injustice is viewed as inevitable or unalterable by human efforts. If I show in chapter 2 that a belief in God's transcendence is crucial to viewing society as an object of critique, then beliefs about God's involvement with the world will have to be adjusted to that belief and that practical function, if they are to be included in a whole body of beliefs supportive of progressive social action.

Chapter 3 establishes the way in which this adjustment takes place. Besides specifying the meaning of God's transcendence, chapter 3 establishes the way a belief in God's transcendence should be combined with other beliefs concerning God's intimate relations with the world to confirm its potential for criticism of sociocultural orders. Chapter 3 specifies, therefore, a shape that the first two factors influencing the practical ramifications of a belief can take if a belief in God's transcendence is indeed to support such criticism.

The resulting body of Christian beliefs, particularly those that concern the status of human beings as creatures of God, is sufficient to make charges of social injustice meaningful as chapters 4 through 6 demonstrate. More specifically, these beliefs supply *reasons* for judging a society to be unjust. As the seventh chapter suggests, the resulting body of beliefs also makes appropriate the attitudes toward oneself and others that are necessary to fight injustice. Thus, the beliefs that foster a critical stance toward a sociocultural status quo do not leave one above the political fray on some spurious platform of neutrality. Instead, criticism will have a clear direction, and commitment to social change will have a clear imperative.

Arguments in chapters 4 through 7 focus primarily on those beliefs that have to do with God's involvement with the world. A belief in God's transcendence does not figure quite as centrally here as in chapters 2 and 3. The beliefs on which I focus in chapters 4 through 7 are, however, the same ones that I will have established earlier when my concern was for a belief's potential for criticizing the status quo. They are the same ones that were produced in weighting a belief in God's transcendence quite heavily.

Most simply, then, the chapters are organized topically as follows: Chapters 2 and 3 discuss how Christian beliefs about God and the world make criticism of the status quo a meaningful enterprise; chapters 4 through 6 show how those same beliefs make injustice an appropriate object of social criticism; chapter 7 shows how such beliefs support the attitudes necessary to fund action for social change. The chapters to come also take up progressively the sort of factors I have isolated in this chapter as influences on the practical dimensions of Christian belief. Chapter 2 begins the process of selecting Christian beliefs for their progressive potentials by commending a belief in God's transcendence for purposes of sociocultural critique. Chapter 3 discusses the meaning of that belief and how it can be combined with Christian beliefs about God's involvement with the world so as to confirm rather than undercut its critical impact vis-à-vis the status quo. Chapters 4 through 7 bring out the influence of situation-specific factors like relative degree of power and powerlessness among the people to whom Christian beliefs pertain, in the process of establishing the way in which specific Christian beliefs can inform condemnations of injustice and attitudes necessary for its remedy.

When all is said and done, political and social radicalism will have found a home in beliefs about God and the world that commonly circulate in the Christian past and present. I will have demonstrated that those beliefs are not owned by forces of reaction, forces cautiously conservative, or forces holding dear the privileges of the few at the expense of the many.

TWO

Self-Critical Cultures and Divine Transcendence

IN THIS CHAPTER I approach the question of Christian beliefs most supportive of critique of the status quo by using the sociocultural perspective on belief that I introduced earlier. This question takes a particular form when expressed in terms of that perspective. I ask here whether, and if so how, Christian beliefs are productive of what I call self-critical cultures.

As I have said, Christians are participants in sociocultural practices as the holders of Christian beliefs. They are inevitably involved in institutionalized forms of social interactions and the circulation of beliefs within them. I now ask whether those social and cultural practices in which Christians participate are likely to take a self-critical shape, to turn a critical eye against themselves, to the extent they are influenced by Christian beliefs. Fundamentally, I am trying to determine whether and in what manner Christian beliefs are able to play a role in sociocultural practices in which established beliefs and social relations are habitually objects of possible criticism. In short, are Christian beliefs able to foster self-critical cultures? If they are, which Christian beliefs might play a crucial part?

These questions about Christian belief presuppose a positive answer to a more general question: Is it possible for the beliefs of any culture to encourage critical reflection on that culture itself and the social relations of which those beliefs are a part? I argue on general sociocultural grounds in the first section of this chapter that self-critical cultures are indeed possible. Although some understandings of the way culture works may discourage recognition of the fact, critical reflection on its own practices is difficult for any society to rule out entirely. Cultures may differ, however, in the resources they present for positively encouraging critical reflection. To make this point, I envision in the second section of this chapter two possible extremes: cultures where established practices are altered almost entirely by purposeful and deliberative means, and cultures where established practices are almost never altered in that way. In the former type of culture, established practices are not merely changed and contested; a society institutionalizes its own means for the purposeful criticism of such practices. In this type of culture, I argue in the third section, a capacity for critical self-reflection is created by a structure of belief that encourages a "view from a distance" on a society's own forms of life. I suggest in the fourth section that this structure of belief may be found in a form of religious culture in which a belief in divine transcendence figures centrally. By this rather circuitous route I establish a resource in religious belief for a culture critical of its own beliefs and of the institutionalized social relations in which it is implicated. The ambiguities of belief in divine transcendence as a resource for self-critical cultures, which I develop in the closing section of the chapter, point to chapter 3. There I discuss what belief in divine transcendence means and how it may be developed vis-à-vis other beliefs in a Christian religious context, if such ambiguities are to be resolved.

THE POSSIBILITY OF SELF-CRITICAL CULTURES

Two understandings of culture exclude the possibility of self-critical cultures. According to one, cultures form homogeneous, monolithic, and organically interconnected wholes. They do not allow therefore for any diversity of opinion or contest over the fundamental terms according to which social interactions proceed. Nor do they allow any breathing room for radically innovative ideas. According to the second, commonly held beliefs, values, and attitudes support established social practices in some fixed and static way. When beliefs support established social practices, they perform only that function, never a critical one. The support offered is never a focus for contest. Finally, practices that gain such support must be monotonously reproduced thereby.

These two understandings of culture are often, indeed, found together.[1] Both take at face value an ideology legitimating the status quo in the cultures they study: "This is the only way to do things, given the way the world is, and there is no other way of thinking about it." Both tend to justify such claims by an inflated notion of the cultural uniformity required for social order: social order is not possible without a consensus in beliefs, norms, and values; social order is not possible unless uncontestable interconnections exist between social practices and commonly held beliefs, values, and norms. Both ignore, therefore, the importance of other modes of social control that are not mediated by beliefs or norms—for example, coercion and the threat of force, a lack of other options, the lure of monetary and status benefits for compliance, isolation from others in similar circumstances, sheer physical exhaustion among an exploited work force. Both of these views fail to look for the cultural diversity and political contest surrounding beliefs, norms, and social practices that might otherwise be obvious to historical investigation unbiased by prior expectations of cultural uniformity. They occlude the way in which patterns of social relations and beliefs are constantly susceptible to construction and reconstruction in ongoing processes of social and cultural interaction.

I am not denying here that social order requires shared background beliefs that are taken for granted by all parties involved, background beliefs that are not, therefore, subject to persistent renegotiation. No coordinated action of any sort among human beings is possible without some commonality of belief establishing what one can expect from others. Institutionalized social relations cannot operate without being interwoven with some pattern of belief distinguishing the true from the false, the credible from the incredible, the real from the unreal. The constituents of such background beliefs may, however, vary from interaction to interaction. The requirement of some background of beliefs does not require the same body of them to reappear each time. Any belief might be subject to renegotiation or contest (given the right circumstances) since all of them are the potentially temporary precipitates of interactions that are ongoing. A background of taken-for-granted beliefs is a presupposition for any conflict to take

1. They are dangers of functionalist forms of cultural analysis.

place regarding others, but in such conflicts it is possible for parts of an existing background of beliefs to be taken down bit by bit. Indeed, such a background was initially constructed piece by piece in negotiations over good sense and meaningful, credible belief. Background beliefs, which are the fallout, the settling out, of processes of interaction in the past, can be shaken up again, so to speak, since the processes that produced them continue. In this way the patterns of social relations that bank on a particular background of taken-for-granted beliefs can themselves be renegotiated and contested.[2]

If this is the way background beliefs are constructed and reconstructed, they are liable to provide quite a bit of room for discursive maneuver. As the precipitates of contestation, beliefs with a prima facie plausibility are likely, first of all, to be shadowed by disqualified and illegitimate ones. They do not have the cultural field all to themselves. Alternative beliefs, which have been defeated and contained by some sort of charge of illegitimacy, are rarely forced entirely out of circulation in a way that would prevent their resurgence as dangerous memories informing present possibilities or future hopes. Moreover, every belief with a prima facie plausibility inevitably produces a vision of what it logically excludes—a photographic negative of itself on the level of belief. Thus even if the losers of every cultural contest are driven from the field, every taken-for-granted belief is still susceptible to logical reversal. A platform for contesting the status quo can be formed by simply denying the beliefs at issue or reversing the way they assign value to things.[3]

2. I am not saying that in virtue of such processes of formation the renegotiation of established social relations and taken-for-granted beliefs is always a real possibility in any society. I am merely saying that it is a possibility for any society unless a society takes steps to block it. (Most societies indeed make efforts to do so by ideological and institutional means.)

My ideas here are not based on any one social theory. They have been informed directly, however, by the following disparate works of social theory: Raymond Williams, *Marxism and Literature* (Oxford: Oxford Univ. Press, 1977); Roberto Unger, *Social Theory* (Cambridge: Cambridge Univ. Press, 1987); Thomas McCarthy, *Ideals and Illusions* (Cambridge: MIT Press, 1991); Joan Cocks, *The Oppositional Imagination* (London: Routledge, 1989), pt. 1; James Scott, *Domination and the Arts of Resistance* (New Haven: Yale Univ. Press, 1990); Chris Weedon, *Feminist Practice and Poststructuralist Theory* (Oxford: Basil Blackwell, 1987); Jürgen Habermas, *The Theory of Communicative Action*, trans. Thomas McCarthy, 2 vols. (Boston: Beacon Press, 1984); Michel Foucault, *Discipline and Punish*, trans. Alan Sheridan (New York: Vintage, 1979); idem, *The History of Sexuality*, trans. Robert Hurley (New York: Vintage, 1980).

3. "The world upside down" of Renaissance carnivals is a conspicuous case of the latter tactic. See James Scott, *Domination and the Arts of Resistance*, 166–72.

Second, because they are the result of contestation, beliefs with a prima facie plausibility are unlikely to be entirely compatible with one another or with established social practices. Gaps in the coherence of background beliefs prevent them from exercising an all-determining influence over discourse. Ill-defined longings that run contrary to socially approved forms of interrelations can come to the surface in such gaps. Moreover, background beliefs in such a situation can simply be played off against one another. For example, a view of women as wives and mothers might conflict with a view of women as autonomous individuals. The one view can be used to criticize the other and the practices it informs. Or background beliefs can come into conflict directly with taken-for-granted social practices. Thus beliefs about liberty, which were established in contests between American colonialists and England, might come to sit uneasily next to U.S. institutions based upon slavery and provide grounds thereby for their ultimate criticism.[4]

Finally, for all the reasons adduced in the last chapter, beliefs that support certain social practices can be uncoupled from them—given new twists of meaning, aligned differently with others, granted a new practical force when employed in different circumstances.

At all these different junctures taken-for-granted beliefs and social practices can become objects of critical reflection. Rather than being presuppositions for disputes about other matters, taken-for-granted beliefs or social relations become at all these different sites the focus themselves of explicit contention. They become matters requiring the support of reasons, and matters susceptible of criticism.

I have not yet established the possibility of genuinely self-critical cultures by these means, however. The ongoing construction and reconstruction of accepted beliefs and social practices, and the kind of sociocultural disorder that is likely to be their result, make possible sites where the sort of critical reflection I seek can occur. Avenues for critical reflection on established beliefs and social practices are available at those points. But what actually prompts critical reflection to be pursued there? What, if anything, positively encourages critical reflection at such junctures? I have not yet shown that established beliefs

4. For a sophisticated argument in support of such claims, see David Brion Davis, *The Problem of Slavery in the Age of Revolution* (Ithaca, N.Y.: Cornell Univ. Press, 1975).

themselves do any work of that sort. On the basis of what I have said so far, it appears instead that critical reflection on taken-for-granted beliefs and practices is the result of different beliefs (and practices) working at cross-purposes with each other. This sort of process with this sort of outcome does not appear to be one that any established belief (or body of beliefs) itself directs. If that appearance is correct, then established beliefs do not turn a critical eye on themselves and the social practices in which they are implicated. One belief (or body of beliefs), and the form of social relations with which it is associated, is being criticized by others.

One might try to argue that the sort of reflexivity I am after is impossible. A culture cannot turn back against itself and the social relations it informs by raising fundamental critical questions. The taken-for-granted beliefs of a culture are presumed in any arguments about truth, meaningfulness, and propriety. Those beliefs are the prerequisites for such arguments, the basis or standard against which such arguments proceed. As such, they cannot make themselves the objects of the same sort of critical scrutiny. The same beliefs cannot be the background beliefs establishing the lines along which critical reflection proceeds and be objects of that critical reflection at the same time. One can argue on similar grounds that when established beliefs support the plausibility of established practices those beliefs cannot also encourage criticism of them.

I say these arguments have similar grounds because they both pass off a formal argument for a substantive one. They argue from circumstances that have to hold everywhere—reflective criticism must always have background beliefs, established social relations must always seek intelligibility in terms of established beliefs—in order to beg the question about the specific shapes that beliefs and social relations can assume. Such inferences are fallacious because from the start everything depends on the particular beliefs or social relations at issue. Thus the ubiquitous circumstance of taken-for-granted beliefs gives one no reason to think that such background beliefs cannot be of a sort to encourage critical reflection on the beliefs that a society takes for granted. For example, beliefs that were taken for granted in the Enlightenment were of that sort. Similarly, the ubiquitous fact that established social practices tend to be informed by taken-for-granted beliefs gives one no reason to think that particular beliefs of that sort cannot promote social practices that are to be constructed and reconstructed as much as possible by public wrangling. Democratically run governments are supposed to be something like that; and they are quite obviously informed, for example, in a U.S. context, by all sorts of taken-for-granted beliefs.

I assume, then, that genuinely self-critical cultures are possible. Socially accepted beliefs can inform patterns of inquiry and social relation that proceed along self-critical lines. They can promote a form of society with established channels for criticizing what a society takes for granted. Whether socially accepted beliefs do so depends on the particular shape they take. The kind of pattern of sociocultural interactions that established beliefs promote depends on the nature of the established beliefs at issue. Cultures made up of different sorts of belief are likely to differ, then, in the capacities that they exhibit for self-criticism.

The idea of culture-specific resources for promoting self-criticism can be contested, however, on two grounds. First, one can claim that criticism of the status quo is not propelled by cultural resources at all. The impulse for such criticism comes from outside culture. It has its source in bodily based desires or in a capacity to transcend any given situation in one's imagination that is everyone's simply as a human being. The sort of sociocultural disorder mentioned previously simply gives such desires and imaginative longings a place to enter. Criticism of the status quo occurs in places where established forms of sociocultural relation suffer the intrusion of desires and longings out of keeping with them.

Claims of this sort make an indefensibly strong separation, however, between the cultural and the natural (or the culturally unformed). All sorts of supposedly natural endowments turn out in fact to be culturally shaped.[5] The very distinction between the natural and the cultural is the product of particular times and places.[6] How the line is drawn between the natural and the cultural also varies in the same

5. See Clifford Geertz, *The Interpretation of Cultures* (New York: Harper Colophon Books, 1973), chap. 2, for a nice expression of the way in which culture might "go all the way down."

6. See Raymond Williams, *Culture and Society 1780–1950* (New York: Columbia Univ. Press, 1958).

way; cultures differ in what they believe to be susceptible of human influence.[7]

Second, one could claim that such resources are constitutive features of *all* cultures.[8] Though this does not appear to be empirically the case, one could insist nonetheless that it is so. One could argue that the most basic features of cultural life (e.g., the proposing of beliefs about what is the case) bring along the necessary cultural resources, even if they remain implicit and underdeveloped. One could also argue that all cultures are on the way toward making such resources explicit if they are not so now. This first line of argument can be convicted, however, of simply reading into the analysis the particular cultural assumptions of the interpreter. The second line of argument is susceptible to the charge of a question-begging teleology: an "all roads lead to Rome" argument like this does not prove the universality of resources for critical reflection; it gets off the ground only by assuming it.[9]

With these objections out of the way, the crucial task that remains is to delineate the cultural differences at issue. What do cultures look like when they foster critical reflection on their own practices? What do they look like when they do not? How are the belief structures in the two cases different? Only with this information in hand can one talk about how religious beliefs might figure in the process.

TWO TYPES OF CULTURE

I begin by imagining cultures at two extremes: customary cultures at the one end; reflective cultures at the other. At one extreme the transformations that a society undergoes happen by way of unreflective habits. At the other, transformations are promoted by reflection on principles or standards of procedure, and in that way produce a self-critical culture.[10]

7. See Roy Wagner, *The Invention of Culture* (Chicago: Univ. of Chicago Press, 1980).

8. Jürgen Habermas is the most sophisticated proponent of such a view. See his *Theory of Communicative Action.*

9. See Thomas McCarthy, "Rationality and Relativism" in *Habermas: Critical Debates*, ed. John Thompson and David Held (Cambridge: MIT Press, 1982), 57–78, for decisive criticisms of Habermas on these sorts of grounds.

10. Anthropological material distinguishing traditional from modern Western cultures, and oral from literate ones, has helped me form this contrast. See, for example,

What such a contrast means will become clear as I proceed, but to avoid misunderstandings at the start I should say that in distinguishing between types of cultures on these grounds I am not suggesting that a reflective culture changes while a customary culture does not. I am not suggesting that the former is innovative while the latter is not. Change and innovation in cultural formations are inevitable.[11] All that I have said so far about the messy and unruly features of culture points to that fact. But even if one considers distinct cultures as fairly homogeneous and well-defined bodies of more or less logically coherent beliefs, cultural understandings are still always liable to transformation. In order for a cultural formation to sustain itself over time, it must be reproduced in ongoing interactions that put it at risk.[12]

Engaging the background beliefs of a culture in new physical circumstances presents one sort of risk. Circumstances may fail to meet culturally conditioned expectations by providing cases of beings that are anomalous with respect to taken-for-granted categories (e.g., androgynes when categories of sexual difference are limited to male and female) or happenings that are unintelligible on existing cosmological schemes (e.g., as Clifford Geertz reports, the enormous, fast-growing mushrooms that prompted the cultural consternation of the Javanese).[13]

The human parties in the interpersonal relations that are necessary if cultural understandings are to be sustained present another inevitable

---

Ernest Gellner, *The Legitimation of Belief* (Cambridge: Cambridge Univ. Press, 1974); Jack Goody, *The Logic of Writing and the Organization of Society* (Cambridge: Cambridge Univ. Press, 1988); Robin Horton, "African Traditional Thought and Western Science," in *Rationality,* ed. Bryan Wilson (Oxford: Basil Blackwell, 1977), 131–71; idem, "Tradition and Modernity Revisited," in *Rationality and Relativism,* ed. Martin Hollis and Steven Lukes (Oxford: Basil Blackwell, 1982), 201–60.

I have no intention, however, of suggesting any evolutionary progression of cultural forms. Nor do I identify customary cultures exclusively with traditional or oral ones. In some respects late capitalist consumer culture fits the type more easily. See, for example, Herbert Marcuse, *One-Dimensional Man* (Boston: Beacon Press, 1964) and Ernest Gellner, *Words and Things* (London: Routledge and Kegan Paul, 1979), for a critique along these lines of technocratic societies where standards of all sorts have merely an operational sense (i.e., standards are simply what is done). For purposes of my argument here I will be sticking with a rather traditionalist version of customary cultures.

11. See, for example, Robin Horton's somewhat belated recognition of this fact in "Tradition and Modernity Revisited," 218–22.

12. See Marshall Sahlins, *Islands of History* (Chicago: Univ. of Chicago Press, 1985); idem, *Historical Metaphors and Mythical Realities* (Ann Arbor: Univ. of Michigan Press, 1981).

13. Geertz, *Interpretation of Cultures*, 101.

source of risk. Even if a society moves from one cultural consensus to another, differences in the understanding of a society's cultural reserves by participants in such interactions are liable to lead to the renegotiation of those reserves. For example, different understandings of loyalty to country on the part of doves and hawks during the Vietnam War effected a renegotiation of the meaning of patriotism in contemporary American culture: loyalty to country does not mean now quite what it did before. The possibility of cultural revision on the basis of such clashes is at its height when the cultural understandings of the people involved have been shaped in different circumstances and in relative isolation from one another—cases that verge therefore on actual interchange between distinct cultures.

This extreme case of intercultural differences makes a general point about the essential revisability of any distinct culture. In the same way that knowing one language provides the basis for an ever-expanding linguistic horizon in interchanges with foreign-language speakers, any distinct culture forms an essentially expandable horizon of basic categories and assumptions. Cultures are essentially scenes of mediation in which the relatively different may be made intelligible by assimilation to prior cultural understandings but not without some alteration of those very understandings themselves.[14] For instance, the extended kinship structures of so-called traditional societies can be assimilated to the contemporary Western notion of a nuclear family but not without altering the Western notion of what family is all about.

To sum up: the reproduction or maintenance of any culture is liable to be a matter of its transformation, and transformations of culture are the means by which cultures may be extended and therefore sustained. The same cultural processes may be called, then, ones of transformative reproduction or, with little difference, reproductive transformation. It is important for my present purposes to see that this reproduction can occur in either of two ways: in a customary fashion, by way of unreflective habit, or via reflective deliberation.

When culture is reproduced in a customary fashion, its transmission is a matter of spontaneous flexibility and automatic adaptation to circumstances. Habits always exist in the flux of adjustment to

14. See the interpretation of Hans-Georg Gadamer's notion of open horizons made by David Linge in his introduction to Gadamer's *Philosophical Hermeneutics* (Berkeley: Univ. of California Press, 1976), xxxiii–xl.

immediate practical needs. "Custom," as Michael Oakeshott observes, "is always adaptable and susceptible to the *nuance* of the situation," making it "capable of change as well as local variation." "Nothing is more continuously invaded by change" than habit or custom.[15]

When culture is reproduced by deliberate application of some principle or standard of procedure, one would expect transmission of it to hold greater prospects for restraint on invention. An objectified rule or norm has some sort of general status; it is not embedded in specific contexts. One might expect a single norm of that sort to be applicable therefore to many different contexts, and to enforce thereby a fairly rigid conformity to a single way of thinking and acting. One would think that, at the minimum, reproduction of culture via principles or standards would vary little with circumstance.

These anticipations are not wholly warranted, however. No matter how rule governed a course of action and belief, the application of those rules, their interpretation and use in particular circumstances, cannot be similarly rule bound. The reproduction of culture via deliberation requires invention to meet the needs of varying circumstances.[16] As Thomas McCarthy makes the point: Following social rules calls for "not mere conformity but competent practical reasoning to deal with . . . contingencies. . . . There is always an element of the discretionary, elaborative and ad hoc about how we apply rules and schemes, for they do not define their own applications."[17] Without such judgmental leeway, rules are too rigid and oversimplified to deal effectively with the complexity of actual social interactions.

This inventiveness in the deliberative reproduction of culture may not match in degree the flexibility of habitual or customary reproduction. But the most significant difference with customary reproduction is that deliberative reproduction makes possible a different attitude toward the inevitable transformation of culture and a different sort of change. Elaborating upon such differences in the character and understanding of change enables one to distinguish two types of culture—deliberative and customary—on the matter of their respective

15. Michael Oakeshott, *Rationalism in Politics* (London: Methuen, 1962), 64–65.

16. See Stuart Hampshire, *Morality and Conflict* (Cambridge: Harvard Univ. Press, 1983); and Basil Mitchell, *The Justification of Religious Belief* (New York: Seabury Press, 1973).

17. McCarthy, *Ideals and Illusions*, 30.

capacities for sociocultural critique. Cultures marked by deliberative reproduction are not simply self-transformative; they are self-critical.

It is obviously a caricature to draw in this way a typological contrast between sorts of culture on the basis of their respective modes of reproduction. Any culture must include both, for two reasons. First, no culture could sustain itself over time entirely or even mainly by the conscious application of rule or principle. Established courses of action and belief must be primarily habitual; and action and belief become habitual through processes of primary socialization in which training figures prominently. Explicit rules, generalized standards or principles, must be employed for the most part in a regulative rather than a constitutive capacity. That is, rather than being the primary mode of *generating* conduct of a certain sort, they alter, direct, or otherwise shape forms of action and belief that are already habitual. They enter on the scene of reproduction as secondary means of control, particularly in times of crisis, when the risks of cultural reproduction discussed become a reality. Second, it is hard to imagine a society without the reflective capacities at least to formulate norms or standards that sum up and render explicit the forms of action and belief a society judges best. There is a point, nevertheless, to working out the case of unmixed extremes. The clarity of the contrast is a useful heuristic tool in the evaluation of particulars—in the present case, ultimately, the evaluation of the function of Christian beliefs in supporting or undermining established sociopolitical practices.

What are these differences in the character and understanding of cultural change that distinguish deliberative from customary cultures? First one would expect changes of culture in customarily reproduced cultural contexts to be relatively imperceptible. Customary cultures may have greater flexibility, but the more extreme such flexibility becomes the less likely it is to be recognized by participants. There is nothing fixed against which change might be noted.[18] For example, the past is retained in customary forms of cultural reproduction only in the shape of the present exercise of the same habits. As a result, it is very difficult to see that what happens in the present is different from what occurred in the past.

Second, because change is imperceptible, there is the presumption of continuity, even of stasis, for sociocultural formations: "we

18. See Goody, *Logic of Writing*, 137.

believe what we have always believed"; "we do what we have always done." Present performance is authorized by this presumption of past performance: If something happens, that is grounds enough for assuming that it has happened before, and if it has happened before it must be proper now.[19] What is right is what is done, and what is done varies with the occasion in the course of the enforced sort of improvisation found in habitually reproduced forms of culture.[20]

Proper behaviors may be objectified and standardized in the form of stories about ancestors or heroes or gods. In that case, present behavior is authorized not merely, or not at all, as a simple transmission of the past but as its veritable re-creation or reinstitution. The present is not just the continuation of what has gone before, but its identical reproduction.[21] The past is not lost in an immemorial process of transmission so that the present can be justified only by the fact of that transmission. A tradition of inheritance has instead a specifiable origin.

But this objectification of a standard for otherwise unreflective habits merely serves as an ideology of stasis. No more than an unspecifiable past does it foster a recognition of change, of distance. Why not? It is true that rules of conduct are no longer merely embedded in a context as unreflective habits; they have been objectified in the sense that they have been raised out of a course of conduct in the form of stories that may be told apart from that conduct. Rules for conduct are not, however, generalized or made more abstract when they take the form of stories. Stories remain as particular as the course of conduct from which they arise. Abstracted from these contexts, they nevertheless continue therefore to mirror them. If storied cultures are themselves reproduced customarily—that is, if the stories exist only as they are transmitted by unreflective habit—they do not have the fixity in any case to ensure a difference between present practice and what they recount. Stories and conduct tend to adjust together to situation, as any customarily reproduced form of belief or conduct is wont to do.

Third, therefore, cultures that are customarily reproduced tend to be characterized in the main by adjustment to, rather than criticism of, present practices. If the past exists only in its retelling in the present,

19. See James Pocock, *Politics, Language and Time* (New York: Atheneum, 1971), 237.

20. See Goody, *Logic of Writing*, 38.

21. See Pocock, *Politics, Language and Time*, chap. 7.

it can provide no critical edge on present practice. Thus any norm or standard abstracted from the context of conduct—be it in the form of a specified past or a reputedly timeless origin—will lack the capacity to do more than reproduce the shape of present practice. It will retain the particularity and concreteness of those contexts and vary with them as a result of its own customary form of transmission.

Direct opposition to customarily reproduced cultures on the part of individuals is also difficult for a number of reasons. First, it is easy for genuinely subversive or grossly nonstandard behavior to be erased in customarily reproduced cultures. These behaviors are simply swallowed up by the continued practice of the group and forgotten. Subversion has no platform with any degree of permanence.[22] Second, it is hard for any form of conduct or belief to be deviant in a way that would jeopardize the character of a culture that is customarily reproduced. The boundaries of customarily reproduced cultures are so fluid that it would be relatively difficult even to come up with forms of behavior and belief that definitely cross over the line of normalcy. Therefore, it is not just that subversion lacks a platform with any permanence. It is hard to be an outsider and so take the stance of a cultural critic. Customarily reproduced cultures are radically assimilative and incorporative. Even the beliefs and behaviors of another culture—beliefs and behaviors established and maintained in a hitherto separate sphere of coordinated action—are not immune. Habitually grounded behaviors and beliefs are marked by an eclectic syncretism. They have the apparent capacity to invent variations appropriate to any occasion, including those of encounter with the culturally strange.[23]

Encounters with what is genuinely strange or deviant may involve, however, the alteration of a cultural formation—something more like actual change than the mere development of situational variants (more like the case of Native Americans adopting European dress than their changing the sort of plumage used in traditional costumes with the near extinction of American eagles). But such change

22. Goody, *Logic of Writing*, 31, 136, 147.

23. See James Clifford's account of the cultural inventiveness of Native Americans in Mashpee, Cape Cod, in *The Predicament of Culture* (Cambridge: Harvard Univ. Press, 1988), chap. 12. See also critiques of the eclecticism of postmodern cultures by, for example, Gerald Graff, *Literature against Itself* (Chicago: Univ. of Chicago Press, 1979).

will be circumscribed. It is unlikely to signal drastic or system-wide revision. It is unlikely to prompt any reevaluation, therefore, of cultural practices as a whole or the fundamental principles of their performance. What revision there is will tend to be ad hoc and situation-specific in keeping with the ad hoc, situation specific character of habitually grounded cultural reproduction. Adjustments of an established belief or practice in order to cope with new circumstances will be favored over wholesale rejection of a belief or practice. When a belief or practice *is* scrapped, it is unlikely that it will take many others with it. Cultures of this sort are highly tolerant of theoretical inconsistency, since they are sustained through habits or unreflective dispositions. Consistency is not a requirement for cultural maintenance. Moreover, when beliefs are embedded in context and habitually sustained, it is difficult for participants to set them side by side in a way that would make contradictions among them apparent. If beliefs and behaviors are maintained primarily by habit, it is hard for participants to recognize them as any kind of system; it is hard to consider them all together as a whole, and therefore partial alterations of beliefs or actions are unlikely to spread to others.[24]

Even though change in such cultures will tend therefore to be gradual rather than dramatic, a matter of partial adjustments rather than radical revolutions, customarily reproduced cultures are nevertheless susceptible to a certain kind of extreme change: change in the form of an overall degeneration. Because they proceed in a quasi-automatic or spontaneous fashion and case by case, simply as circumstances might dictate, alterations of customarily reproduced cultures are inclined to be thoroughly undirected. The result may not just be theoretical inconsistency; it may be practical incoherence. Differences in habitual response may eventually prohibit coordinated action altogether. Furthermore, the lack of clear boundaries permits the fluidity of syncretisitic assimilation on the part of customarily reproduced cultures and allows for their eventual demise via a loss of identity. It may be by progressive increments, but sooner or later, especially in encounters with other cultures, a habitually reproduced culture is liable to lose its distinctiveness as a particular cultural formation.[25]

24. Oakeshott, *Rationalism in Politics*, 64.

25. See, for example, Marshall Sahlins's account of the demise of the Hawaiian tabu system through encounters with European traders in his *Historical Metaphors and Mythical Realities*, 33–66.

The attitude toward cultural transformation and the form change takes in deliberately reproduced cultures are the obverse of those in customarily produced ones. First, transformations in belief and action tend to be perceptible since there is something relatively unchanging against which to measure them—a norm for belief and action referenced apart from the changing circumstances of habitual belief and action. For example, the character of the action at a particular time can be formulated in a relatively fixed way that saves it from the oblivion of the past. Past action in that way becomes a standard or benchmark against which present change can be charted.

Second, along with a perception of change comes a possible criticism of it. Standards in a more strictly normative sense, standards of propriety, whether they be identified with the past or with generalized rules for proceeding or with atemporal ideals, may have their origin in the flux of habitual performance, but once abstracted from it, they gain a certain distance on it. What is proper will not tend to vary in sync with what is done, since standards of proper practice will not exist merely in the form of customary behaviors. Moreover, such standards are not likely simply to mirror the particulars of established practice since they are in some way more general or abstract than those particulars.

Third, because of the existence of relatively fixed, generalized standards, change does not proceed automatically, apart from conscious reflection upon it. Cultural changes are more likely to be deliberately instituted or to require, after the fact, some sort of justification. Changes in culturally acceptable practices are liable to require either the deliberate reform of existing standards for behavior (i.e., change in their formulation or interpretation) or some principled reason for their inapplicability in present circumstances.

It is because changes in practice require principled reflection on established standards that deliberately reproduced cultures are more resistant to change than customarily reproduced ones. This resistance does not spell, however, any kind of cultural entrapment. Unlike customarily reproduced ones, deliberately reproduced cultures are not encased within the ongoing flux of cultural formations since they do not automatically validate the changes that inevitably mark all efforts to sustain cultures over time. Moreover, when cultural change is deliberately instituted change is likely to be both fairly radical and contagious for the following reasons.

First, since cultural reproduction proceeds by way of reflection rather than by habit, response to changing circumstances will naturally tend to be less exclusively ad hoc or situation specific. Mere adjustments in established beliefs or practices to meet the needs of new circumstances are liable to be replaced, therefore, by substantive revisions or outright rejections of those beliefs and practices. Second, deliberately reproduced cultures do not have the fluidity of customarily reproduced cultures with which to tolerate situational variants by mere addition, by syncretistic incorporation. Inclusion of the different is more likely to require amendments or deletions of beliefs in the interest of consistency. Theoretical consistency becomes a requirement of coordinated action, of sociocultural maintenance, when individuals determine what to do and evaluate what they have done by reflective means. Inconsistency can be perceived because principles of action and belief can be set side by side once they have been abstracted from the particular contexts they inform. In general, reflection upon habitual practices in the attempt to formulate the principles by which they abide is a step-by-step process of objectifying one's own culture. A culture of taken-for-granted beliefs becomes in this way an object of deliberation and possible change. Spontaneous flexibility is sacrificed for the potential of principled self-criticism. The gradual transformations of habitual practices make way for possible revolution. The background beliefs these practical routines presuppose become questionable.

STRUCTURAL FEATURES OF THE TWO TYPES

These differences in the character and understanding of change on the part of deliberative and customary cultures can be correlated with basic differences in the structural organization of their respective belief systems. These different structural properties are the prerequisites, the supportive cultural tissue for self-reflective or customary forms of change respectively.[26] The crucial discrimination here—what distinguishes the structural properties of the one from the other—is

26. Here I am appealing to much the same sociological and anthropological material as Jürgen Habermas and making many of the same basic points, but without any claims for ontogenetic or phylogenetic advance, or cross-cultural normativity for the structural organization of (what I call) deliberative cultures. See his *Theory of Communicative Action.*

the resources they represent for distancing a culture from its own established sociocultural practices, from the routinized or habitual beliefs and forms of social relation with which it is involved. The self-criticism of deliberative cultures requires such distance. The self-transformative character of customary ones does without it.

I do not suppose that differences in such resources of distantiation are merely cultural. They also tend to presuppose certain differences of socioeconomic circumstance. I cannot make much of a case for it here, but the structural distinctions in the organization of belief that I will mention can be tied to what social scientists call social differentiation and to the cultural differentiation attendant upon it. The structural distinctions in the organization of belief systems that I examine are a response to the relative cultural chaos that follows upon social differentiation.

Social differentiation means that (1) different aspects of social activities (e.g., familial, economic, military, governmental) are localized in different networks of social interaction; (2) a society is stratified into economic classes or prestige groups; and (3) occupations are specialized according to a highly refined division of labor. When these forms of social differentiation occur, the distribution of socially constructed and maintained knowledge is markedly uneven. That is, people in different social locations do not believe the same things or hold the same beliefs in the same way—the cultural reserves of a society are differentiated. The structural distinctions within belief systems that I discuss work to make this sort of cultural differentiation intelligible and restore intellectual order.[27]

The first structural feature of belief systems that provides a resource of distantiation involves a discrimination among three world-concepts—external reality, the social order, and personal subjectivity—and a separation of their respective validity spheres.[28] Cultures that are simply self-transformative tend to mix natural and social categories,

27. For example, the epistemological use of a distinction between appearance and reality, which I will discuss, helps make sense of a lack of unified belief by suggesting the possibility of different perspectives on the same reality. The last two paragraphs are my more technical formulation of Ernest Gellner's sociology of modern intellectual history. See his *Legitimation of Belief.*

28. The term "world-concepts" and the three different forms of world-concept I cite come from Jürgen Habermas. See again his *Theory of Communicative Action.*

in keeping with the taken-for-granted self-evidence of habitual practices. The unquestioned inevitability of social proceedings are to be accepted as one accepts the givens of the natural environment. The human order is naturalized; nature is anthropomorphized. Nature and society are more or less undifferentiated orders within a single ontological sphere. When natural and social worlds are distinguished, the latter loses its self-evidence as a natural given. The social order is de-reified, to use Peter Berger's term.[29] Social arrangements can be viewed as specifically human constructions that are not ingrained in the very nature of things. The alteration and manipulation of these arrangements become thereby a theoretically possible aim of action.

Similarly, in order for rebellious eccentricity not to be ruled out, as it is in customary cultures, a sphere of individual experience must be distinguished from the social world. Persons cannot be identified with their social roles, their feelings equated with socially stereotyped expressions. In order for individuals to be the source of critical possibilities, their wishes must not be swallowed up in the relentless tide of habitually reproduced group practices. They must be able to withdraw themselves from their place within established social practices and view such practices from the outside. Self-critical cultures make the requisite distinctions between individual and social spheres: they institutionalize individuality. Individuality is institutionalized culturally in the sense that the background of taken-for-granted communal convictions in such cultures is neither extensive enough nor concrete enough in its particulars to cover the life experiences of its membership. Thus these cultures force the recognition of a specifically individual sphere of experience and decision.[30]

Once these world-concepts have been distinguished, it is possible to segregate their distinct validity claims—the sincerity or authenticity of personal expression, the rightness of social behavior, the truth of claims about the world. The difference between the last two sorts of validity claim is particularly crucial for the formation of self-critical cultures. It spells an ideal of objectivity in which facts and a domain

29. See Peter Berger, *The Social Construction of Reality* (New York: Doubleday, 1966), 89–92.

30. See Emile Durkheim, *The Division of Labor in Society* (New York: Free Press, 1933), for the beginnings of such an account. See also Steven Lukes, *Individualism* (New York: Harper and Row, 1973).

of true descriptions concerning them can be distinguished from values and the human order in which they have a place. Truth has its own criteria of assessment that are, ideally, not to be mixed with those of socially oriented values or concerns for utility. Something is not more likely to be true simply because it is espoused by a powerful or prestigious member of the community, because it occupies a long-standing or hallowed place in a society's tradition of belief, because it helps to maintain the social order, or because it boosts morale. Truths need not be socially serviceable. They may provide instead a platform for social criticism.

An interest in social order, conversely, need not hamper criticism of what is believed to be true. When beliefs are formed according to unmixed criteria, criteria formed, that is, without reference to social concerns, the number of beliefs that are socially entrenched tends to decrease. In other words, fewer beliefs are part and parcel of a society's orderly functioning. Social order will not be jeopardized, therefore, should such beliefs be radically emended or dropped.[31]

A second group of cultural distinctions that provide a resource for distantiation are those that construct notions of something outside or beyond established beliefs or normative arrangements. First, a sphere of reality is distinguished from that of ideas about it. Distinct orders of fact, on the one hand, and interpretation, on the other, take the place of a relatively undifferentiated cosmological-ideational order inclusive of words, thoughts, and things.[32] Second, a notion of de facto norms—of what is acceptable behavior in a particular social group at a particular time—is distinguished from that of de jure norms—from what by rights should occur. The *fact* of social arrangements, in

31. Notice that from my methodological point of view, the distinction between truth and social value is a particular cultural formation that permits a relative distinction among criteria of validity. I am not assuming that truth is ever finally separate from power relations or that it needs to be in order to be a resource of social criticism. Furthermore, although the distinction between truth and social value *permits* criticism of sociocultural orders, it does not require such criticism. The claim for truth separate from norms of social validity can clearly be used to hide the fact that what is proposed as true serves particular interests. This is just another way of saying that the distinction itself between truth and social validity is implicated in struggles for power. It has therefore an ambiguous function, making possible both the criticism and the support of social orders.

32. See Michel Foucault, *The Order of Things* (New York: Vintage, 1973), chap. 2.

other words, is distinguished from what *ought* to be. Socially valid norms become distinguishable from ones that are ideally valid.[33]

The existence of such distinctions blocks the automatic self-validation of established beliefs or social arrangements. One cannot assume that one's words and ideas are bound up with the way things are. A linguistically formed worldview cannot be identified with the world order itself in any way that would prevent the former from being recognized as a particular interpretation of the latter, and consequently as something open to critical revision.[34] A concept of reality is available with which to perceive variations in worldview as different interpretations of natural and social orders that are subject to reflective assessment. One can ask whether what one takes to be true is *really* so. Similarly, once social and ideal normative validity are uncoupled as distinct categories, the mores of a particular society are not validated simply by virtue of being established. One can ask whether what is commonly perceived to be proper is really so. Socially valid norms as well as worldviews become subject to argumentative assessment. In both cases, what is, the setup or the given, is kept from forming a limit on the possible. A difference between appearance and reality—between the really true and the apparently true, the really proper and the apparently proper—becomes a potential measure of discontent.

Once distinctions are made between reality and interpretations of it and between ideal and socially valid norms, notions of reality and an ideal norm can be used in either of two ways: in a transcendent and regulative way, or in an immanent and constitutive way. In the latter case, the notion of reality or an ideal norm is substantively filled, so that it may function as a criterion or *discrimen* in the process of evaluating a particular belief or normative claim. For instance, when reality is defined for such a purpose, the distinction between reality and one's idea of it amounts to a distinction between differently evaluated interpretations. That is, in the process of reevaluating a particular account of reality—"we believed that this was the way things are but now we know better"—one account of reality is set against another. One version is identified with the way things really are, the other with a mere idea about reality. Similarly, in the case where a distinction

33. See Habermas, *Theory of Communicative Action*, 1:88–89; 2:73.
34. Ibid., 1:50.

between ideal and socially valid norms is used to reflect critically upon a particular normative claim, the distinction is a way of making a point about the relative value of different socially valid norms. That is, in arguments that conclude "we thought that was the best way for people to treat each other but now we know better," the distinction between ideal and socially valid norms simply serves to privilege the presently agreed-upon socially valid norm.

In a transcendent and regulative use of notions of reality or an ideal norm, their content remains unspecified. Such notions are zero semantic categories or surds, placeholders for a reality or ideal independent of our conceptions of it.[35] They mark a reference to a reality or norm beyond our ideas of either, by repelling differentiating descriptions, by eschewing the adequacy of any proposed account of what they are. As a result, notions of reality or the ideal cannot function as criteria in the evaluation of particular beliefs or norms. Nothing can be done with them for particular purposes. Because they have no content, they cannot be implemented as standards in the process of evaluating particular beliefs or norms. They may work, however, to ground a general ethic of cognition or normative judgment. They have a general procedural or regulative use in preventing claims of dogmatic finality for any belief or normative claim. That is, they prevent an immanent and constitutive use of such distinctions from permanently privileging any one account of reality or any one account of an ideal norm. A distinction between reality and one's idea of it or between the ideal and a socially valid norm is used in such cases, not to make relative discriminations among ideas of reality or among socially valid norms, but to discriminate between *all* ideas or socially valid norms and some reality or ideal beyond them. The general point is simply that ideas and norms at any particular time are subject to revision.

The transcendent use of these notions for regulative purposes extends, moreover, beyond this mere indiscriminate reminder of the ultimate inadequacy of every cognitive or normative proposal. The notions provide a general direction for forming judgments among proposed truths or norms. As I have suggested above, reality and an

35. See Thomas Nagel, *The View from Nowhere* (Oxford: Oxford Univ. Press, 1986), chap. 6; and Wayne Proudfoot, *Religious Experience* (Berkeley: Univ. of California Press, 1985), 124–36, for suggestions of how transcendent notions can be rule-governed cultural constructions of this sort.

ideal norm cannot constitute criteria for judging proposed truths and norms apart from some conception of what they are like; apart from ideas about them, reality and an ideal norm have no standing that would enable them to be used themselves as such criteria. In other words, one cannot assess the relative adequacy of different accounts of reality by comparing them to reality itself, or the relative adequacy of different normative proposals by comparing them with the ideal good itself. But the notion of a reality or an ideal norm beyond one's conception does set guidelines for the sort of criteria that should be brought to bear in making such judgments. If belief systems cannot be judged with reference to a reality absolutely independent of human conception, they can at least be judged according to a best approximation for particular purposes, that is, according to evidence or criteria that are relatively independent of human conception in the sense that they are independent of any of the particular belief systems under investigation. (For example, even if description of empirical data is never theory-neutral but always influenced by some understanding of the nature of reality, such description should not be informed by any one of the competing scientific theories to be assessed with reference to the data). Similarly, if social norms cannot be judged with reference to an absolutely ideal norm, they can at least be judged according to criteria that are relatively unprejudiced by the social interests of the particular parties in disagreement. In sum, the transcendent use of notions of reality or an ideal norm translates into a procedural recommendation of openness to criticism by what is independent relative to the particular socially valid norms or interpretations of reality under consideration.[36]

36. See Gellner, *Legitimation of Belief*, esp. 19–23, on this last aspect of a regulative use of notions of the transcendent. In this paragraph and the previous one I have been splitting the difference between those, on the one hand, who make an acultural and rather flat appeal to transcendent truths or norms as prerequisites for social criticism (e.g., Habermas, Christopher Norris, Peter Dews), and those, on the other, who deny altogether the legitimacy, sense, or usefulness of transcendent notions as cultural constructions (e.g., Richard Rorty in some moods; Wittgensteinians who decide in advance, on general philosophical grounds, the limitations of cultural good sense instead of really leaving "everything as it is").

See Habermas, *Theory of Communicative Action*; Christopher Norris, *Contest of Faculties* (London: Methuen, 1985); Peter Dews, *Logics of Disintegration* (London: Verso, 1987). For Rorty's vacillations (or change of heart) regarding the transcendent force of notions like truth, compare his "Solidarity or Objectivity" in *Post-Analytic Philosophy*, ed. John Rajchman and Cornel West (New York: Columbia Univ. Press, 1984), 6 ("There

RELIGION AND THE TWO TYPES OF CULTURE

What place might religion have in either of the sorts of culture just sketched? It is not uncommon to associate religious belief systems simply with what I have been calling customary culture. I need to address the reasons for such an association. If valid, they would make it unnecessary to investigate further whether Christian belief in particular can inform a culture of self-criticism. Like all other religions, Christianity would simply be allied with ideologies of stasis.

One might hold, with Jürgen Habermas, an evolutionary view, in which the structure of religious belief systems is said to be progressively replaced by more reflective relations to culture. One assumes thereby that religious beliefs are proposed and maintained in a way that discourages their argumentative assessment. One cannot get behind what is proclaimed to be sacred. The questioning of religious belief is a form of sacrilege. Religious belief is a classic instance of normatively ascribed consensus whereby established beliefs are simply presumed true.[37]

On this evolutionary view, it is true that the structure of religious belief systems might itself be altered in the progress toward argumentatively based belief. The authority of the sacred is no longer in that case a taken-for-granted given, but something for which one argues on the grounds supplied by a religious worldview. This represents a "communicative thawing of traditionally solid institutions based on sacred authority."[38] "Convictions owe their authority less and less to the spellbinding power and aura of the holy, and more and more to a consensus that is not merely reproduced but *achieved,* that is, brought about communicatively. . . . by way of intersubjective recognition of validity claims raised in speech acts."[39]

is nothing to be said about truth save that each of us will commend as true those beliefs which he or she finds good to believe") and "Pragmatics, Davidson, and Truth" in *Truth and Interpretation,* ed. Ernest Lepore (Oxford: Basil Blackwell, 1984), 334–35, where he notes a "cautionary" use of appeals to the truth in which one reminds oneself that the world may not be as one's justified beliefs say it is. For Ludwig Wittgenstein's claim that philosophy should leave "everything as it is," see his *Philosophical Investigations,* trans. G. E. M. Anscombe (New York: Macmillan, 1953), paragraph 124.

37. See Habermas, *Theory of Communicative Action*, 2:77–111, on the "linguistification of the sacred," for a recent, highly sophisticated version of this view.

38. Ibid., 2:91.

39. Ibid., 2:89.

One might argue, however, that the basic structure of religious belief systems remains unchanged in this process, and hence such belief retains its alignment with customarily reproduced cultures. A religious worldview puts systematic restrictions on the argumentative assessment of action and belief by failing to distinguish among expressive, cognitive, and normative spheres of validity.[40] The highest principle of such systems—God, in theistic ones—fuses notions of the true, the good, and the perfect.[41] Religions refuse a discrimination between cognitive and normative spheres of validity in their demands for a world order that is ethically meaningful.[42]

One could also dispute that religious beliefs can be part of self-critical cultures, on the basis of historical evidence. The authoritarian and dogmatic character of religious forms of justification, in the West at least, was proved historically in the internecine religious conflicts of sixteenth- and seventeenth-century Europe. In this context, the way that religion informed competing political agendas made it impossible to resolve conflicts by rational means. Such resolution required the formation of a distinctively political vocabulary of natural rights, social contracts, and public welfare. Rational assessment had to be set against religiously backed convictions. Proponents of a strictly political form of argument might have been wrong to think of their project as one that proceeded above history and independent of cultural inheritance: what they succeeded in doing was to institute a rational *tradition* for settling public disputes. They were not wrong, however, about the need for their project if a rational tradition of argument was to be set up. Reworking available cultural resources, the proponents of political argument arranged for the first time a cultural context, of a fundamentally nonreligious sort, that permitted self-correction.[43]

None of these arguments, however, produces strong enough a priori reasons for thinking that an investigation of possible religious

40. Ibid., 2:189, 194.

41. Ibid., 1:246, 248, 348.

42. Ibid., 1:160–63, 202–3.

43. See Jeffrey Stout, *The Flight from Authority* (Notre Dame: Univ. of Notre Dame Press, 1982), 235–42, on the historical significance of religious wars. He is following here Quentin Skinner, *The Foundations of Modern Political Thought*, 2 vols. (Cambridge: Cambridge Univ. Press, 1978). See also Stout, *Flight from Authority*, 44–46, 74–76, on the notion of a rational tradition. With characteristic caution Stout does not flatly proclaim the bankruptcy of religious resources in the setting up of self-critical traditions. He merely strongly suggests it, and awaits, as he should, a sustained argument to the contrary.

forms of self-critical culture is a waste of time. Aside from the problematic character of any evolutionary view of cultural development, the particular one I mentioned that distinguishes religious cultures from those that are reproduced and maintained by communicative acts appears to be based on an overly simplistic and narrow account of religious appeals to sacrality. The argument is a grossly general one that takes a particular sort of religious belief system for the whole.

One might respond to this rejoinder by claiming that an unquestionable sacrality for at least some beliefs or actions is the baseline of a religious worldview, however religions may differ in the extent and fervor of such attributions. But the burden of proof remains on the respondent to show that this unquestioned status exceeds in extent or character what any deliberative culture assumes. Even the most deliberative of cultures poses beliefs and actions for argumentative assessment against a background of what is not in question. It is true that in reflective cultures the background can be put into the foreground in a piecemeal fashion, but in all cultures at least some of these background beliefs are so basic that a culture lacks criteria for their meaningful assessment.[44]

The argument that the basic structure of religious belief systems puts systematic constraints on reflective assessment seems fallacious for a number of reasons. First, religious demands for the coordination or integration of norms and worldview do not necessarily indicate any failure to distinguish between types of claims or their criteria of assessment. Only the latter failure would conflict with structural prerequisites for a self-critical culture. A distinction between the natural world and social values is presumed whether one's theory of their relation detaches one from the other—on the assumption, perhaps, that the natural world runs contrary to an interest in human good—or brings them together in the belief, for instance, that the natural order is under the rule of a divine moral agent. In other words, a

44. See Habermas's own assimilation of these Wittgensteinian points in *Theory of Communicative Action*, 1:335–37; 2:109, 219–22. See Alvin Plantinga, "Is Belief in God Rational?" in *Rationality and Religious Belief*, ed. C. F. Delaney (Notre Dame: Univ. of Notre Dame Press, 1979), 7–27, for an argument that certain religious beliefs are foundational in a Wittgensteinian sense. I do not believe that this argument is successful for reasons that are not germane to the present discussion. It is enough for my purposes here simply to throw doubt on a priori arguments for religious dogmatism, so as not to preclude further investigation into possible religious resources for self-critical traditions.

distinction between the orders of value and fact does not require their *detachment*. To assume so is to overlook the logical relation between these two orders explicated in the first chapter: normative claims are reasonable and motivated with reference ultimately to theoretical claims about what is the case. This does not involve a failure to distinguish between theoretical and normative claims; it merely presupposes a coordination of the two rather than their disjunction. To conflate such a distinction with separation is to demand a peculiarly quixotic character for normative proposals in reflective cultures—an existentialist nobility in extremis where people grit their teeth and carry on in a world that makes a mockery of their own desires and best intentions to further a human good. It should be clear that the mere differentiation of world-concepts or validity spheres does not involve such a demand. Furthermore, a simple coordination between normative proposals and claims about the world of the sort found in religious belief systems does not all by itself prejudice the issue of cultural self-criticism or self-validation. Everything depends on what one believes the world is like. A norm of self-criticism might be confirmed by the claims at issue. How can one know in advance that religious beliefs about what is the case rule out normative recommendations of critical reflection?

Finally, historical grounds for denying that religious systems have the resources to form rational traditions are just that—historical grounds, without the logical force to preclude such a possibility. Historical evidence can perhaps demonstrate that religious belief systems have never *yet* formed a rational tradition of reflection, but it cannot rule out such a possibility in the future or absolutely. In singling out religion for special opprobrium, historical arguments of this sort also overlook evidence of irreconcilable contests of opinion among purely politically motivated parties who produce reasoned defenses of their convictions. Indeed, post-Enlightenment forms of public discourse are commonly indicted for the same sort of impasse of which religion is accused.[45] Were one to decide the question on historical grounds alone, one might be able to conclude that religiously backed convictions are no worse off than any other sort. There is a dogmatic potential, at

45. See Alasdair MacIntyre, *After Virtue* (Notre Dame: Univ. of Notre Dame Press, 1981).

least, in appeals to reason and in purely political arguments, just as there is in religious conviction. While a religious authoritarianism that prevents the application of critical intelligence may be properly faulted for dogmatism, appeals to reason may be equally dogmatic. Such appeals may claim a spurious universality for reasonable notions and presume a commonality of criteria for determining what is or is not reasonable in ways that invalidate from the start the possible rationality of conclusions differing from one's own. If one assumes, despite historical confirmation of this sort of dogmatic potential, that reasoned reflection has the capacity to undercut dogmatism, why categorically deny the same of religious forms of justification? Why, more specifically, cannot religious beliefs support rather than deflect the exercise of critical intelligence?

One should not beg the question, therefore, of religion's association with customary cultures by overlooking the possible complexity of religious systems and the diversity of the historical evidence. Instead, one should try to determine the particular sort of religious belief that can be correlated with the features of customarily reproduced cultures discussed previously.

Able to be so correlated is a mythological sort of religious belief that concretely articulates a sacred cosmos or divine sphere so that nature and society are fused as homologous orders. Two aspects of mythological religious constructions are important here. First, a storied depiction of gods or sacred forces permits an overall structure of repetition linking the natural, the social, and the divine. Second, contemporary natural and social events are not merely correlated with such a storied world by way of symbolic representation, but enter within it as the actual reinstitution of events depicted.[46]

The ideology of stasis identified with customary cultures is one consequence. Continuity is understood in terms of repetition, reactualization, and return. People do now what totemic ancestors or heroes or divinities in alliance with cosmic forces did before. They do more than merely repeat the same sort of acts. They make those very

46. I am interested here in a type of religious belief that can be associated in an unambiguous way with the structural features of customary cultures described above. Of course, other forms of religious belief short of this have at least an obvious potential for such an association (e.g., the myriad forms of immanentism in Christian theism), but an argument of the sort I am making here for any one of them would be much more complicated and difficult.

acts present again in their own acts, or by so acting enter within an ahistorical cycle of eternally recurrent, exactly repeated "events."[47]

The reification and presumed inviolability of social constructions, which occur when the world-concepts of nature, society, and individual experience are not distinguishable, are another consequence. The natural, the social, and the sacred are fused in mythological religious constructions in so far as human actions (e.g., institutionalized or coordinated action systems of building, founding, healing, marrying, ruling) and the corresponding social roles are thought to embody a cosmic and sacred order. For example, kinship structures are not merely representative of human social organization. The whole of being—from animals to personalized gods—is organized in a structurally similar manner. Participation in a human institutional order *means* therefore participation in a sacred cosmos.[48] A particular institution like marriage may be a reenactment on a smaller scale of the union of heaven and earth that myth represents as the origin of a sacred cosmos.[49] Rites of building or founding may repeat those acts of the gods through which the world was constructed from the body of a sea dragon or giant. The first act of building may be, therefore, to drive a peg into the exact spot where "lies the serpent that supports the world." In this way the cosmogonic act by which a god "smote a serpent" is repeated.[50] Those with political power may simply *be* gods, or just participate as human beings in a sacred order to the extent that they literally reenact the gestures of the gods or mythological heroes.[51]

The human world is in this way embedded in a cosmic order that is itself sacred or that exists on a single plane of reality with gods or divine forces. In either case, human orders are grounded by way of participation in a transhuman realm so as to be spared, by definition, the contingency and variability of mere human constructions. Human orders are bound up with the very nature of things—a nature of things

47. See Mircea Eliade, *The Myth of the Eternal Return* (Princeton: Princeton Univ. Press, 1954).

48. Peter Berger, *The Sacred Canopy* (New York: Doubleday, 1969), 34.

49. See Eliade, *The Sacred and the Profane* (New York: Harcourt, Brace and World, 1959), 145–46, on the Upanishads.

50. Ibid., 52; idem, *Myth of the Eternal Return*, 19.

51. See Talcott Parsons, *The Evolution of Societies* (Englewood Cliffs, N.J.: Prentice-Hall, 1977), 54, on Egyptian kings.

that is, moreover, embued with the ultimacy and inviolability of sacrality. The way human beings do things is the way of the world; to deny the former is to deny the very being of the cosmos. The sacred character of such a cosmos bestows a further ultimacy of reality, value, and validity upon it and the human orders it comprehends. Consequently, the human order is taken for granted as an inevitable aspect of an atemporally repeated or eternally reproduced sacred order. From mythological constructions it derives an aura of overpowering permanence and stability. In other words, the mythological process of locating a social world within a cosmic and sacred frame promotes the reification of those social arrangements as nonhuman, potentially coercive, and unchangeable givens, for which human beings are not responsible and about which they can do nothing.

By reifying it, mythological religious constructions legitimate a social order. Because a structure of repetition blends a particular social arrangement with cosmic and sacred orders, a religious worldview in such a mythological mode can do nothing but support institutionalized social norms. The stories of the gods, heroes, and cosmic forces may supply paradigms for proper action on the part of human beings—human actions may fall out of, and therefore need to be brought back into line with, what is recounted there—but the concrete articulation of such a sacred cosmos allows for a one-to-one match between established social practices and these normative accounts. The participation scheme that links a microcosm of human events with the macrocosm of a sacred universe does not force any distance between ideal model and realized social fact.

Mythological religious constructions have no capacity to challenge the ultimate validity of the norms, values, and practices of the society they inform, since they do not establish any reference point for critique beyond such structures.[52] Particular forms of conduct may fail to meet the social standards for behavior that mimetically reinstantiate a sacred cosmos. Such conduct is indeed susceptible to religious critique. But this religious criticism will assume the overall validity of the group's social standards. It will criticize a particular act

52. Mythological religious constructions that undergird a particular ethos and form of social organization can obviously challenge the propriety of *another* society's practices and values. The reader should remember that the issue here is a culture's capacities for *self*-criticism.

with reference to the taken-for-granted normative system of the society whose overall order conforms to a sacred paradigm.

A human world of both socially acceptable beliefs and behaviors becomes uncriticizable, by religious means or otherwise, in the degree to which it is thought along mythological lines to be pervaded or suffused by divine or sacred forces. The social order also seems to be uncriticizable because mythological religious constructions block the distinction between spheres of social order and individual experience necessary if an individual is to withdraw from his or her place within established social conventions and institutional arrangements, and gain some critical leverage on them. The inexorability of the social world on a mythological worldview extends to the socialized identities of individuals within it. Social roles have the inviolable inevitability of cosmic facts and sacred realities. It would make no sense therefore to try to alter or rail against them. Moreover, the individual tends to a strong self-identification with social roles since one's socialized identity is not merely a social fact but a cosmic truth and a sacred trust.[53]

If this way of correlating mythological religious constructions with the features of customarily reproduced cultures makes sense, one would expect the general form of religion that plays a part in self-critical cultures to differ from the mythological sort in two important respects. First, one would expect the account of divinity or a sacred sphere to remain relatively unarticulated. At the extreme of what one might expect, no concrete story about the character of a divine or sacred realm is found. Without such a story, any structure of repetition linking the natural or social worlds with the sacred is precluded from the start. A divine order will not be able to mirror, therefore, any particular social arrangement or buttress thereby assumptions of the latter's self-evidence. Moreover, an ideology of stasis will be much harder to ground in such circumstances with reference to a sacred origin or atemporal paradigm.

Countering the construction of concrete stories about a divine or sacred realm is a second feature one would expect of religions that inform self-critical cultures: a belief in a nonparticipatory relation between divinity, on the one hand, and natural and social orders, on the other. In short, divinity is believed to be transcendent. No natural

53. Berger, *Sacred Canopy*, 37–38, 95.

force or human role can be identified as divine or sacred. Divinity is something "other." Natural forces and human beings have a distinct, specifically nondivine ontological status.

The terms that properly characterize human beings and natural forces should not therefore be applied to a divine or sacred realm. A gap in being between the divine and the this-worldly justifies a gap in expression. The ontological transcendence of divinity justifies its cognitive transcendence. At the minimum, concrete terms appropriate for the description of natural forces and human actions are devalued and, more often than not, replaced by less colorful, abstract characterizations. Talk of differentiated, multiple, or changing forms, which is appropriate language for discussing human beings or natural forces, is inappropriate for a transcendent God. Abstract terms (e.g., of unity and simplicity) are to be preferred to concrete stories if the divine is not what human beings and natural forces are. At the maximum, one might have a simple prohibition on expression. No language is appropriate since all language is human language designed for discussion of human beings that are not God. This second feature and the first one are closely connected in this way: divine transcendence is a reason why accounts of divinity remain relatively unarticulated.

A belief in God's transcendence does not absolutely prohibit talk about a divine or sacred realm in the terms used to discuss the natural and social worlds. It does prevent, however, their fusion as homologous orders. Thus, if divinity is understood in the categories of human relation, a belief in God's transcendence might block the seriousness with which the same terms are applied to both divine and human realms. Though used for both, the categories properly apply only to one. For example, if God is a king then no human being is; or, if kingship is a term that properly describes a form of human power, then God is not really a king in the ordinary sense. Either way, a concrete story about divine kingship need not valorize human orders of power as they stand.

Divine transcendence is therefore the crucial factor blocking a homologous fusion of social, cosmic, and sacred orders and this fusion's conservative social effects. A failure to articulate a sacred or divine order will prevent this fusion, but divine transcendence will also, whether or not, or in whatever manner, a story about divinity is told. I turn, then, to the exact way in which such a belief might figure in self-critical cultures as I have described them.

In all the ways I will mention, belief in divine transcendence is a force for distantiation and for distinction among social, natural, and personal worlds. First, natural and social orders become objects of reflection in themselves from a platform supplied by that belief. In other words, the cultural construction of a divinity that lies beyond them permits a view from a distance. Natural and social orders can be considered as wholes with respect to a divine reference point existing over and against them.

Second, this reflection upon natural and social orders potentially involves their criticism. Divine transcendence fosters a critical distance. Once evacuated of sacrality by the claim of divine transcendence, natural and social orders cannot claim an unquestionable inevitability. Because the transcendence of divinity desacralizes natural and social orders, neither has the prima facie ultimacy to block critical questioning.

Extant social organizations are not themselves sacred, and therefore inviolable, if the true locus of sacrality is a transcendent God. Nor are they bound tightly with any sacred cosmic order. Beliefs, social norms, and institutional arrangements may still be located within a cosmic framework so as to be taken for granted as natural givens. But that cosmic order itself no longer has any inevitability or ultimacy. The truly ultimate and supremely real confronts it in the form of a transcendent divinity or sacred realm. An ontological realm different from the cosmic order relativizes the cosmic order. The cosmos does not exhaust the real, nor can it claim to be even the highest form of reality.

A belief in divine transcendence generally fosters the structural features of self-critical cultures I have mentioned. First, the notion of divine transcendence makes possible a distinction between moral and natural orders so as to de-reify the former. If social orders are not part of a sacred cosmos, it is at least possible for one to see them as mere human constructions, the historical products of human working and not inexorable aspects of the nature of things. The notion of divine transcendence opens up in this way the possibility for a distinction between what is naturally given and what is socially required. The natural and the social are also likely to come uncoupled as a result of the fact that any relation of a nonparticipatory sort between social and divine realms can bypass the natural world. A nonparticipatory relation between social orders and divinity does not take place via a sacralized cosmos. Indeed, it need not take place via the cosmos at all. Relations of a nonparticipatory sort between the natural order and divinity, and between the social world and divinity, may proceed independently of each other.

Second, for a similar reason the notion of divine transcendence permits a distinction between a social world and a world of individual experience. The nonparticipatory relations that individuals might have with divinity are not forced to proceed by way of a sacralized social order. In other words, an individual need not gain a relation to divinity by virtue of the sacred or divine character of her or his own social identity. An assured, unquestioned self-identification with a social role gives way, because the individual has now a distinct, potentially quite different identity in relation to the divine.

Third, the notion of the divine or the sacred as a fundamentally transcendent locus of ultimate reality, truth, and value provides a paradigmatic center for distinctions between what is taken for real and what is genuinely so, between the purportedly true and the actually true, between socially valid norms and ideal values. This notion forces a generally applicable distinction between appearance and reality. If divinity is the locus of what is ultimately true or good, and the human cannot be identified with the divine, appeals to a transcendent God are a possible focus for criticizing rather than reinforcing what passes for right belief and action in a particular society. Religion supplies an alternative locus for the true and the good with which to undermine social canons of good sense and proper behavior. Socially entrenched beliefs, norms, or institutional arrangements need not be ultimately legitimate. The transcendence of divinity suggests that human notions and norms might be judged and found wanting, inadequate and in need of change. A divine or sacred realm exists whose ways need harmonize with neither human opinion nor social expectation.

Human understandings of the real, the true, and the good are also wanting to the extent they presume an ultimate validity for themselves. Because ultimate truth, value, and reality reside in a transcendent realm, pretensions to ultimate finality for human understandings of what is real, true, or good are destroyed. The notion of divine transcendence tends to compel in this way a recognition of (1) the limited and finite nature of human ideas, proposals, and norms; (2) their historical and socially circumscribed bases; and (3) their essentially fallible and defeasible character. The transcendence of God functions as a protest against all absolute and unconditioned claims.

Belief in a transcendent divinity might have the sort of constitutive and immanent use to which I have referred. Religious forms of culture can specify what a divine standard of truth, reality, and goodness is. That standard then becomes available for a religious critique of the norms and beliefs of a wider or foreign social order. Thus within the same society the values and affirmations of religious subgroups may run up against those of nonreligious ones. Conflict of this sort becomes possible when religious aspects of life are concentrated in distinct institutions with personnel and operations that are relatively independent of others—especially those of government and enforcement agencies. Without involving conflict between distinct social subgroups, religious beliefs may simply run contrary to what is taken for granted as good sense in the society from which a religion draws its membership. Conflict of this sort is most likely to happen when a religious worldview is a response to intellectual and social crisis within a socially established outlook, or among such outlooks. Cultural disintegration and intra- or intercultural contention prompt religious solutions to problems of meaning or suffering that go beyond the common sense and common values of the social groups concerned.

The critical potential of a belief in God's transcendence is arbitrarily restricted, however, when only nonreligious spheres fall under the awning of such critique. A religion maintaining a belief in a transcendent God is potentially critical of all human interpretations of reality, truth, and goodness, including religious ones. Indeed, complaints against religious claims are the most direct implication of a notion of divine transcendence as a critical principle. If divinity is transcendent, then descriptions of divinity are most obviously inadequate; descriptions of divinity are brought first and foremost under a relativizing knife. Religious claims are the first human claims that must be recognized to be conditioned, limited, and fallible. The kind of critique that a religion with a belief in divine transcendence directs against nonreligious values and affirmations is therefore properly self-referential. Belief in a transcendent God turns back against itself and forms thereby a self-critical cultural tradition.

THE AMBIGUITIES OF DIVINE TRANSCENDENCE

I have specified, then, an intrareligious resource for sociocultural critique—belief in divine transcendence. In forming the final conclusions in this chapter, I cannot overlook, however, the ambiguities of this resource. The notion of divine transcendence has a genuine but ambiguous potential for purposes of sociocultural critique. Whether the belief functions for purposes of sociocultural critique, whether it is drawn upon for such purposes, remains an open question for two general reasons.

First, the critical force of belief in divine transcendence is historically conditioned. Only certain historical circumstances favor the actualization of that belief's critical potentials. The social circumstance that social scientists term sociocultural differentiation is most propitious.

The simple existence of societies holding beliefs and values different from one's own is not enough to shake their taken-for-granted certainty. Several strategies for maintaining the sacrosanct character of one's own beliefs and practices are readily available in such circumstances. A society can take measures to exterminate those groups with which it disagrees; it can try to ignore them, discount their beliefs and practices as those of barbarians or social deviants, or explain their positions as simple errors from within its own taken-for-granted worldview. None of these strategies is possible, however, where differences of belief and practice are the result of an internally differentiated sociocultural order, where, that is, such differences do not occur between relatively isolated, independently operating groups, but are based upon differences in class affiliation, institutional membership, or occupation within a single, complex sociocultural order. The beliefs and practices of others cannot be discounted by attributing them to deviants or strangers, since the beliefs and practices at issue are maintained by productive members of one's own society. Exterminating groups of people with beliefs and values different from one's own becomes self-destructive when such groups constitute, along with one's own, the functionally interdependent subgroups of a single society. Ignorance via segregation or exile of offending parties is impractical for the same reason. Finally, claims of simple error, prejudice, or partiality become less plausible against subgroups of one's own society since such groups are often of similar prestige and commonly share or rotate their memberships.

By cutting off in these ways the usual strategies of response to differences in beliefs and practices, circumstances may open one to the suspicion that one's own beliefs and practices are wrong or improper. This suspicion affects one's religious views. The kind of religious fallibility that the notion of divine transcendence implies will therefore make sense in such circumstances. A general critique of socially established beliefs and norms on grounds supplied by a belief in divine transcendence will also find ready soil in this sort of social context. Because of sociocultural differentiation, such a society's beliefs and values are prone of themselves to a crisis of plausibility and legitimation.

Second, apart from any consideration of historical context, belief in divine transcendence has a number of ambiguities of its own. If we make the rather uncontroversial assumption that sociocultural differentiation is a feature of most modern societies in which Christianity is an influence, this second set of ambiguities becomes the more pressing focus for discussion in this book.[54] I need to adumbrate these further ambiguities with some care.

First, the fact that positing an ideal norm or truth allows human beings to claim it as their own renders the critical potential of a belief in divine transcendence ambiguous. The human tendency to pretend a universal, absolute, or unconditional character for one's own beliefs and values may be undercut by the notion of a transcendent locus of ultimate truth and goodness; but the presumed existence of such an ideal locus serves as a constant temptation for the same inclinations. Specifically religious forms of fanaticism or dogmatism may result. One claims to speak for or as divinity. Surreptitiously or otherwise, one fails to feel the critical force of a belief in divine transcendence when it comes to some particular sphere of human claim.

Second, the transcendence of divinity, especially if it is understood in terms of distance or absence vis-à-vis the human order, can undercut its own critical potential for sociocultural critique by suggesting that the norms and truths that divinity represents are irrelevant

54. For a discussion of the contemporary U.S. context as one of sociocultural differentiation, see ibid., chaps. 5–7.

to human concerns. If divinity is transcendent, divinity has its own truths and norms; humans have theirs. The transcendence of divinity leaves the human order alone in that case to abide by its own standards of what is true and good; the norms or standards applicable to human concerns are specifically human ones and not divine. While the ideal truths and values of a divine sphere are clearly different from what passes for true or right in the social world, they lose in this way any critical leverage over that world.

This is an irrelevance of complacency in the human, which presumes a fairly positive evaluation of human spheres on their own terms. An irrelevance with more negative grounds is also possible, however. Human orders may be so completely devalued, in comparison with the transcendent ideals of truth and goodness that God represents, that applying divine standards to such orders is more hopeless than ungermane. Divine standards are pointless in a world that has fallen so far. This is an irrelevance of despair in the human.

Indeed, the more radical the transcendence of divine norms or standards vis-à-vis human orders, the more likely is despair over whether such standards can do human orders any good. The critical potential that is gained for a belief in divine transcendence on one front seems ironically in this way to be lost on another. The greater the distance between human truths and values and divine ones, the greater the critical potential of an appeal to a divine standard: a more extensive revision of human beliefs and values would be necessary to bring the human into line with the divine. The greater the distance, however, the harder it is to see how divine standards might apply to human circumstances, the harder it is to perceive the means with which the social world could be altered to conform to those standards—in sum, the more likely a belief in the irrelevance of divine standards for human society out of despair over the possibility of ever implementing them there.

Third, belief in the transcendence of divinity might renege on its critical potential by feeding into standard skeptical arguments for abiding by convention.[55] If the transcendence of divinity means that no one can claim to know what is right or true with any confidence,

55. See Richard Popkin, *The History of Skepticism* (Berkeley: Univ. of California Press, 1979); Terence Penelhum, *God and Skepticism* (Dordrecht: D. Reidel, 1983); Pocock, *Politics, Language and Time*.

then it might be best simply to conform to the customs and traditions of belief of one's social group. The transcendence of divinity would in this way support a skeptical equipoise of arguments pro and con a particular ethos or worldview, leaving one holding the same beliefs and values but nondogmatically, without any assurance of their probity. Since one cannot know what truth, goodness, or reality look like to God, one is forced to make do with how they appear to one. Skepticism about human capacities to know the true and the good, skepticism brought on by belief in divine transcendence, would prohibit in such circumstances any serious explication of divine ideals or standards for critique. No account of divine truths or norms could be proposed for use in criticizing socially entrenched beliefs and values.

Assimilating the results of a belief in God's transcendence to the effects of classical skeptical arguments in this way is probably inappropriate, however. The claim of divine transcendence is not reducible to a simple agnosticism concerning the reliability of all human claims; it is the assertion of their imperfection and susceptibility to critique, vis-à-vis a realm of ultimate truth and goodness that exists whether human beings can articulate it or not. The claim of divine transcendence does not leave one, therefore, with a simple equipoise of arguments pro and con human conventions, but with a positive knowledge of their fallible, correctible character. Criticism of human conventions is therefore not a matter of illegitimate arrogance or dogmatism, as it is for classical skepticism. Judgment of, and possible dissatisfaction with, those conventions is just what an appeal to a transcendent divine locus of truth or goodness requires.[56]

But what sort of appeal to a transcendent locus of truth and goodness is available for purposes of critique? Do not the skeptical consequences of belief in divine transcendence prohibit, as has just been charged, any commitment to a particular concrete explication of divine standards for such purposes?

Even if that were the case, it is not clear that critical reflection and revision of human conventions require such a commitment. Like the regulative use of an appeal to reality or truth or goodness per se, a regulative use of a belief in divine transcendence can propel the hard task of arguments pro and con between ultimately provisional human

56. See Penelhum, *God and Skepticism*, 34.

claims without any specification of what truth, reality, or goodness look like from God's point of view. It is that sort of argument—one among provisional human claims—that should be directed against human convention. An account of a divine truth or goodness can indeed be proffered, but it must enter within such arguments as one human and therefore fallible account of truth or goodness in competition with others.

One might suggest, however, that under such conditions arguments will remain without direction. Where should one start, how should one proceed, without the material guidance of some privileged account of a divine standard of truth and goodness? Without some clear sense of direction, criticism of human conventions cannot get off the ground, even if one believes such criticism is appropriate. Another sort of despair of irrelevance sets in: a despair over the point of argument if no clear indications of divine standards exist.

At the end of the description of the structural features of a self-critical culture, I did try to show how a regulative use of an appeal to the true and the good could provide a general direction for such arguments. I have not developed that claim, however, for belief in God's transcendence and worries might remain in any case.

In fact, none of these ambiguities and worries regarding the critical potential of a belief in God's transcendence is resolvable without attention to a particular religion. To resolve them, one would need more information about what divine transcendence implies, and one would need to know about the rest of the religious beliefs with which a belief in divine transcendence is conjoined. In the next chapter, therefore, I turn to a belief in God's transcendence as a possible resource for sociocultural critique within a specifically Christian religious context. The additional Christian beliefs under consideration are limited, as suggested in the first chapter, to basic ones concerning God's relation to the world as creator, governor, and redeemer. By specifying the meaning of divine transcendence and considering these other beliefs, I try to determine whether and to what extent the critical potential of a belief in divine transcendence may be realized in Christianity.

THREE
Sociopolitical Critique and Christian Belief

IN THIS CHAPTER I examine resources for sociopolitical critique that may be found in Christian beliefs about God's nature and relation to the world. To begin with, are there such resources? Do these Christian beliefs suggest that social relations can be assessed critically through the use of human intelligence? Were they to do so, one would expect them to conform to the type of religious belief associated with self-critical cultures in the previous chapter. Christian beliefs about God and God's relation to the world should avoid articulation of a divine realm to match human social orders and any claim of a participatory relation between God and creatures that might support such a match.

I admit at the outset that Christian accounts of God and God's relation to the human order do not always correspond to this sort of religious belief. Eusebius's "Oration in Praise of the Emperor Constantine" (335 C.E.) is a good case in point. According to this apologist for a Christian empire, there is a clear story to tell about a divine realm and it mirrors Constantine's relations with his subordinates. "Ministers of heavenly hosts," "armies of supernal powers," and "countless multitudes of angels" bask in the glory of the divine commander to whom they owe allegiance, just as the retainers and subjects of Constantine bask in the glory of his human imperial rule.[1] Following a microcosm-macrocosm scheme of reiteration, Constantine "directs his gaze above,

1. "Oration in Praise of the Emperor Constantine," trans. E. Richardson, in *Nicene and Post-Nicene Fathers*, ed. Philip Schaff and Henry Wace (New York: Christian Literature Co., 1890), vol. 1, chap. 1.

and frames his earthly government, according to the pattern of that divine original, feeling strength in its conformity to the monarchy of God."[2] These microcosm-macrocosm relations appear to be relations of participation. They are justified by a claim that Constantine shares the status of divinity in the planning, and perhaps the execution, of his own government. Thus, according to Eusebius, Constantine possesses divine as well as human knowledge. He shares in the glory of the Word in the same way that the Word shares in the glory of the Godhead and is therefore gifted with a "divine faculty" that brings a sacred wisdom.[3] For an understanding of proper human relations, therefore, Constantine is as good as God. This sort of participatory relation between a human emperor and God, via a divine reason or Word of God, legitimates a whole host of human-divine reiterations. It makes an imperial form of rule, in all its aspects, sacrosanct.

A certain strand of the Christian tradition, however, affirms quite strongly the transcendence of God, which is the crucial counter to a microcosm-macrocosm relation between sacred and social realms. Agnostic or apophatic trends in Christian theology, in which doubts are expressed about the adequacy of human language for talk about divinity, block or undercut the significance of any account of divinity that might match up with socially established relations among human beings. Prohibitions against idolatry stress the ontological nonidentity of God and things or persons of this world. Divinity is not the natural and social world, because of the inherent limitation, finitude, or dependence of that world, on the one hand, and because of its corruption or defect, on the other. The primary reason for not identifying God and the world is the latter's created nature, its ontological status distinct from God's and suitable for limited, dependent beings. A secondary reason for a distance between God and the world is the corruption of its proper character or right relation to God as a result of sin or the fall.

If one can assume that Christianity contains a resource for the critique of social and cultural orders in virtue of such a belief in God's transcendence, a further question, raised at the end of the last chapter, concerns the ambiguous potential of that resource. Will the critical

2. Ibid., chap. 3, section 5.
3. Ibid., prologue, sections 2 and 3. See chap. 3, section 8.

potential of a belief in divine transcendence be blocked in Christianity by an identification of human constructions with divine standards or by the sense that such standards are irrelevant?

The meaning of a Christian account of divine transcendence does something of itself to counter the sort of irrelevance of divine norms or truths that presumes complacency with the self-enclosed standards of a human order. God's transcendence would suggest that sort of irrelevance for the standards of truth and goodness that God represents if it were understood in terms of an absence or isolation of God from the world. Such a construal is ruled out, however, in the Christian tradition by affirmations that God is intimately related to the world as its creator, providential guide, and redeemer. A strictly oppositional account of God's transcendence—God is simply not what the creature is—might also suggest that sort of irrelevance. But again, such a construal of God's transcendence is blocked by beliefs regarding God as creator. Developing a notion of God's transcendence by way of a simple opposition to the characteristics of nature and human society would hamper belief in God's intimate relations with them, and is accordingly improper. Without such an oppositional characterization of God's transcendence, it becomes possible to imagine that, while they are not *of* the world because of God's transcendence, the goodness and truth that God represents are nevertheless *relevant* to it.[4]

Christian beliefs about God as creator stand behind, then, those accounts of divine transcendence that prevent divine standards from appearing irrelevant to this world. The created world is intimately bound up with divinity as the one upon whom it depends for its existence, character, order, and redemption. Therefore, God—and the truth, reality, and goodness that God represents—have to have something to do with the world. The world is brought under a divine standard of truth and goodness as God's creation, as the site of God's working. The world should therefore bear the marks of that standard; it should show itself to be oriented to them.

In other ways, however, beliefs about God's creative relation with the world can undercut the critical potential of a belief in God's

4. See my *God and Creation in Christian Theology: Tyranny or Empowerment?* (Oxford: Basil Blackwell, 1988), chap. 2, for an account of the logical relations between affirmations that God is creator and affirmations that God is transcendent, and for an account of how divine transcendence might be characterized in a nonoppositional way.

transcendence. They do so when they suggest that somehow or somewhere human standards of truth and goodness are to be identified with those of divinity. A simple identification of God and creatures or of divine and human orders in microcosm-macrocosm fashion is unlikely since either would obviously conflict with the belief in God's transcendence assumed here. But an identification of divine standards for truth and goodness with human notions of them can nevertheless be reintroduced by other means (which I will specify). When that happens beliefs about God's creative relations with the world confirm a second worrisome potential of a belief in a transcendent God mentioned at the end of the previous chapter. Seduced by the confident presumption that those standards at least exist, one is tempted, despite God's transcendence, to identify one's own account of truth and goodness with the standards for them that God represents. With such an identification come obvious restraints on the use of critical intelligence to assess human notions of truth and goodness.

Belief in God the creator does not have to have such results, however. The general idea of God as the creator of the world exhibits, in fact, an ambiguous import. One way of understanding belief in God the creator (which I will specify) clearly confirms the critical potential of a belief in God's transcendence. When understood in that way, belief in God the creator is itself a resource for sociopolitical critique. Furthermore, a variety of more specific beliefs about God's creative relations with the world are found in the Christian tradition, and these differ in their respective capacities to support or undercut the critical potential of a belief in God's transcendence.

In the first section of this chapter I discuss this ambiguous potential of Christian belief about God the creator, tackling the belief in its most general form first, and then in a variety of more specific versions: an orders-of-creation view of God's relation to the human world; claims for a divine mandate of social norms or a direct divine commission of social roles; and finally an account of God's all-encompassing providential agency as the creative underpinning of human action. The last is the account of God's relation with the world that is most readily conformable to a belief in God's transcendence as a resource of sociopolitical critique. That is, an account of God's universal providential agency most effectively prevents identification of a divine truth or goodness with human notions of truth and goodness, while fostering the exercise of critical intelligence in determining what is proper for human beings to believe and do.

Besides Christian accounts of God's relation with the world and the meaning of God's transcendence, another doctrinal resource exists for blocking the sort of irrelevance of divine standards of truth and goodness that is bound up with complacency in the human: Christian accounts of sin, mentioned previously as a secondary reason for belief in God's transcendence. These accounts are the focus of the second major section of the chapter.

As a reason for belief in God's transcendence, Christian accounts of sin have the clear capacity to confirm the critical potential of that belief. Indeed, they enhance it in a way that thwarts any irrelevance rooted in complacency. If the world is in sin, it is not just an imperfect place compared to a divine standard, compared to the truth and goodness that are God's and perhaps properly God's alone. There is something profoundly *wrong* with the human world. Besides any failure to manifest the truth and goodness that might be properly God's alone, the human world, because of the existence of sin, does not meet divine standards for even a human order. One ought not say, therefore, that, given the transcendence of God, the human world *could* be critically assessed and challenged, thereby leaving open the question whether it *needs* to be. The human world should be challenged as an order infiltrated by sin. One cannot remain complacent about the world in which one lives.

Notions of sin have their own dangers, however, that might stand in the way of realizing the critical potential of a belief in God's transcendence. Unlike accounts of God's relation with the world, notions of sin do not suggest of themselves any identification of divine and human standards. (Though they can be corrupted, as can the notion of God's transcendence generally, by accounts of God's relation with the world that make such identifications.) Instead, notions of sin risk an irrelevance of despair—the second type of irrelevance mentioned at the end of the previous chapter. In a world of sin there might seem no point in availing oneself of the resources for criticism that a notion of divine transcendence presents, or no way to do so effectively. In the section where I discuss Christian notions of sin, I therefore have to specify ones that counter such despair. Only in that way can I hope to succeed in showing that potentials for sociocultural critique are realized in Christianity.

In the final section of this chapter I continue this discussion of possible reasons for despair by addressing the question of a skeptical malaise brought on by the very account of God's relation to the world that I favor—an account of God's universal providential agency. If human ideas of God's providential intentions can never be equated with God's own, how can human beings ever hope to be effective agents of God's purposes? In this way I address the last more general worry about realizing the critical potential of a belief in God's transcendence that I raised at the end of the previous chapter: the problem of aimless or directionless critique. The inability to bracket this worry entirely marks a transition to the next chapter.

THE DOCTRINE OF CREATION AND SOCIOPOLITICAL CRITIQUE

When understood most generally, a Christian belief in creation confirms the critical potential of a notion of divine transcendence by relativizing the status of natural and social worlds. First, neither the natural nor the social world is absolutely good in itself; each gains its value in virtue of a relation to the God upon whom it depends for all that it is, and to that God's creative intentions with respect to it. Second, the natural and social worlds are not simply there to be accepted as inexorable and unconditioned givens; they are viewed instead as the products or works of God. As the products of a free God, moreover, natural and social spheres must be recognized as contingent rather than inevitable developments: God does not have to create any world at all or the world as it happens to exist. Because the world continues to depend for its existence on the intentions of a free God, natural and social worlds should be seen as alterable—at least by God. Indeed, if God's intentions extend in that direction, natural and social spheres may even suffer such change by way of critical assessment and action by human beings.

The created status of natural and social worlds can also, however, undercut the critical leverage of divine transcendence. The validation of what exists is a consequence of the doctrine of creation: whatever is, is valuable. Creatures may not have value *apart* from their relation to God—they are not anything, after all, independently of God's creative will for them—but in *relation* to God they are indeed valuable. What exists owes its existence to God, and God and God's will for the world are good. The mere existence of something becomes grounds therefore for assuming its value. Drawing out the apparent implications of this point, one could conclude: The facts of this world have God's sanctity transferred to them as the direct manifestations of God's creative intentions; they are not, therefore, appropriate objects of critical assessment or challenge.

Such conclusions are incorrect, however, for a number of reasons. First, a sanctification of what is, on the grounds offered, is in outright conflict with the transcendence of God. Sanctification of what is, on these grounds, becomes a form of idolatry. Second, the assumption here that God's intentions are directly manifest in the world is fallacious: it ignores the possibility of sin emerging from a distinct created order of existence and the Christian claims of its actual pervasiveness. Given the possibility of sin, determining whether an existing state of affairs matches God's own intention for the world is a difficult matter for human judgment. Such a match cannot be presumed from the mere fact that something exists. Finally, even if existing states of affairs are part of God's creative will for the world and therefore valuable, it is improper to infer their sanctity from that fact in any way that would exclude principled proposals for alterations to them. Even if what a good God intends for the world is valuable, what God intends may include a changing and perhaps humanly alterable course of events. To assume to the contrary that alteration of what is cannot be part of the world God brings to be is either to deny God's freedom vis-à-vis God's creation—that is, God's freedom to bring about something different from what already exists—or to confuse the inviolability and immutability traditionally affirmed of God with the character of the created world.

Orders of Creation

In the first, more specific type of Christian account of God's relation to creation, the use of the doctrine of creation to sanctify what is extends directly to relations among human persons, to their socially institutionalized arrangements, for a directly conservative social effect.

God creates not merely the natural world and human beings but also the extant order or relations among them whereby differentials in power and function have been established. As the direct manifestations of God's creative will, existing social orders are not historical matters of human working, to be set up and perhaps taken down by human effort. Conventional differences are instead deemed natural in so far as they are a part of an order of creation (a *Schöpfungsordnung*); they are as fixed and ineluctable as any feature of the world God creates. In apologizing for German nationalism in the first half of the twentieth century, Emanuel Hirsch, the famous Nazi sympathizer, could therefore say, "The people, the race, is a creation of God. God wishes mankind to live in the division of nations."[5]

In this way appeals to God's creative will produce a confusion of natural and human orders that I identified as a structural feature of customary cultures. Social relations are assimilated to natural facts. They are simply part of the way the world works. They are therefore not the sort of things one should think about changing.

The existence of a standard outside socially established ones—the other structural feature of deliberative cultures besides the dissociation of natural and social spheres—is also blocked on an orders-of-creation outlook. A divine standard for human life no longer has a platform outside established human orders; it is to be equated with them. The family, the nation, the relations among feudal "estates," must incorporate and encapsulate the standards God establishes for human life as the purportedly direct manifestation of God's creative will for human life. De facto norms become in that way de jure norms. Whether or not they are the sort of things one can think about altering, it is simply improper to challenge them.

Given these parallels with the structural features of customary cultures, it is not surprising that an orders-of-creation outlook hampers the use of critical intelligence in assessing the validity of particular social arrangements. If the shapes that human relations take are the direct creations of God, then the mere fact of an institutionalized order, the mere fact that a particular form of social relation has become established over time and taken for granted, suffices to justify a claim

5. Hirsch, *Das Kirchliche Willen der Deutschen Christen*, quoted by Reinhold Niebuhr, *An Interpretation of Christian Ethics* (New York: Seabury Press, 1979), 92.

for its immutable validity. If a social order works, if present social arrangements have proven their stability by functioning effectively to maintain order, there are no further critical questions to ask of it. At best, the present functioning of a stable social order sets narrow limits on the critical questions that it is appropriate to ask of the elements that make it up. Whether certain forms of social relation are necessary for social order as it presently exists (whether, e.g., obedience on the part of wives is necessary within a generally patriarchal social order) is the only critical question an orders-of-creation view authorizes one to pose.

The theological arguments that support inferences like these are fallacious, however, along the lines already discussed for a socially conservative use of the doctrine of creation in general. From the premise that a good God creates the world, an orders-of-creation viewpoint argues that any established social order must be part of God's creative will for the world and therefore good. This argument ignores the potentially sinful character of human intervention in a socially established order. In order to block the possibility that human failings vitiate present social arrangements, an orders-of-creation outlook tries to insulate those arrangements on some basic level from human efficacy generally; it is part of such a position to use the notion of God's creation of social orders to deny their historical character as products of human working. This denial is improbable to any modern person who recognizes the way human relations are socially constructed; it conflicts with modern historicist sensibilities. But such a denial is also theologically problematic for a number of reasons.

This denial overlooks the fact that on Christian principles God's creative will for human society may be a creative will for the human interactions that set it up and alter it over time.[6] There is indeed no reason generally to restrict what God creates to the static, to the inert and the constant, as socially conservative orders-of-creation theologians are prone to do. If such a restriction is behind their denial of human initiative in the construction of social orders, then such an argument is unsound. Assuming that social orders are fixed, and therefore not the potentially alterable products of human working if they

6. See my *God and Creation*, chap. 3, for this sort of account of the relation between God's creative will and human working.

are created by God, violates either God's freedom vis-à-vis creation, by denying the contingent character of a social order God creates, or God's transcendence, by insisting upon the immutability of any social order created by an immutable God.

Finally, denying that social orders are the products of human working because they are created by God becomes question begging in any situation where it is recognized that social orders have in fact been changed by human initiative. Since the newly set up social order is the product of human working it cannot be the social order God creates, but a transgression of it, a sinful social order—that is what a socially conservative orders-of-creation theologian would argue. Any new and radical alteration of a previous order is criticized simply because it is new or different. If, however, the constancy of a social order is the only grounds on an orders-of-creation outlook for calling one form of social relation rather than another an order of creation, then nothing can stop someone from arguing that the fact of change disqualifies the old order. After the new social order has been established, solidified over time, it can also claim to be called an order of creation. Claims for the old order are especially hard-pressed where one can argue that it, too, like the new order, came into being in some not-too-distant past as the result of human action.

Tactics in argument of this sort can set off a futile search for an original social past: newness is merely reinstitution of an original social arrangement created by God. In times of rapid social change, arguments back and forth like this become tragicomic: the Nazi state *restores* the social orders of creation lost in the days of the Weimar Republic and is therefore to be applauded; the Nazi state *violates* the orders of creation of an aristocracy-dominated Old Prussia and is therefore to be condemned.[7]

7. Paul Althaus, for one, came close to the first position; Bonhoeffer, to the second. For a discussion of the general dynamic, see Robin Lovin, *Christian Faith and Public Choices* (Philadelphia: Fortress Press, 1984), chaps. 3 and 6. Unfortunately, from a post-World War II standpoint, no German theologian proposed that the social freedoms and the institutionalized avenues for dissent found in a democratic Weimar Germany were orders of creation—they were not "ordered" enough apparently. Orders-of-creation theologians tend to favor authoritarian forms of social relation, ones in which lines of authority are sharp and fixed and unconfused. Social relations of that sort tend to be stable at least, and therefore seem, for an orders-of-creations point of view, to be the appropriate products of God's own creative intentions. Orders-of-creation theologians stop short at totalitarian states (like Nazi Germany) because that form of state organization usurps other authoritarian orders of creation—for example, aristocratics no longer have clear authority over commoners, or husbands over their wives in such states.

The question of an orders-of-creation viewpoint never asks during all this disputation is whether any of these social orders supposedly created by God is any good. Inconclusive efforts to determine whether a social order was established by God or by human beings take the place of substantive arguments over a social order's morality or immorality, justice or injustice. By propelling argument away from such substantive issues, an orders-of-creation position bankrupts the exercise of critical intelligence.

Natural Law

The natural law tradition in Christian theology represents another sort of account of God's relation to creation that can be used to skirt the critical force of a notion of God's transcendence, although it has a greater critical potential than an orders-of-creation viewpoint. In a natural law tradition, instead of being viewed as the direct creation of God, legitimate social orders are considered to be human constructions following what the essential created natures of human beings dictate about the proper ends of human life. In the classic Thomistic version, the law for proper human behaviors, which actual social orders are to follow, is grounded in the created capacities and inclinations of human beings for certain ends or goods of a natural or supernatural sort.[8]

Such a notion of natural law has clear critical potentials; like the notion of divine transcendence it fosters certain forms of critical reflection upon social constructions. The formation of norms for human behavior on a natural-law basis requires the exercise of critical intelligence. Right relations among persons are not simply to be read off directly from the extant relations of a social order, as is the tendency in an orders-of-creation theology. A natural law must be derived from, or be at least justifiable by, reflection upon essential capacities or structures of human beings. Natural law insists, therefore, upon a rationally explicable and defensible normative code.

8. Even more so than for the other types of position I examine, there is an enormous variation in natural law theories—within Roman Catholicism itself, let alone between Roman Catholic and Protestant theologies. In the interest of clear types of positions, I assume a classical Thomist version here, with only incidental reference to the more "historicist" forms of natural law theory in contemporary Roman Catholic theology. That is, I am not including as a feature of this type any idea that the human nature on which natural law is based is itself essentially variable or a product of historical development.

Critical intelligence not only establishes the character of natural law; it is also exercised when determining the propriety of institutionalized relations among persons in a particular society. The created natures of human beings and the goods appropriate to them provide a resource for criticism of socially valid norms and established social orders. If social orders frustrate the achievement of the ends for which human beings are created, they are to be condemned. The positive laws that human beings construct for themselves must be assessed, judged to be proper or not, in the light of their compatibility with laws appropriate for the essential created character of human persons.

The norms used for such assessment are accessible to all human beings using their natural rational capacities. Every human being, whatever her or his social standing or institutionalized role, is in basically the same position to judge whether extant social relations conform to a natural law. What is right is therefore not fundamentally a matter of social judgment, of judgment according to socially entrenched norms or norms maintained by the politically and socially powerful. Every individual is given a mandate to break free from such socially constrained judgments of right and wrong.

In sum, for natural law theory a de facto norm—what is considered proper behavior in a particular place and time—is not necessarily a de jure norm—what is genuinely right. A standard for assessment exists outside the changing happenstances of human life and judgment. That standard is ultimately God's law, the eternal law, the orders for human life that God had "in mind" in creating human beings. What God intends for human life is not identified with extant social orders; it is not located or incorporated there, as in an orders-of-creation view. Between what God intends and human society as it exists lie the God-given natures of human beings and the efforts of human beings to set up habitual or institutionalized relations among persons on such a natural basis. Because it is conveyed by these intermediaries, God's law for human life is genuinely beyond society as it exists. Because God's law is beyond human society, the sanctity of God's law is not immediately transferred to socially established norms. Socially established norms are instead criticizable.

Human sociopolitical relations are recognized to be conventional. They are not natural givens of the world that God creates, as in an orders-of-creation theology. Indeed, they are not set up by God in any way that would bypass human working. Because human effort and decision have established human society, any extant order is contingent and therefore alterable by further human efforts.

These critical potentials are dampened, nevertheless, by a natural law theory in the following ways. The distinction just mentioned between the conventional and the natural, between norms for human society and the facts of the natural world, does not go all the way down according to a natural law theory; that is, the distinction is not applied at every level of the law. Extant human laws are not the direct creation of God; human beings are actively involved in constructing the laws of their society and therefore these laws are contingent. All this is taken back, however, when it comes to the natural law itself. Natural and social orders are not uncoupled: a law for human society is written into the very nature of things, according to the very definition of a natural law.

To the extent that human orders participate in the natural law, the distinction between natural and social orders, and the latter's contingency, are taken back for them too. Human orders may not be part of the natural world God creates, but, if they are proper orders according to a natural law, they are nonetheless embedded in it as the human relations that the essential character of human being demands. To the extent that human orders conform to a natural law, they are therefore unalterable; human orders are alterable only where they are not based simply upon natural law, upon the essential character of human nature.

The critical potentials of a natural law theory are taken back in a second way. Although God's law for human life is located beyond de facto laws, God's law is not located beyond the God-given natures of human beings, which are the basis for natural law. The natural law simply is the law that God intends human beings to follow since it is the law written into the very nature of things that God creates. God brings human beings to be according to the plan for human life that God formulates in God's wisdom, that is, according to God's eternal law. That eternal law is therefore directly manifest in the essential structures of human being that God brings about. The law for human life written into the very nature of human beings, the natural law, is the immediate expression of God's own law. It participates in God's law; it encapsulates it. For all intents and purposes, it stands in place of it.

The attributes of God's own law for human life are consequently transferred to the essential structures of human being and the natural law grounded in them. If God's law is directly expressed in human nature and natural law, the latter are immutable and unconditioned, indissoluble and absolute. In short, they are themselves divine.[9] So are the practices of human society to the extent that they participate in natural law. If the laws of human society express the requirements of essential human nature, if they express a natural law, they are to that extent immune from challenge. In this way the critical potential of an appeal to a divine law beyond the human is undercut. A natural law theory fails to follow through on an idea of God's transcendence just as it fails to follow through on a distinction between the conventional and the natural. An exception is made for natural law itself and thereby for positive law (i.e., the laws that human beings posit or construct) in so far as they are proper human laws according to the standard that natural law poses.

This failure to follow through on God's transcendence has its effects, too, on the critical reflection that goes into formulating the natural law and evaluating positive law on its basis. Critical reflection has the tendency to end when a decision is reached. The absolute, unconditional character of natural law is inclined to infiltrate judgments concerning it. Identifying one's conclusions about what is humanly fulfilling with a natural law acts as an obstacle to further challenge and criticism. What is added to any judgment that a positive law is fulfilling for human beings is the claim that things simply have to be this way given the way human beings are constructed. The character of what one seeks—an unconditional law for human affairs—tends to override in this way an awareness of the tentative, merely human processes used to reach it. This is especially so since, according to natural law theory, correct judgments on this score are not supposed to be very difficult to make: correct judgment is the matter-of-course result of following the natural inclinations of human reason.

Natural law theory has the admirable intention of blocking human temptations to make what is right be whatever human beings might make of it. There is a divine law for human affairs, so natural

9. See, for example, Josef Fuchs, *Natural Law* (New York: Sheed and Ward, 1965), 8–10, 60–65, 124.

law theory declares, that remains absolute and unchallengeable whatever human beings might think, whatever human beings might do. In order to make such a point, however, natural law theory takes the unfortunate route of identifying God's will for human life with the natural inclinations and structures of human being and the social relations they appear to demand. Those inclinations and structures seem appropriate objects for such an identification, given a desire to distinguish God's will from human whim, since, as natural, they are not the sort of things that human beings can do anything about. If people are honest with themselves, they must recognize the demands that such features of human life pose and conform their formulations of human law to them.

Such an identification is unfortunate for several reasons. First, it pushes natural law theory either to ignore or to run roughshod over the contingencies of human life. If God's will for human life is absolute and immutable, the inclinations and structures of human beings that are the basis of natural law must be absolute and immutable, too. Human nature at its roots, and therefore the essentially satisfying ends of human life, must be the same in all times and places, even if they do not appear to be so. Natural law theory in this way forces judgments of universality even when careful attention to the facts of human history might suggest such judgments are spurious. Moreover, natural law and the positive laws that participate in it must be protected from the contingencies of human life, immunized from alteration by them. Once one identifies natural law with certain positive laws, one can simply refuse to admit that the contingencies of human life have any effect on them. In this way absolute claims are made for contingent and historically variable facts of human life. Thus Thomas Aquinas's own natural law theory ends up sanctifying the contingent particularities of thirteenth-century feudalism. If positive laws seem unmistakably influenced by historically circumscribed concerns, they can simply be isolated from a natural law's jurisdiction. Positive laws of that sort are nothing but human constructions, operating independently of nature or divine law, according to their own criteria and modes of procedure appropriate for a merely mundane set of concerns.[10]

10. See Quentin Skinner, *Foundations of Modern Political Thought*, 2 vols. (Cambridge: Cambridge Univ. Press, 1978), 2:154–61, for development of the Roman Catholic natural law tradition in these directions.

Second, such an identification is unfortunate because it fosters presumptive constraints on human fulfillment. Natural inclinations and capacities that could enable any number of forms of human development are instead viewed as necessitating only certain ones. Were natural inclinations and capacities not restrictive in that way, the coerciveness of an external divine law would be threatened. Natural law theorists often work actively, therefore, to alter the appearance of latitude in the development of natural capacities or inclinations.

Finally, such an identification is unfortunate because it turns against any fundamental intent in natural law theory to maintain the sovereignty of God's eternal law. While God's law for human life could be manifest in the form of an immutable human nature, God's law does not have to manifest itself in that form, as a natural law theory assumes, in order to be itself immutable. God's plan for human life might be more appropriately realized in human beings whose essential natures develop over time, possibly through their own exertions. If God's plan for human life were of that sort, and God, as the sovereign creator of all, brings about a world of changing human capacities to match it, then God's plan is still as immutable as any natural law theory could wish. Such changes do not *alter* God's plan; they *conform* to it.

There is no reason, moreover, to restrict God's plans to what even a changing human nature is capable of achieving. To assume that God's plans for human life must be manifest in natural human capacities is to restrict arbitrarily the way in which God's will for human life can show itself and the directions it can take. Natural law theory imposes such restrictions when it insists that God's redemptive plans for human life fit within the teleology of the human natures God creates, when it insists that God's will as redeemer respect the achievements of God's will as creator, building upon those achievements in some way rather than contravening them. Such continuity in God's plans for human life might turn out in fact to be the case. If the same God is at work in all aspects of human life, the expectation of such continuity is in order. To presume such continuity, to demand it of God in the name of human nature, however, seems clearly to be a misplaced respect: respect for human nature takes the place of respect for God and God's free will.

God's Mandate of a Normative Order

The next Christian account of God's relation to the world identifies what God wants for human life with a divine mandate or command of particular courses of human action. Such mandates or commands are usually brought back ultimately to the Bible, to the ethical teachings or moral codes found there, although the specifics of those mandates or commands may vary with the circumstances and not be deducible per se from general biblical principles.[11] Whatever their exact provenance, divine commands are the simple reflection, without metaphysical or natural underpinnings, of God's will for human life.

When human norms are based upon a divine mandate or command, they therefore have an immediate relation to God's will. The relation of a human normative order to the divine will bypasses the created order altogether. A fissure opens up between the categories of the normative and the natural, with the potential to confirm the critical force of a notion of divine transcendence beyond what is possible according to an orders-of-creation or natural law viewpoint.

Norms based on a divine mandate break the embedding of human codes in a natural created order (natural law) or their identification with it (orders of creation). Human codes simply are not part of the very nature of things. Consequently, proper human comportment does not have the fixity of the natural world. The way the natural world works does not stand in the way of the alteration of human codes. For example, the inviolability of a normative code cannot be assumed from the fact that the basic structures and inclinations of human persons apparently remain the same. According to a divine mandate perspective, God can issue a new command for human affairs without requiring the world to be turned topsy-turvy, without requiring the basic structures and inclinations of human nature to be altered. A change in normative codes would certainly seem, therefore, to be an easier proposition according to a divine mandate theory than according to a natural law one.

In another way, however, the immediacy of the relation between human norms and divine mandates undercuts the critical potential of

11. See James Gustafson, *Can Ethics Be Christian?* (Chicago: Univ. of Chicago Press, 1975), 148–68, for a discussion of this diversity of opinion about whether divine norms are deductive or situation-specific inferences.

a divine mandate theology. Socially entrenched norms are not necessarily identified with God's will for human life, as they are in an orders-of-creation perspective. God's will takes the form of a command or mandate that comes in between God's intention for human life and extant institutional arrangements. God may give a normative code to human beings, but human beings have to work to conform their relations to it. One cannot presume that the institutionalized orders human beings produce are in conformity with such a norm, even when human beings intend to abide by it in their efforts to construct and maintain appropriate human relations. Moreover, God has the freedom to mandate a course of human behavior that does not correspond with the way human beings have customarily gone about things.

Socially entrenched norms may, however, correspond with God's own mandates. This correspondence is indeed likely on a selective basis, if God's commands are evident (say, on biblical grounds) and human beings are open to them in their social relations. When such a match occurs, no criticism of socially entrenched norms is possible. The notion of a divine mandate thoroughly undercuts the critical leverage of God's transcendence in that case—a particular social code or order is simply identified with God's command. Such a social code or order takes on the sacrality proper to divinity, the unquestionable ineluctability that is a sovereign God's right. Because God's commands have no metaphysical or natural underpinnings, no reasoning about the natural character or inclinations of human persons has an inroad here, as in natural law theory, to counter such an identification. The transcendence of God, which might mitigate against human pretensions to have formulated or responded to such a command properly, is easily overlooked in the interest of establishing concrete directives for human life and conforming social relations to them by following God's will.

God's Ordination or Commission of Human Institutions

One can talk in the Christian tradition not only about a divine mandate of human norms; one can also speak of a direct divine ordination or institution of the power differentials and status and occupational arrangements of a social order. In other words, God is directly behind the institutional arrangements in which people find themselves, rather than indirectly, by way of a command of the norms according to which human beings are to go about arranging their own lives. God's will for human society is not found in the more remote form of mere divine commands to which human beings are to conform, but is inherent in the very social roles and functions that God sets up, or at least directly authorizes, for the purpose of maintaining a proper order among human beings. The locus classicus of such a position is Romans 13. The powers that be are ordained by God; sociopolitical authorities are established by the will and hand of God and therefore have a legitimate claim on one's obedience.

Like a divine command position and unlike that of orders of creation or natural law, the notion of a divine appointment of human roles and relations severs the connection of those human orders with the natural world God creates. Social orders are specifically human orders. Rather than being part, or a necessary consequence, of the way the world is, they are the result of a special divine commission. Human orders owe nothing to nature and everything to God. They are artificial, therefore, in a way that is inconceivable from an orders-of-creation perspective or from an outlook that sees humanly instituted social orders as participating in a natural law. Though they may be artificial, human orders, according to a divine ordination position, are not conventional. As the results of a divine commission, they are not viewed as contingent products of human decision. *God* sets them up and authorizes them as God's will for human affairs.[12]

The notion of a divine institution or commission has a certain critical potential. First, the derivative status of human authority opens that authority up for criticism. Human powers and authorities may be authorized by God, but they have a derivative authorization. The higher authority of God stands beyond a human one. The latter is consequently not self-validating.

Second, even though a particular status position or role gains an irrefragable authorization in so far as it is instituted or commissioned by God, this sort of authorization is not owned or possessed. As a gift of God it can presumably be taken away. Power or status positions

12. See Skinner, *Foundations of Modern Political Thought*, 2:154–55, 161, for indications of this sort of either/or in a divine ordination position: social orders may be set up and authorized by *either* a divine *or* a human procedure.

and occupational roles are not fixed in the nature of things as the rational developments of an order intrinsic to the God-given character of human persons. They simply arise by divine appointment, which God could just as easily rescind. This is the critical potential of a distinction between the human and the natural worlds on a divine commission outlook.

The crucial question is whether a particular social order is in fact backed by a divine commission. This question is a live one, however, only if a gap is possible between the sociopolitical powers that God sets up and authorizes and ones with only a human basis and backing. This gap tends to be elided on a divine commission outlook. The tendency is to move without sufficient justification from the claim that God institutes power and occupational relations for the sake of order in human life to the conclusion that God ordains this particular institutional and social order. If socially and politically powerful roles and status positions have been established, then they are ipso facto entitled to claim a divine commission. The tendency is to work backward from the mere fact of an established social organization to a claim for its divine apppointment.

Such a tendency is fomented by the general inclination of a divine commission outlook to deny the conventional character of political and social authority, to deny the role of human decision in its establishment. It is also encouraged by the fact that likely avenues for the reflective assessment of a divine commission have been cut off. Natural differences are no help in determining whether a particular social order is divinely instituted. For example, the equal intelligence of men and women has no bearing on the question of whether patriarchy is a divinely commissioned social arrangement. The subordination of women might be part of such a commission even if it has no basis in a difference of natural capacities. The harmonious integration of functions in a social order is not a telltale indicator of a divine commission either, since God's institution of human orders is not identical with a reason at work in things.

I have asked whether the notion of divine commission allows for any critical leverage with respect to an institutional arrangement as a whole, but one can also ask about its capacity for criticizing particular claimants to roles or statuses that are believed to be divinely commissioned. The critical potential is greater here but still ambiguous. Even though an office may be divinely appointed that does not mean that the officeholder is. The idea that institutional orders are based upon a divine commission instead of a created order forces a distinction between person and office: status, power, and occupational relations float free of differences in personal qualities. A divine commission authorizes the office, not the particular person that holds it; a divine commission grants authority to an officeholder only *through* the holding of that office upon which one has no claim by right of one's person. One has a claim upon a particular status or social standing in virtue of one's deeds, in virtue of one's performance, not in virtue of what one is. A claimant to an office can therefore lose the title to it by not fulfilling the appropriate functions. God may institute a particular social role but along with it go certain duties or obligations or proper tasks—duties to God or to one's fellow human beings. The authorization of a divine commission is lost to an officeholder by the nonfulfillment of such tasks. Monarchy might be considered a divine commission, for example, but a tyrant will forfeit such authorization. Kingship may be divine but it still might be legitimate to kill a king.[13]

Resources exist, therefore, for criticizing abuse of the power or authority one holds by way of a divine commission, but this is purely a policing function that leaves the institutional order itself intact. If slaveholding is thought to be a divine commission, for instance, one should be good to one's slaves; the institution of slaveholding remains, nevertheless, sacrosanct. One may have responsibilities toward one's slaves, but one does not have any obligation to end their servitude. Slaveholders may be criticized for neglecting the former sort of responsibilities but not the latter. Criticism of the way a social order works is thus kept on the level of superficial reform. It cannot generate enough steam to bring into question the very institutional setup within which it is possible to be either abusive or good to one's slaves.[14]

A further ambiguity concerns whether, according to a divine commission view, claimants to a role or status position are to be self-policing or susceptible to challenge from without. If a claimant does not succeed in bringing himself or herself into line with the duties of

13. Ibid., 2:222–24.

14. See Donald Matthews, *Religion in the Old South* (Chicago: Univ. of Chicago Press, 1977), chap. 4.

a position, what does the theory of divine appointment permit in the way of external challenge? Such a challenge could be suppressed by truncating the reference of a notion of divine appointment. Only the king, say, has been divinely ordained. Even if a king performs his duties badly, therefore, no one else in the realm has anything like the authority of a divinely commissioned office to call him to account. If only the office of the claimant is divinely commissioned, and especially if that office is believed to be the only sort of ordering principle for human life that God could conceivably ordain, challenges to a claimant may simply appear to be too dangerous; they seem to threaten anarchy.

Should the notion of a divine commission be extended to a number of social offices, criticism of a tyrant (for instance) might be itself based on a divine commission. Inferior magistracies, say, might also be divine commissions, and such magistracies' commissioned functions might include keeping watch on the potential for abuse of power by kings.[15] Once God's ordination is extended to a variety of social offices, it becomes possible to see that the order God ordains might comprise a self-reforming network of mutually accountable offices. There is no either/or, in that case, between order grounded in a power that God appoints and anarchy resulting from a challenge to it.[16]

When the application of a notion of divine commission is extended in this way, a divinely commissioned office loses the sort of critical leverage it could have over others without it. A single divinely commissioned office can no longer lodge an uncontestable demand for change against the rest of a social order that has not been so appointed. But an extended application of the notion does increase the possibilities for critique generally in that it tends to prevent the sanctification of the standpoint of any one. The exercise of every divinely commissioned office becomes susceptible to challenge by others.

15. Both Luther and Calvin admit this possibility. See Lovin, *Christian Faith and Public Choices*, 92–93. Some French Huguenots took up the argument in the late sixteenth century. See Michael Walzer, *The Revolution of the Saints* (Cambridge: Harvard Univ. Press, 1965), 66–92; also Skinner, *Foundations of Modern Political Thought*, 2:323–25. Some Lutherans used it in declaring war against the Emperor Charles V as leader of the Roman Catholics in 1546; see ibid., 195. Martin Bucer and Anders Osiander were early Lutheran theological advocates of it; see ibid., 204–5.

16. See Reinhold Niebuhr, *The Nature and Destiny of Man*, 2 vols. (New York: Charles Scribner's Sons, 1964), 2:267–69, for a discussion of this middle ground.

The pertinence of such a challenge by other divinely commissioned offices is increased to the extent that the challenged officeholder has duties to other members of society as well as to God. An external challenge in that case does not simply present a reminder to another officeholder to be true to his or her own commission in obeying God's command. It represents the demand that such an officeholder be true to those others to whom his or her duties extend. A duty toward others implies accountability to them and to the other offices whose duties extend to their defense. Such accountability provides a pointed justification, therefore, for challenging poor performance on the part of a holder of a divinely appointed office.

It is true that as a holder of an office that God commissions one's primary duty is to God. One does whatever one does *because* God has commissioned it to be done. That fact does not prevent, however, *what* God commissions from including responsibilities toward others. Indeed, the entirety of such a commission might concern responsibilities of that sort; and in that case obedience to God would involve nothing beyond the fulfillment of one's duties toward other human beings.

Even when one recognizes that duties to human beings are part of other divinely commissioned offices, one might still appeal to one's own primary allegiance to God as a way of avoiding an obligation to correct the wayward holders of them: "I will do what God requires of *me*; if other people renege on their obligations to others, that is a matter between them and God, and no concern of mine." Such an appeal may find religious confirmation in an individualistic focus on self-correction or self-discipline, or in a belief in an either/or between God's work of judgment and correction and our own. Such an appeal overlooks, however, the possibility that one's own divinely commissioned responsibilities might include a duty to uncover and work against injustice wherever it occurs.

Finally, one must note that a divine appointment view favors *institutionalized* resources for bringing an officeholder to account. It is the holders of divinely commissioned offices who have the responsibility for challenging the performance of others. A notion of divine commission does establish a distinction between person and office, between one's standing as a private person and one's public persona, but it is only as a public person, that is, in virtue of one's particular social identity, that one brings a king or prince, for example, to task.[17]

Since it is already-established roles and offices that stand in a relation of mutual correction, reform tends to remain mere reform. It is hard for social critique on this basis to extend to any radical revisioning of a current institutional setup. Indeed, critique always presumes that setup. The holders of powerful office can be criticized only if and to the extent that a society itself institutionalizes the roles that permit it. Resistance to the powerful is appropriate only where and in the form in which it is authorized by those with the legal power to grant such authorization within a particular society.[18]

One might think that a divine commission view holds resources for critique on the part of individuals standing apart from any institutionalized scheme of things. If one's role is a matter of special divine commission, and is not part and parcel of one's natural endowments as a being with a certain place within the created order, one is permitted to have some sense of a natural self apart from an institutionalized social order. This sense of oneself is not, however, a platform for radical social critique, according to a strict divine commission outlook. First of all, this natural self is devalued relative to one's social identity, since one's relation to God according to a divine commission theory comes by way of the latter and not the former. Second, one tends to identify with one's social role rather than take any critical distance on it. One may not be tied fast to a role in virtue of one's natural qualities—on the human plane, one may ascribe one's role to accidents of birth or circumstance—but such a role can easily take on the character of an equally inexorable fate when seen as an appointment ordained by God. Third, public concerns from a divine commission point of view are bound up closely with social roles and statuses. One's natural self is tantamount to one's private self; relations with others that concern power and status form an artificial sphere of divine appointment.

God's Universal Providential Agency

One other Christian understanding of God's relation to the world—the fourth and final example—is useful to explore in this connection. This last account of God's relation to the world combines the

17. See, for example, Skinner, *Foundations of Modern Political Thought*, 2:205, on Martin Bucer's denial of rights of resistance to "private men."

18. See Lovin, *Christian Faith and Public Choices*, 92–93.

critical potential of the previous two types of accounts while avoiding their defects. Like a divine command view and unlike a divine ordination outlook, it breaks connections between the natural and the social in a way that respects the working of human beings in the construction and maintenance of institutionalized social relations. Contrary to a divine command view, however, it breaks any easy identification of human and divine norms by way of a mechanism like the one at work in a divine commission account: God's will for human affairs cannot be easily identified with any particular human claimant to it because of the extent of God's working. Unlike a divine commission view, however, God's working is not manifested exclusively in human roles and the institutionalized relations that bind them. God manifests God's will for human affairs in the actions of human beings whatever the nature of their social standing, and whether they act in virtue of such standing or in a private capacity.

This account of God's relation to the world affirms God's universal providential agency. According to this outlook, God is bringing about God's intentions for human affairs, and indeed for the whole world, by working in and through all human agencies and natural events. I need to specify the features of this perspective carefully to make the case that it, more than any other outlook discussed so far, confirms the critical potential of a notion of divine transcendence.

On the face of it this outlook might seem difficult to distinguish from the others. It may in fact be combined with them, but several unusual features give it a distinctive critical potential. First, the emphasis in this outlook is on God and the relation of the created world to God, rather than on the product of God's creative will, be it orders of creation, natural human capacities, or commissioned offices. Second, God's working of something is not understood to exclude a human working of it. On an orders-of-creation view, the point of saying that human relations are a matter of a God-given order of creation is to block the idea of their human construction. Similarly, a divine command or commission means that the respective norms and offices are not of human provenance. Certain human relations and offices, and norms for human life—the ones constructed by God without human interference—can simply be identified, therefore, with what God wants. On the other hand, where human working is believed to enter, God's influence tends to exit. Thus human beings seem solely responsible for action in accord with a divine command, or for the application of natural law to the mundane needs of forming and sustaining an ordered commonwealth. According to a view of God's universal providential agency, however, God's working does not replace human working. When God works in and through human acts these remain genuinely human. Neither does God's working stop where human working begins. By doing what they do, human agents are the very agents of God's own intentions for human life.[19]

Such an account of God's universal providential working follows from a certain account of God as creator—indeed, it is a generalization of that idea. In a narrow sense, the claim that God is the creator of the world means that God is the giver of existence; God is responsible for the fact of one's existence in contrast to what one is or does or becomes. But in a broader sense of the claim, God is the creator of the world whatever the aspect of created existence at issue (e.g., existing, acting, relating to others, finding a new life in Christ). As the creator of the world, God holds up into existence the whole of nondivine existence, a whole plane or level of nondivine being, inclusive of every item or order that is or happens within the world in every respect. Talk of God's universal providential agency does not designate a new mode of divine activity, therefore, but indicates a particular consequence of the same creative activity of God: interactions and interrelations among creatures, including those that involve the doings of human agents.

According to this account of God as creator of the world, all that a creature is—including human powers and operations—is owed to God as the creator of the world. In the same way that creatures are given an existence of their own in dependence upon God's creative will for them, they are given powers and operations of their own, powers and operations that are creaturely and not divine, although they reflect God's creative intention for order within the world.

The first feature of this account of God's providential agency mentioned above—the emphasis on God and God's relation to the world—confirms the critical potential of a notion of divine transcendence in two ways. First, it shifts attention away from any finished character of what God brings about and toward the ongoing dependence of any such order upon God's creative will for it. Human social

19. See my *God and Creation*, chap. 3.

relations are contingent upon God's creative intention, and nothing rules out God's creative intention for a world of human social relations that change over time. God is free to will a world in which human efforts alter human social orders.

Since they are the consequences of God's creative intention for the world, social orders have no standing independent of God's intention sufficient to shut out God's will for an alteration of their direction. Whether human orders are based on natural capacities or identified with created orders is of comparatively little moment. Whatever the case, a sovereign and free God holds sway over them.[20]

On such a picture of God's providential working, one does not start and end speculation about human social relations with what one takes to be the given products of God's creative will. Consequently, norms and institutional arrangements are not as likely to seem the fixed, ineluctable workings out of a given natural or social world. Each norm or particular social arrangement is directly based on God's providential will for it. It is what it is primarily because of that divine will and in relative independence of any constraint that the rest of the natural or human world may present. In other words, it is what it is in virtue of God's will, not because, apart from any direct intention of God, it is a requirement of an already established natural or social order.

The stress here is on God's active power in bringing to be what is. The stress is therefore on the manifestation of God's will in a moral *ordering* rather than in a moral *order* with some static and immutable character.[21] The dynamic character of what God wills is brought to the fore in this account of God's providential influence. This account highlights how God's will is behind the very activity of human agents through which social organizations are established and possibly transformed.

The same general emphasis on God and God's relation to the world confirms the critical potential of the notion of divine transcendence in a second way: by locating God's rule or governance of human affairs, not in those social relations themselves or their natural grounds,

20. Of course, this is not to say that no continuity will characterize God's creative intention for the world, just that the fact of continuity and its exact character cannot be presumed.

21. See Gustafson, *Can Ethics Be Christian?*, 108.

but in their relation of dependence upon God. God may hold sway over the world in and through natural events and human interactions that are institutionalized; but it is God who so holds sway, not those institutions or that natural order. No institution or social arrangement can therefore be identified with the rule of God. Nor is God's rule the rule of a reason within the world. God's rule is in God's ruling; it resides in the relation of dependence upon God whereby everything that exists falls under God's creative sway.

One's primary obedience is therefore to God, in such a way that it cannot be replaced by obedience to some institutional arrangement or divine representative. Obeying God does not necessarily mean obeying established social or political authorities. It cannot be limited to that obedience; that obedience is not an absolute condition for obedience to God.

One need not be obedient to God by way of obedience to any particular human norm or office. Obedience to God has a more immediate character. That is, it does not appear to be dependent on the intervention of created intermediaries in the form of, for example, established social norms or institutions. Were those particular norms or institutions not to exist, God's providential influence would be exercised all the same. The importance of sustaining and protecting intramundane orders is thereby relativized. Efforts of that sort cannot be an unconditional obligation on the religious grounds that such orders simply incorporate God's will for human life.

If following God's will cannot be equated with following the obligations set by a particular sociopolitical order, then it is possible for one to obey God's will as a private person. The consequences of this point are directly contrary to the ones discussed for a divine commission outlook. Institutional orders themselves, not just the actions of social functionaries, can be the object of critique. Moreover, critique does not require authorization from a social order itself.

The second general feature of this account of God's providential agency—the idea that God works in and through human agents—confirms the critical potential of a notion of divine transcendence by blocking the transfer of the unquestionable sanctity of divine authority and goodness to any human understanding or instantiation of moral propriety. The latter remains genuinely human. When God is at work in and through human agents, those agents remain fallible and limited and corruptible. As the products of human agents of that sort, social norms or arrangements are appropriate objects of criticism by a divine standard. Those norms and arrangements are not insulated from such criticism as they might be if the human contributions to them were segregated from divine influence, along some parallel or sequential line of working next to God's. A divine standard of goodness and value is clearly the sort of standard to which human orders should be held, if God is at work in and through human agents.

That God works God's providential will through created agents could presumably counter, however, the critical force of a notion of God's transcendence. If God's providential hand is behind everything that happens, should not the proper response be passive acquiescence? Whatever happens is ipso facto good; it has God's blessing. God is at work in the forces that bear down upon us. One should simply consent, then, to the way the world works and to this influence of others upon one in light of the fact that it is God who is at work in them.

Counsel against such consent need not imply a refusal to recognize the conditioned character of human life as one of mutual response and interaction. Nor need it imply a refusal to recognize that God's providential sway holds even with respect to those who make life difficult for oneself and others.[22] What decides the question of acquiescence or dissent is one's active responsibility for intervening and altering the direction of human affairs. A notion of God's providential will cuts off the possibility of such responsibility and thereby fosters acquiescence only if one exempts oneself from God's providential intentions and identifies them too closely with what has happened through the efforts of other human beings prior to one's own active entrance onto the field. The universal compass of God's providential intentions conflicts with such an exemption. The fact that it is limited and potentially corrupt human beings who are under the sway of God's providence prohibits so close an identification of God's will with the will of others.

22. H. Richard Niebuhr and James Gustafson are two moral theorists who orient their ethics in order to avoid such a refusal. See James Gustafson, *Ethics from a Theocentric Perspective*, 2 vols. (Chicago: Univ. of Chicago Press, 1981-84); H. Richard Niebuhr, *The Responsible Self* (New York: Harper & Row, 1963). For my own opinion of this course of action, see below, pp. 240–1, 241 n. 4, and my "A Theological Case for Human Responsibility in Moral Decision Making," in *Journal of Religion*, Special Issue on Realism and Responsibility in Ethics (forthcoming).

The difficulty in identifying God's will with the will of others is part of a general difficulty in determining God's intentions on this account. Presumably one would need such a determination to decide whether it is appropriate either to change or to sustain the present course of human affairs in obedience to God and as an agent of God's providential intentions. How might such a determination be made and what might any proposed method of determination suggest about the propriety of passive acquiescence before the will of others?

In the history of Christian appeals to God's providence, success has often been proposed as an indicator of divine backing. This sort of indicator might seem to favor acquiescence in the face of established forms of human governance, but it is not enough to block action against them. One could accept such an indicator and still contest the propriety of even the most well-established forms of human rule, set up and successfully sustained against any number of previous challenges by opposition groups. Were present opposition groups to succeed now they could legitimately claim for *themselves* the title of instruments of God's will. Rulers have the authority of God, Calvin says, only so long as they reign, and "are able . . . to retain under their hand and at their appointment great multitudes of men." Should God deliver up such rulers to their opponents, legitimate rule shifts to them.[23] If success is the indicator of divine backing, that backing is therefore always a *post facto* ascription. It is no help in determining beforehand whether God's providential will is behind an effort of resistance.[24]

Besides being predictively impotent in this way, success is simply not a very plausible indicator of divine intentions under real conditions of sociopolitical life, where, more often than not, established power relations are not homogeneous across differences of locale and appear (in any case) to be the temporary precipitates of ongoing conflict. The success of opposed forms of governmental organization at different times and places suggests a curiously incoherent form of divine government—at least if one continues to make an immediate identification of God's will with successful political agencies.[25]

23. See Walzer, *Revolution of the Saints*, 38, citing Calvin's commentary on Daniel.

24. Ibid., 61.

25. See William Lamont's description of confusion on this score by those hoping to identify the agents of the expected kingdom of God during the English Civil War, in his *Godly Rule* (London: Macmillan, 1969).

This is the fundamental problem with success as an indicator of divine backing—it assumes an immediate identification of God's will with the political projects of particular groups. According to the notion of God's providential will that I am using, the extent of God's providence is universal in scope. In conflictual circumstances it encompasses, therefore, all parties. If every one of the parties in political conflict is under the sway of God's providential will, it follows that none of them is the agent of God's will straightforwardly. None of their own intentions or goals can be simply equated with God's providential will.

God's rule is consequently not one of immediate enactment but one of ultimate fulfillment. God may be at work in human agents, but God's will is not fulfilled directly upon the enactment of any particular human plan or project. It encompasses the whole at any particular time and the indefinite extension of the future with its possible reversals and setbacks. God's will is fulfilled in that, in possible contradiction to the intentions of human agents, the consequences of their acts will eventually, and in the light of a wider context of human action and natural events, conform to God's intentions.

Belief that one's opponent is an agent of God does not provide a sanction, therefore, for that opponent's intentions and plans. As a human being and as an agent who sins, one's opponent may be furthering God's will by the unintended consequences of his or her action, or may be setting up temporary barriers to the achievement of God's will by acts that must be contested or whose effects must be overridden by the actions of other human beings in order for them to be brought back into line with God's will. Belief that one's opponents are acting under God's providential will does not mean, therefore, that one must bow down before their projects as before a divine plan or relinquish all thoughts of resistance. But neither does belief that God's providential will includes one's own agency provide simple sanction for one's own plans and intentions. Belief in God's providence, especially in times of multiple and conflicting claims of God's guidance, dovetails with the notion of God's transcendence to shift questions of right away from any of these simple claims of being God's agent and toward more particular judgments of relative conformity to God's will.

Those judgments are, however, difficult to make. The shift means that such conformity cannot be assumed in virtue of one's status as an agent of God, that God's plan is not directly discernible in the intentions and plans of God's agents, that God's will cannot be read directly off the happenings of this world. Judgments of right that must be defended replace mere presumption.

One might try to get a sense of the sort of world God wants to bring about by isolating principles and precedents to be found in the Bible, then using this information to defend the rightfulness of one's intentions and acts as a response to present circumstances. According to the view of God's providential agency discussed here, however, the emphasis on God's active and free sovereignty makes at least the application of those principles and precedents problematic. The force of precedent in particular is undercut; God may be working differently now than before. For instance, God as a God of justice may work to deliver an oppressed people from the hands of their oppressors, but God's working may go on to include the chastisement of the same people for their own lack of love. A call to rectify the failings of others at one time cannot exclude the propriety of repentance for one's own failings and a call to self-correction at another.

In general, the idea that God's influence is present in a moral ordering, rather than a moral order, shifts questions of the discernment of God's intentions to contemporary events. Biblical evidence may suggest that God acts as a judge in the employment of human agents or as a redeemer of those who suffer unjustly, but one must attend to the particulars of present circumstance to uncover the meaning of this judgment or redemption for one's responsibilities here and now as an agent of God's will. Such responsibilities are dependent, at least in their concrete character, upon circumstances and thus may change with them.

Interpretation that involves a clearly fallible exercise of critical intelligence will therefore enter onto the scene. Is one's opponent an agent of God's judgment calling one to repentance and the effort of self-correction? Does the cruelty of the opponent's own intentions run contrary to a merciful God's will and therefore challenge one at the same time to an act of resistance? Because of the limitations of human beings and the existence of sin, there is no systematic correlation between divine and human agency with which to simplify such judgments. Because of this lack of systematic correlation, because of the emphasis on contingent events, and because of the intervention of situation-specific interpretation, judgments of what it is right to do as God's agent take on a fluid and flexible character. They do not have the hard-and-fast character of universal pronouncements but the tenuous, circumscribed nature of judgments that hold in relation to some circumstances but not necessarily in relation to all others.

Judgments of what it is proper to do as God's agent are still principled judgments of the sort required for self-critical cultures. They are made with reference to a standard over and above the simple facts of what happens in human life. But they neither prejudge such developments of human life nor occur independently of a careful consideration of what such developments might mean for an understanding of one's responsibilities as God's agent.

SIN AND SOCIOPOLITICAL CRITIQUE

A reference to sin has come in and out of my treatment of the various accounts of God's creative relations with the world and their respective capacities to confirm or to undercut the critical potential of belief in a transcendent God. Christian notions of sin have a certain independence of those accounts and their own set of complexities that warrant separate consideration.

As a reason for affirming God's transcendence, notions of sin naturally have a tendency to confirm the critical potential of a belief of that sort. I have provided some evidence for this tendency in the previous section on Christian notions of God's relations with the world as creator. Indeed, as mentioned in the introduction to this chapter, notions of sin increase the critical potential of a belief in God's transcendence by suggesting the positive need for critique of the human world.

These supportive and augmentative functions can be blocked, however, in two general ways. First, notions of God's creative relation with the world can undercut the critical potential of a belief in sin just as they can a belief in God's transcendence. Sinful orders are too closely identified with what God intends for the world as its creator and governor, and thereby the critical potential of such an affirmation of human sin is undermined. The specifics of such an identification vary with the type of belief in God's relation to the world that is brought into play, but the mechanism and effects of such an identification are much the same.

I already gave one example of such an identification of human sin with God's will when discussing God's providential agency. One might be tempted to say that God wills the hateful intentions and barbaric acts of the sinful, rather than admit a more indirect and complex relation between God's intentions and the sinner's, between the immediate results of a sinner's plans and what God can bring out of them. If one succumbs to this temptation, however, one lapses into a straightforward form of incoherence. On the one hand, it becomes difficult to see how so-called sin can be genuinely wrong—after all, it conforms to God's will. On the other hand, if one wants to say that sin remains sinful, it becomes difficult to see how God remains good in willing it.

A similar sort of identification of sin with God's intentions for the world can take place within a natural law or divine ordination outlook. One would think that the admission of the sinful condition of human action would break any identification of extant human orders with the natural law that God is behind as the creator of the world, or with institutional arrangements that God ordains, and call down upon those orders a judgment of impropriety. One can block that sort of judgment, however, either by saying that extant social arrangements are themselves a divinely instituted response to sin for its punishment of control, or by saying that those orders are themselves the way in which the divine reason of a natural law works itself out under conditions of sin in order to ensure some measure of peace and tranquility. Extant human orders clearly do not have the perfection that would allow them to be identified with the natural law or with the orders that a good God would ordain ideally for human life, but one can still claim in this way that they are the direct expression of a divine reason or a divine will. Compulsory conformity to law, inequalities, the institutionalized violence of slavery and military force can all be justified, therefore, as the best that God can commission or the reason of a natural law can demand under conditions of sin. Apparently senseless injustice, which is hard to pass off as a positive corrective for sin, can still be identified with God's will and a rational natural order for human life, to the extent it is viewed as a punishment for sin.

That extant orders are implicated in the sinful conditions to which they respond is downplayed by this identification of those orders with the divine will or natural law. In other words, that these orders themselves are the result of sin tends to be submerged in the perception of their remedial or punitive function, when they are viewed as expressions of a divine reason or will. Since they are divinely ordained or the expression of a natural law, extant human orders, though sinful, tend to be exempted from God's judgment. The negative side of God's relation to creation—God's judgment of iniquities—is superseded by the positive side of that relation—God's relation to the world as its creator and governor—when sinful orders themselves are thought to be the manifestations of God's own work as creator and governor. A divine judgment upon sin is lost when the results of human sin are considered a matter of divine ordination or an adaptation of natural law. Christian talk about God creating and governing a world that is nevertheless under divine judgment becomes disordered. Instead of maintaining that what God brings about falls under the judgment of God as a result of human sin, one says that God is bringing about the very sinful orders that are suitable for divine judgment.

Moreover, the creative power of God to redeem a sinful world tends to be subordinated to the existence of sin when that world is lent the sort of religious justification I have been discussing. Thought stops with the divine ordination of, or creative relation with, extant human orders under conditions of sin, instead of going beyond the fact of that existence under sin to a need for redemptive change. The divine ordination of an imperfect order seems to be God's response to sin in this world rather than any ordination of human offices to change the sinful conditions that make that imperfect order necessary. The result is that extant human orders seem more like necessities under conditions of sin than temporary makeshifts, and more like absolute necessities or necessities pure and simple, since sin appears an inevitability of this life.

Finally, because there appear to be two sets of God-given laws or commissions for human life, those appropriate for a world in sin and those appropriate for a world without sin, the former remain relatively untouched by the latter. Social relations proper for a world *without* sin lose any critical leverage over a world *with* it. The natural law or divine commission of offices for this world's originally created state may prohibit the very forms of social relation that a sinful world requires in the interest of relative peace and order (say, coercive means of government). But that is no reason for supposing that forms of social relation under conditions of sin should be altered; that fact supplies no particular impetus for changing them, in other words. The order of a sinful world remains undisturbed by any disjunction or apparent conflict of that sort.[26]

The second general way in which the critical potential of a belief in sin can be undercut is one for which accounts of God's creative relations with the world bear no responsibility. Affirmations of sin can undercut their own critical potential by encouraging a belief in the irrelevance of divine standards that is based upon despair. In a number of ways Christian notions of sin can suggest that critical reflection about the human world has no point. First, an account of sin can suggest that a sinful human world is irremediable even by God. Second, and more commonly, Christian notions of sin can suggest that sinful social relations are unalterable by *human beings*. In any case, there is no point to criticism because there is no way for human beings to implement that criticism effectively. Human action to remedy social fault is either inappropriate altogether or, at the very least, an exercise in futility.

To show that Christians can be prone by their beliefs to be critical of the sociopolitical practices in which they are involved, I have to isolate Christian notions of sin (and the associated ones of salvation) that suggest that purposeful human action for social ends is indeed a relevant and potentially effective response to sin. I have to show that at least some Christian accounts of sin make plausible active efforts to bring social orders into line with a divine standard, rather than resignation before their perceived faults.

The possibility that a Christian account of sin will suggest that social corruption is utterly without remedy, even by God, is rather slim. It can happen, however, where the two grounds of divine transcendence mentioned in the introduction of this chapter—sin and the distinct ontological status of creatures—are equated. If sin is either identified with, or a necessary concomitant of, the mere existence of nondivine beings, then the corruption of the created world seems to be simply without remedy. Because creation and fall are collapsed into one, the human world is *essentially* corrupt: human beings, as creatures,

26. See Reinhold Niebuhr, *Nature and Destiny*, 1:292.

cannot be anything but corrupt; even God has no choice in the matter. If human beings are to remain creatures, not even God can offer them hope of any radical improvement. Such equations of sin and creaturely status are rather rare, however, in Christianity.[27]

The possibility that *human* action for social change will be rendered inappropriate or futile by a Christian notion of sin is a more serious problem, especially since such a possibility often increases the more a Christian notion of sin buttresses the critical potential of divine transcendence by suggesting the urgency of a critical perspective on society. The greater the degree or extent, or the more radical the nature, of sin the greater and more radical the nature of the change that is necessary to remedy it. Mere reform that would leave basic social or natural structures intact might not be enough, for progressive emendation of those structures continues to stand under a judgment of sin. Instead, a revolutionary transformation from the bottom up is required. The more radical the change necessary, however, the more likely is despair over the means by which to bring it about; the more sensible it will seem, therefore, to abdicate human responsibility for it—in short, the more such change is liable to seem the province of God alone. On the one hand, extant social orders might be abominated; on the other, their sinfulness is so serious and so deep that human beings cannot be expected to do anything about it.

To argue that Christianity realizes the potential that a belief in God's transcendence has for sociopolitical critique I have to affirm both the relevance of human action in altering sinful social relations for the better and the urgent need for such a change. I do not want to trade the one off the other—for example, denying the depths of human sinfulness in order to make human action in response to sin a meaningful possibility. Ideally, the change required should be radical and human action for it at least possible. What account of sin makes sense of such a position?

It is important to see that claims about the depths of sin are not the only beliefs on the general topic of sin and salvation that suggest the impropriety of human action vis-à-vis the transformations required

27. Hegel provides one case in point. The human world does improve according to his account of it—indeed, it improves of necessity. But one could say from a more traditional Christian perspective that such improvement is possible because human beings are not to remain nondivine creatures; they are improved by being divinized.

of a human world. What is crucial is the existence of a large gap (for lack of a more descriptive term) between a saved state and the state from which one is saved. The extent of the gap is determined by the general way one conceives of the relation between those two states, not simply by the extent of sin. For example, one can think of a saved state primarily, even after the fall, as an elevation from a created to a supernatural plane. The distinction between these natural and supernatural levels of existence is often rather extreme and clearly suggests, therefore, the inability of human beings to bridge it without divine help and some radical transformation of natural human capacities. One can also conceive of salvation as the healing of a defect. Human beings in that case could presumably work with their remaining intact faculties, or with the possibilities for justice that a defective but not absolutely corrupt institutional order offers, to bring about reform. Finally, one could view salvation, as a transformation that marks a discontinuous break with a prior sinful state. If the break is of that sort, it is difficult to see on what human basis it might be initiated. This is the one account of the relation between a saved state and the state from which one is saved that does indeed make a strong claim for sin.

Given my aims in this chapter, I prefer the last account, despite its apparent difficulties, since if human action were pertinent it would be of a radical, even revolutionary sort. On the first account of the relation between saved and pre-saved states I mentioned, although the gap between these states is radical, one can conceive of a supernatural plane of existence as merely added onto a natural one: the elevation of nature to a supernatural plane would in that case be an essentially conservative process. Salvation means elevation to a supernatural plane, but created nature itself remains fine as far as it goes; nothing about it fundamentally needs to be altered—by human beings or by God. On the second account of the relation between saved and pre-saved states, human beings help to bring about a saved state by working within present social arrangements, with the means at hand. This saved state cannot therefore be radically different from the one that preceded it; human action is action for mere reform.

These additional complexities suggest that the need for *God's working*—whether because of sin or the simple limitations of created nature—gets in the way of a belief that human action is appropriate in bringing about the ends for the human world that God intends. According to the assumptions about God's creative working that underpin my account of God's universal providential agency, it is not necessary, however, to deny the involvement of human agents for the ends God works. God bridges the gap that human beings, without the help of God, cannot hope to bridge—because of sin or the simple limitations of human nature. But *with God* human beings may be acting for the ends, for the saved state, God intends.

God's working with human beings may happen with or without conscious human cooperation, in the same way considered previously in the discussion of God's providential working. Human beings working according to their own intentions and plans under conditions of sin may be brought, despite themselves, into line with God's own intentions and plans for their salvation. For example, human beings may try to merit their salvation by performing good works, and these efforts may turn out, in fact, to be a preparation for grace, but only in so far as God providentially brings one to despair by way of them. Human preparations can also be more positively related to God's ends—according to a very traditional account of salvation a decision to attend to God's Word can be considered a positive preparation for conversion—but these preparations can themselves be considered the work of God's grace in so far as God's creative will is behind this very human action of attention. Even if the ends for human life—say, the vision of God—are beyond natural human capacities, human beings may still act for them if God transforms their natures, giving them, in the case of a beatific vision, superhuman intellectual capacities.[28]

Because God can bring human action along to a place it could never have gotten alone, it is proper to say the following. No matter how wide the divide between a saved state and the state from which one is saved, human action can also be a part of the process by God's grace. No matter how deep the world's sin, if that sinfulness does not make the world unredeemable by God, it is also not enough to exclude the pertinence and general contribution of human working. In order to make sense of human working for the ends God wills one need not limit the extent to which the exigencies of sin demand God's own

28. See again my *God and Creation*, chap. 3, for an attempt to show the coherence of this general sort of position.

working. One need not claim that things are not all that bad in order to ensure that human beings have a contribution to make in bringing about the improvements to human life that God desires.

I have the conclusions I wanted, then. Radical change of human orders may be necessary and human action for such an end may still be pertinent. To show that Christian beliefs can realize a capacity for sociopolitical critique I need to do more, however, than demonstrate the pertinence of human action for the ends God intends as savior and redeemer. I need to demonstrate that Christian accounts of sin and salvation permit the relevance of specifically *ethical* human action for *social* ends.

The general way in which sin and salvation are understood does a great deal to determine whether *ethical* conduct in service of the ends God intends for human life makes sense. Thus, sin might be defined as ignorance, and salvation as the knowledge of God. Or, sin might be understood as the breaking, and salvation as the reinstitution, of a right personal relation with God on an affective plane (e.g., as the breaking and reinstitution of a loving or trusting relationship with God). Sin might be understood as separation from God and salvation as one's deification or taking on of divine attributes. Finally, sin might be understood as the lack of a right moral relation to God, as disobedience, and salvation as a restitution of one's moral fabric, as personal holiness or some newly found inclination to carry out God's law or command. The last sort of commonly proffered Christian definition of sin and salvation is most obviously encouraging of ethical conduct in furthering the ends that God intends for human life.

One need not hold onto that account exclusively, however. Obedience to God's commands might be conditional upon the attainment of one or more of the other three—knowledge, love or trust in God, deification—attainments that ethical conduct does nothing of itself to further. In that case sin and salvation might be understood primarily along one of those other lines. The important point for my purposes is that ethical conduct is also somehow involved, as, say, a necessary concomitant of sin or salvation understood along one of these other lines. Thus it is common to say that a trusting relation with God, if genuine, will necessarily issue in good works. Overcoming estrangement from God could also obviously have that implication.

Obedience or holiness as a primary characterization of one's saved state is not, moreover, an unambiguous purveyor of sociopolitical critique. Obedience to God's commands will not lead to undercutting established social relations if those commands should concern action in fixed social roles or already stereotyped behaviors of any other sort. Obedience to God or holiness as a primary mark of a saved state can also be made a matter exclusively of private, self-concerned acts. For example, one's own life may be the object of attention—one is concerned to correct it—but the lives of others are their own concern. Or, if one is concerned with the moral character of others, that concern may be limited to their individual acts and fail to include the institutionalized relations that are the backdrop for those acts. This worry leads to the second consideration mentioned above: Does ethical action in service of the ends God intends for human life include a *social* dimension?

The location of sin and salvation does a great deal to determine whether correction of social corruption is appropriate to furthering the ends God wills for human life. A number of ways of specifying those locations have the capacity to block social concern. Thus, if sin is located exclusively in *this* life, and salvation is located exclusively in some *other* world (heaven or a constantly deferred future eschaton), or in some *other* life (after death, say), ethical conduct is unlikely to concern the correction of existing social orders. Salvation may indeed have a social dimension, but one that is not to be realized here and now; any social aspect of salvation does not concern society as it presently exists. Other specifications of the location of sin and salvation are simply prone to deny or underplay the social reference of those notions. If sin and salvation have an individual rather than a social locus, ethical conduct may focus primarily on forms of self-correction rather than institutional change. If salvation is located in a religious realm distinct from a more secular or worldly human arena, human action in service of God's ends for human life may involve a moral policing of monastic or church life, but it is unlikely to have much concern for the political arrangements of society at large—except in so far as they affect such religious realms. Moreover, if sin and salvation are purely spiritual matters, a religious sanction is lacking for ethical attention to the bodily and material suffering that certain sociopolitical orders promote. A spiritual/temporal distinction is liable, indeed, to eviscerate the critical force of ethical mandates altogether, by stressing the importance of the religious attitude with which one undertakes a course of action without regard for what that course of action or its effects might be.

For ethical conduct in the service of the ends God wills for human life to extend to criticism of existing sociopolitical orders requires a more all-encompassing account of the nature of salvation. An account of the requisite sort is promoted by my position on the universal range of God's providence, based as it is on the idea that God's creative will holds into existence everything that is, in every respect that is good. God, as the creator and governor of the whole—of the material and the spiritual, of the individual and the social, of present and future worlds, of human life and death—can offer, and can call human beings to work for, an end of human life that concerns all of these. In short, God's saving will can be as wide as God's creative or providential will.

Expanding the scope of the ultimate ends of God's working in this way has its own problems, however. Criticism of sociopolitical orders on the grounds that God's saving intention for the world extends to orders of those sorts can be cut short where salvation is simply *identified* with a rectified world order. New and improved sociopolitical arrangements would at some point no longer be themselves criticizable. Such an end to critique would be no tragedy if the sociopolitical arrangements at issue were in fact what God wills as the end of human life, if they amounted say, to a perfectly fulfilling world for all human beings. The danger, of course, lies in premature claims that a world of that sort has been realized.

The account of God's universal providential agency previously offered blocks such premature claims to some extent by suggesting that there may always be something more to God's will for human life than social improvements according to human plan. Even if human beings are somehow incorporated within God's plans for an ultimate end of human life, that fact never gives one adequate grounds simply to equate the products of human planning with God's saving will. Human beings remain limited and fallible in the conception and execution of their plans for social change; their action for such ends may be sinful. God may therefore realize God's will for a redeemed human order in a way that runs contrary to human expectations for social life, perhaps by countering what human beings believe to be their own successes, or by way of the unintended consequences of human social engineering.

The bare idea that God realizes God's intentions for a redeemed corporate life *in this world* presents a danger, however, especially since my account of God's providential agency provides no clear way of identifying the "more" that is to be God's contribution to such a redeemed corporate life. Improved social relations that human beings had some hand in may, for all one knows, have also been brought about with the help of God; it is possible on these grounds to identify some new order of social relations with God's will for a redeemed human life. The new order, then, becomes uncriticizable.

The only way to cut off this possibility altogether is to claim some ultimate distinction between what God intends a redeemed human life to be and anything that can be accomplished in this world. Salvation concerns this world, it has to do with it, but it does not take place entirely within it. Salvation is an eschatological end of history, in the sense of history's telos or completed good but also in the sense of its termination in something beyond it.[29]

I should also say that for my purposes salvation does not have to be restricted to an institutionalized social locus. It does not even have to be centered there. An initial focus on a personal rather than a social sphere is compatible with a concern to criticize extant social orders so long as that focus expands from there to include social action and the transformation of the world. Christian theologians often distinguish between stages or degrees of a redeemed life—for example, between justification and sanctification, or between intermediate and final states of grace. Transformed social relations might be somewhere down the road in such a salvific process. Even if salvation is used in a narrower sense and transformed social relations are not strictly part of it, social relations of a certain sort might be its consequences. Salvation is such cases might not be something that occurs or is produced in social relations, but it could at least be manifested there. For example, where moral transformation of one's person is salvation's first stage, or is simply identified with the meaning of salvation, a saved state might easily issue in changed social relations with others. To take another example: Salvation as a new-found love of God may

29. See Reinhold Niebuhr, *Nature and Destiny*, 2:287.

have as its consequence love for God's own wishes for the world, a love for the creatures that God loves, including those human beings who suffer under unjust sociopolitical regimes; it may issue therefore in action on their behalf. Similarly, salvation as the reinstitution of a trusting relationship with God may suggest the propriety of obedience to God's law, a law that may demand service to one's neighbors in the promotion of a social good.

Indeed, any ethical claim that salvation makes on individuals is more likely to issue in an active criticism of social orders when the means to grace are identified as personal rather than institutional. It is difficult for ethical demands on graced persons to include, for example, the reworking of church orders, if those orders are believed to be the means to that grace. A belief in institutional agencies of a coming kingdom of God—at least when these agencies are identified with established institutions of present social orders—cuts off the radical criticism of such orders that might otherwise attend human working for a salvation that is to include the transformation of the world.[30] When a salvific relation to God is immediate between an individual and God, the human agencies that are to implement the ethical mandates of that salvation are independent of established social orders; thus nothing stands in the way of an active hostility toward them.

DESPAIR AND THE POSSIBILITY OF AIMLESS CRITIQUE

The despair in which Christian notions of sin are implicated cannot be limited, however, to the kind just discussed—a despair based on a sense of the inappropriateness or inefficacy of human action. Even when action for social ends makes sense as a response to a sinful world, one might despair of ever being able to begin action in the absence of concrete directives for it. One can only begin to act when one has some way of determining what it is one should do. The kind of agnosticism about God's intentions for human life that is part of the account of God's providential agency offered previously might appear to cut off the possibility of such directives and thereby foster a skeptical malaise. The existence of sin combines in that account with the limited

30. See Lamont, *Godly Rule*, on the way in which the revolutionary potential of seventeenth-century English millenarianism was held in check by these means.

and fallible perspectives of human agents, and with the universality of God's working, to prohibit any simple identification of God's will. This conclusion blocks the sanctification of established social or political forces as the agents of God's will. But it may seem to do so at the expense of any guidelines at all for human action. A skeptical morasse would in that case lead back again to inaction before established social and political powers.

A theologian fearful about the absence of such guidelines should not, however, go back on the conclusions drawn in the first section of this chapter and try to show how the beliefs discussed there mandate a particular social or political agenda. For example, the theologian should not try to identify God's will with a certain type of institutionalized order. Such an identification would prevent criticism of the order specified, and the loss of such a critical potential is simply too great a price to pay for a secure sense of direction for present action. Instead, the theologian should recognize the propriety of theology's failure at least to supply *specific* recommendations for action. Such a recognition would itself help ease a tendency to despair over their absence. The claims about God's nature and relation to the world that I have examined are not enough to settle political arguments all by themselves. Nor should they be. A theology comprised of such claims is not a totalizing discourse; it does not offer a complete guide to action or answer all the questions in any field of human investigation.[31]

Rather, theology makes room for low-level, specifically political, economic, and sociological arguments, which may produce definite but obviously fallible and contestable conclusions and recommendations. When specific directives are required, judgments about extant social orders that simply make reference to God's transcendence or creative agency have to give way before more mundane analyses of what is specifically right and wrong with them and what to do about it. Arguments focus in that case on existing sociopolitical frames of reference, using the regular criteria for such judgments. Indeed, theology, on my account of it, does more than merely permit these sorts of argument—it positively requires them in so far as salvation is brought about by, or manifested in, the work of fallible human beings,

31. See Clodovis Boff, *Theology and Praxis*, trans. Robert Barr (Maryknoll, N.Y.: Orbis Books, 1987), 89, et passim.

acting from the particular standpoint and perspective they occupy within the world they hope to help transform.

A theologian fearful about the absence of guidelines does not have to try to designate the particulars of God's intentions for human life on grounds like those discussed in the first section of this chapter, since other, general guidelines are available that are adequate to prevent despair. First, as mentioned previously, general moral requirements are part of the Christian moral heritage and its reading of the Bible (e.g., one should love and serve God and neighbor, help the needy and the downtrodden). Second, without attempting to identify God's will for human life, one can derive a general, formal account of the nature of social sin and an alternative to it from the simple fact of a transcendent God's relation to the world as its creator. This is my own contribution to the prevention of a skeptical malaise over the direction of human action in chapters 4 through 6.

General directives like these do not, however, issue directly in specific proposals for political action in response to sin. They remain general proposals. Indeed, Christians, should not want them to issue in specifics. Were that to happen, Christians could not retain their freedom with respect to specific proposals generated; nor could such proposals be effective in meeting the exigencies of particular circumstances. To take more specific shape these general directives require what José Míguez Bonino calls historical mediation.[32] Thus, on the basis of biblical injunctions, one might have the sense of what side to be on (the side of the poor and the oppressed) and some sense of what one should do (work for greater justice and love in social relations). Determining what the particular circumstances demand in keeping with those commitments and the means to implement the resulting recommendations requires, however, a straightforward, empirically based political and economic analysis.

Theological guidelines of this general sort do not prejudge the conclusion of such analysis. For example, besides an expectation that because of sin some parties will take advantage of and abuse others in present social circumstances, such guidelines do not decide which groups are downtrodden or specify the mechanisms of their hurt. These

32. See José Míguez Bonino, *Doing Theology in a Revolutionary Situation* (Philadelphia: Fortress Press, 1975), 97.

matters vary with circumstances. Sociopolitical or economic analysis reserves its own right to judge them.

Such analysis does not, however, proceed in complete independence of the theological claims about God's nature and relation to the world that I have examined in this chapter. Here again, such beliefs are able to specify a general direction for action and analysis. Without developing the implications of these beliefs any further, it is clear that they exercise a regulative or transformative influence over sociopolitical judgment. They influence the way in which one makes and holds sociopolitical judgments and acts on them. Because of God's transcendence, because of the creaturely status of human beings and their sin, because human plans are never quite God's own, one must recognize that all sociopolitical judgments and attempts to act on them are susceptible to revision. These claims foster a general ethic of cognition and action in which one leaves oneself open to criticism. Sociopolitical judgments can never claim finality.

More positively stated, these claims suggest the immediate possibility of a more accurate judgment or a greater good. As agents of a salvation that concerns this world, human beings are obligated to act on such a possibility. The ideal for this world that God intends may never be identical with anything human beings can achieve, but what that means positively is that human beings are always called to realize a greater good.

The negative import of this general ethic returns again, however, at each point at which one hopes to have achieved a greater good. As a result, although concrete analysis of what that greater good is and how to implement it might start from within an existing sociopolitical framework, one cannot assume that it will not extend in a radical direction to bring about the questioning of an entire social order. Moreover, although these theological claims suggest that a greater good or more accurate account of the truth exists, they do not provide any assurance that human attempts to attain that good will be successful. One cannot assume that progress is being made.

In sum, then: One must continually strive for a greater good in the belief that the development of a more just social arrangement has no limits; human beings can never pretend to have achieved a final good, because of their finitude, their sin, and because of the lack of any identity between what God and human agents will. In acting for a greater good, one must be constantly vigilant, however, for the possibility of an equal or greater imperfection or corruption. A vertical tension with a divine good that no human action can achieve prohibits a complacent faith in change as an unproblematic mark of progress.

This general ethic is a genuine contribution of belief in God's transcendence. It is not the same as a simple recognition of the fallible and limited character of human claims and achievements. It is not equivalent in function to a simple naturalism that makes no mention of God in its concentration on the purely human, on the historically conditioned finitude of human life. This religiously based general ethic has certain dangers that naturalism does not. The belief in a more-than-human divine goodness and truth makes possible a human claim for their instantiation; such a claim is prohibited only by the notions of divine transcendence and creative agency identified in this chapter. The continual disparity between a divine goodness and truth and what human beings achieve could also presumably lead to the pointlessness of human striving, unless belief in that divine truth and goodness translates into an obligation to realize a greater good or truth. On the positive side of things, however, belief in a divine goodness and truth suggests at least the existence of a definite end or goal of human efforts. In contrast to the expectations of a pure naturalism, one believes in some ideal to approximate even if one has no assurance of progress toward it by one's own efforts alone. Finally, such a belief may prohibit what a naturalistic viewpoint has no resources to prevent: complacency in the seemingly inevitable limitations, corruptions, and compromises of human life. A divine standard stands outside those happenings of human life to prompt their critical appraisal.

CHRISTIANITY'S CRITICAL POTENTIAL AFFIRMED

I have specified in this chapter the critical potential of a Christian belief in God's transcendence and shown the way that potential can be realized given a wider framework of Christian beliefs about God's relations with the world and the world's existence in sin. Neither an overidentification with divine standards, nor their irrelevance, nor despair stands in the way of that belief's capacity to promote critique of the sociopolitical status quo. In the process of making my case, I have demonstrated how Christian beliefs about sin and salvation, and about God's relation to the world as its creator, governor, and redeemer, can work either at cross-purposes with, or in confirmation of, the resources for sociopolitical critique that I located in a belief in God's transcendence.

When accounts of God's relation to the world did not undermine the critical potential of belief in God's transcendence by suggesting an identification of the divine and the human, belief in God's transcendence seemed itself a major influence on those accounts. Belief in God's transcendence modified belief in God's relation to the world so as to block its tendency to produce self-satisfied judgments about the probity of established human orders. Belief in God's transcendence infiltrated accounts of God's relation to the world and pushed them in the direction of (1) an agnosticism regarding human claims to know what is really true or right, and (2) a denial of any simple identity between what happens in this world and what God wants. Accounts of God's relation to the world have also seemed, however, to have their own critical resources, most fully when they stressed (1) the active sovereignty of God in that relation rather than the apparently fixed products of God's creative will, and (2) the universal, comprehensive range of God's working, rather than its association with particular human agencies or institutions.

I have identified three distinct resources within Christian belief for criticism of established social orders: belief in God's transcendence, an account of a free God's world-encompassing providential agency, and a strong emphasis on sin (with the qualifications made in the second section of this chapter). The three together form a progressively unfolding focus for critique of established sociopolitical orders. If God is transcendent and human orders are therefore not themselves divine, those orders do not have the unconditional sanctity that characterizes God's existence and nature. If human orders are what a free and sovereign God brings about, not only are they not sacred, they are alterable and contingent. If the world is in sin, human orders not only *can* be altered, they *should* be. Given the general parameters for accounts of sin established in the second section of this chapter, it makes sense, moreover, to believe that human beings might be empowered to make such efforts.

Despite the fact that the version of belief in God's relation to the world that I have specified has its own critical capacities, it serves generally to make the critical potential of a belief in God's transcendence less anarchic. If God is the creator of the world, one cannot simply launch a prophetic No! against any and every social order on the grounds that it is not God and not what God intends the world to be. As the world God creates and guides and redeems in Jesus Christ, the world is forever God's place no matter how distant it seems from the standards of truth and goodness that God represents. God is at work there for the ends God intends. Indeed, God is at work for those ends in established forms of social relations, no matter how great the efforts of human beings to stymie them. Therefore, according to the account of the relation between divine and human working that I have been favoring, one cannot rule out the possibility of human working within such a social sphere to bring human life closer to such ends. Because the world continues to be the place of God, belief in God's transcendence does not require one to leap out of one's cultural and social setting even when insisting upon the need for its radical transformation. One can work for the ends God intends within one's cultural and social context, while knowing that such efforts may very well require the radical transformation of that context itself. A potentially context-transforming critique that does not force one to try to be an exile from one's own sociocultural location—that is the sort of critique that the version of Christian beliefs that I have specified suggests. These beliefs suggest a genuine *culture* of self-criticism, in other words. If the arguments in this chapter are sound, Christianity has the resources to be such a self-critical culture; and Christian beliefs favor generally the idea of social and cultural contexts that are susceptible to revolutionary transformations from within.

In this chapter I have discussed doctrinal grounds for criticizing established sociocultural orders. I have not asked, however, what a sociocultural order might be being criticized *for*. Despite the third section of this chapter, one might be left therefore with the sense that any critique will lack direction. I have also said that a sociocultural order might deserve criticism in so far as it is a place of sin, but my treatment of Christian notions of sin neglected to identify what sin is. Unless social critique is simply a matter of change for change's sake, might not there be doctrinal resources for determining the general character of sociocultural orders that demand to be changed? In the course of the next several chapters I try to identify this character as one of institutionalized intolerance and oppression. The project requires the question: What do beliefs about God and creation suggest about the nature of proper relations among persons?

FOUR

Christian Belief and the Justification of Hierarchy

IN THE PREVIOUS chapter I asked whether traditional Christian beliefs about God and the world present resources for criticizing established sociopolitical arrangements and, if so, whether the critical potential of those beliefs stands a chance of being realized given the dangers that surround an appeal to transcendent standards in self-critical cultures. I answered these questions in the affirmative with reference to a certain body of beliefs—beliefs that center around God's transcendence and that include an account of God's universal providential agency, along with a healthy respect for the depths of human failing and the social character of at least its effects. A culture in which those beliefs about God and the world figure has the potential to be self-critical. The prevailing ways in which power is managed and wealth and prestige distributed cannot claim any inviolate, sacrosanct character. Instead, a standpoint for their potentially unfavorable evaluation exists outside them in God. Sociopolitical arrangements are alterable by human effort in so far as they come under God's providential rule, and are ripe for improvement as a domain infected by sin.

Beginning with this chapter I need to move beyond these generalities, however. I need to specify criteria for the actual use of such resources to criticize a sociopolitical order. There are a number of reasons why such criteria are necessary and why my account has yet to supply them.

On the basis of the conclusions in chapter 3 I can say only that a Christian culture of self-criticism may lie anywhere along a continuum between two out-of-bounds extremes. If a Christian culture is self-critical, the one extreme of blanket approval for sociopolitical arrangements is ruled out. If a self-critical Christian culture is to remain an established culture in its own right, the other extreme of anarchic repudiation of any and all forms of social order is also ruled out. Where a self-critical Christian culture falls between these extremes becomes a matter of the relative weight or emphasis given to the various beliefs within the body of those I have specified, with their differing capacities to undermine or undergird prevailing practices. For example, if God's transcendence is weighted more heavily or given greater emphasis than God's efficacious working within the world, a theologian in Nazi Germany may be inclined to charge the state with idolatry. Where the weighting is reversed, a theologian in the same circumstance may be inclined to look for some good in the *Volk* as an agent of God's providential will for the world. What considerations are behind differences like these?

The relative weight or emphasis given the particular beliefs at issue may be a matter of principle for a particular theological tradition. (Indeed, such principled differences in emphasis may be what *establishes* the distinct theological traditions that are possible on the basis of the beliefs I have specified.) Thus it may be characteristic for a particular tradition of Christian belief (e.g., neo-orthodoxy) to emphasize the transcendence of God and the fallenness of human beings whenever possible. Such a theological tradition will therefore fall closer to the critical end of the spectrum permitted by the body of beliefs I have identified. But even in that case the critical capacity of such an emphasis remains just that—a mere capacity, a mere potential. What criteria determine when that potential is to be actualized, that capacity exercised? Unless the critical potential of the Christian beliefs I have specified is to be employed indiscriminately, some criteria are necessary to determine the particular sociocultural circumstances in which such criticism becomes especially relevant or urgent.

Even if the critical capacity of Christian cultures is employed indiscriminately, exercised across the board on the assumption that any social arrangement can stand improvement, such criticism becomes empty and abstract without standards establishing a specific reason for criticism and a general direction for human betterment. Even if one believes that all social relations are in a state of sin, such a charge is impotent unless one can specify the nature of the sociopolitical fault that warrants attack and some vision of an alternative. What might be the source of these specific reasons for criticism and of this vision?

I have already said that the Christian beliefs about God and God's relation to the world that I have identified will not provide in and of themselves any analysis of specific economic, social, or political ills afflicting human institutions. Ascertaining in a concrete way what is wrong with a particular social order and how to fix it requires a straightforward sociopolitical analysis. The admission of theological insufficiency on this score is exactly what these Christian beliefs themselves suggest.

Christian belief in God's transcendence and in the working out of God's will in the lives of human beings presents, it is true, certain general reasons for criticizing established orders. I can conclude from arguments in the previous chapter that certain ways in which one might view these orders will render them targets of criticism. If a social order is deemed self-evident and unalterable, that is a reason for considering it suspect. Justifications of a social order that involve some claim of an identification between the human and the divine also supply a reason for criticism. Finally, a social order becomes subject to attack to the extent it is believed to exist in isolation from God's creative influence on the world—because it is thought to be either unredeemable in its depravity or an autonomous realm of purely human doing.

Some of these criticisms seem, however, to be fairly useless. They hold only for situations in extremis, for the relatively uncommon circumstances of utter desperation or utter idolatry. The potentially universal applicability of others threatens to render them trivial. For example, is there any society, where habitual or customary practices do not at some point take on the character of self-evidence? Moreover, all these criticisms are alarmingly superficial. Social relations seem to be criticized more for the way they are considered than for what they are. For instance, would a social policy of murdering Jews be any less objectionable if it were subject to an "eschatological proviso," held onto tentatively as a revisable human project on the part of Christians who hope to do God's will even as they admit their own sin?[1] For a

1. The Confessing Church movement in Germany in the 1930s might be crit-

critique that burrows deeper, the character of relations between persons has to be the explicit subject matter under consideration. Are there any specifically Christian criteria for a critique of that sort?

Specific judgments about appropriate and inappropriate relations between persons are an explicit part of the biblical stories and the Christian moral heritage, in which one is counseled, for example, to love one's neighbor, and to alleviate the suffering of the poor, the widow, and the orphan. One could easily avail oneself of proscriptions and prescriptions like these for the purposes at hand. Here and in subsequent chapters I contend, however, that the very body of beliefs I have said inform a Christian culture of self-criticism also imply principles for evaluating the interpersonal relations a society institutionalizes. Beliefs about God's transcendence and universal providential agency have the capacity to identify the general shape of sociopolitical fault or sin. The principles that result can mediate between very basic Christian doctrines about God and the world and specific Christian moral injunctions to be found, for example, in the Bible. They also mediate between those basic Christian beliefs and nontheological, sociopolitical analyses of particular situations. Such principles provide some direction for what to make theologically of those sorts of analyses. For example, if beliefs about God and God's relation to the world suggest that certain forms of social relation are inappropriate, the theologian should be especially attentive to what sociopolitical analysis reveals about the specific shape and nature of such relations in a particular context.

In the following chapters I argue that the sort of beliefs in God's transcendence and providential agency I have been talking about cut off the legitimation of (1) fixed hierarchies of superiors and subordinates, (2) oppressive relations of domination or exploitation, and (3) intolerance toward others. These beliefs promote, instead, the idea of

icized on this score. Thus the quasi-religious pretensions of the state are challenged in the Barmen Declaration with little direct attention to the actual policies of the state regarding, for example, racial purity and violence directed against political dissidents. See Robin Lovin, *Christian Faith and Public Choices* (Philadelphia: Fortress Press, 1984), chap. 5. I argue later for a connection between a theologically illegitimate hubris and a social policy that warrants the sacrifice of others' lives, but the point I am making now still stands. The term "eschatological proviso" is associated with the political theology of Johannes Metz. See Johannes Metz, *The Theology of the World*, trans. William Glen-Doepel (New York: Herder & Herder, 1969), 114–24.

universal community, of equal regard and respect for others in all their diversity.

An argument of this sort is a tall order since beliefs about God's transcendence and relation to the world as its creator have a long history of being implicated in the opposite sorts of social programs, in which power and privilege are distributed in systematically inequitable fashion and treatment of those who differ from a rigidly exclusive norm is oppressive and disrespectful. I have no intention of downplaying such facts. My strategy, rather, is twofold. First, I intend to analyze carefully the exact way in which such beliefs are used for such purposes, with the hope of either distinguishing the beliefs at issue from the account of a transcendent God's providential agency developed in the previous chapter or showing that the latter account, though indeed employed for such purposes, is held inconsistently in doing so. I follow this strategy of analysis when discussing in this chapter the propriety of hierarchical social arrangements from a Christian point of view. The second strategy involves working from my own fully developed account of a transcendent God's relation to the world and showing how the conclusions of, for example, egalitarianism and tolerance in human social relations, follow by short, logically incontrovertible steps. I follow this strategy in chapters 5 and 6.

Hierarchy, oppression, and intolerance, as foci for either Christian approval or critique form the three topics to be addressed. Each successive member of this series of topics takes the issue to a more fundamental level of analysis and clarifies more intensely, therefore, the possible benefits or horrible deficits of the beliefs at hand. I start with hierarchy in this chapter, move on to oppression in chapter 5, and to intolerance in chapter 6.

By hierarchy I mean a particular social arrangement defined by fixed orders of superiors and subordinates establishing unequal access to such things as rewarding work, goods and services, economic and political power or prestige. Traditional Christian beliefs about God's nature and relation to the world can justify hierarchical relations among persons in a number of ways. I need to separate out these logically distinct forms of justification from the often confusing and imprecise history of theological rhetoric on this topic, in order to make clear where appeals to God's transcendence and providential agency fit into this rather ignominious Christian heritage. In the process, the meaning of those beliefs delineated in the previous chapter will be clarified and elaborated.

THE MODEL OF AN INTRADIVINE ORDER

In one form of justification, Christian theologians claim that hierarchical relations among human beings match an order of similar relations within a divine sphere and are thereby justified. The quotations from Eusebius in the previous chapter suggest a justification of this sort. There is a heavenly hierarchy of angelic hosts over which God presides—say, thrones, seraphim, and cherubim, in some descending order of superiority and subordination established by their respective excellences of being or function. Human hierarchies replicate such a heavenly model—be it a divine emperor before a multitude of angelic armies and ministers, a divine lord surrounded by a feudal court of ranked angels and archangels, or an absolute sovereign served loyally by magistrates of his own appointment.[2]

The account of divine transcendence in the previous chapter breaks this modeling relation between divine and human orders. Moreover, such a modeling relation is difficult to reconcile with a serious commitment to monotheism. Where such a commitment exists, any relationship of God with "heavenly hosts" cannot be considered to constitute an intra*divine* order, but indicates at most God's relationship with a particular *created* sphere. The one God according to the Christian tradition is not, of course, spoken of as an undifferentiated monolith: one can talk of intradivine relations within the Trinity. Orthodox trinitarian speculation, which refuses to rank persons of the Trinity, will not, however, supply appropriate material for this sort of replication strategy for justifying human hierarchies. The fact that it does not might be one reason why Christian supporters of imperial hierarchy in the fourth century C.E. tended to be Arians.[3]

2. See David Nicholls, "Images of God and the State," *Theological Studies* 42 (June 1981): 203; idem, *Deity and Domination* (London: Routledge, 1989), 234–35.

3. See Nicholls, *Deity and Domination*, 235. Even orthodox trinitarian speculation has its dangers, however, as a source for models of human relation—particularly when the focus of that speculation is the economic trinity. For example, talk of God the Father's relation to his Son Jesus slides easily into valorizing an order in which the latter is perfectly subordinate in judgment and will to the former. Karl Barth's account of male-female relations on this basis is infamous. (See *Church Dogmatics*, ed. F. W. Bromiley

CHAIN-OF-BEING AND CHAIN-OF-COMMAND JUSTIFICATIONS OF HIERARCHY

Another theological strategy for justifying hierarchical relations among human beings does not claim a mirroring relation between distinct divine and human orders but simply includes God within a single hierarchically arranged universe. This idea of the universe was prevalent especially in medieval and Renaissance times, and is fittingly captured by Arthur O. Lovejoy's title *The Great Chain of Being*. Everything that exists is ordered according to a hierarchical principle, and God is simply the first in some line of superiors and subordinates in being or function, or merely the supreme head of some organic whole of dependencies constituting the universe. The same purportedly divine reason is at work everywhere to form a single, all-inclusive structure of repetitions or correspondences that can be characterized as hierarchical. Separable orders of angels, human beings, animals, plants, and inanimate objects have their respective places fixed in a hierarchically arranged pyramid under God, according to the excellence of their respective natures; each of these orders in turn is arranged hierarchically according to its particular superiors and subordinates. Thus God is greater than the angels; the angels form a hierarchy of cherubim, seraphim, and archangels; the angels are naturally superior to celestial spheres, which differ in status as would king (the sun), queen (the moon), and common people (the stars); an ecclesiastical hierarchy is superior to political government that includes kings and lords and subjects. Therefore God is to the angels as angels are to human beings, as the king is to his vassals, as the lion or eagle is to the lowly grasshopper or snail, as a man is to a woman, as a father is to his household, as the head is to the other members of a living organism, as the soul is to the body.[4] Human relations cannot hope to escape arrangements of superiority and subordination, given the nature of the universe.

---

and T. F. Torrance, trans. A. T. MacKay et al. (Edinburgh: T & T Clark, 1961), 3/4:116–240). In the conclusion of the book as a whole, I express some general reservations about a strategy for countering Christian justifications of hierarchy that does not reject the whole idea of a mirroring relation between human and divine orders outright but simply focuses on a different account of God's nature.

4. See W. H. Greenleaf, *Order, Empiricism and Politics* (Oxford: Oxford Univ. Press, 1964), chap. 4; Michael Walzer, *Revolution of the Saints* (Cambridge: Harvard Univ. Press, 1965), 151–71.

A similar procedure for justifying human hierarchy replaces this talk about a chain of *being* with an account of a chain of *command* running from God, the supreme commander, through the human powers that are God's lieutenants, to the lowliest human subjects obedient to the orders of those in between.[5] This sort of substitution is common where God is understood to relate to the world primarily by an exercise of power and will (e.g., in Calvinist traditions). A hierarchical structure of *being* is no longer, as it was in the chain-of-being strategy, the basis for a hierarchical arrangement of *power*. A hierarchy of power is simply the means God employs to carry out God's plans for creation. Hierarchy thus loses the inevitability it had as an inherent feature of the universe; the character of the universe to which God once conformed is now an order that God controls. There is at least the possibility therefore of some variability in the roles and role relations through which God distributes human power and prestige. The particular power and status distributions characteristic of human society need not repeat or bear an exact correspondence to those of other created spheres.

The results of a chain-of-command justification of hierarchy are much the same, however, as those of a chain-of-being justification. God's influence on and relation to the created world proceed by way of an order of superiors and subordinates. Religious subordinates, say, laypersons, are related to God and obey God's will for spiritual affairs by obeying their religious superiors, the members of an ecclesiastical hierarchy, who have been empowered by God for that purpose. Political subordinates obey God's will for human government in so far as they loyally follow the commands of their political superiors (e.g., the king and his ministers). One can understand the following comment by Martin Luther to make the point nicely for relations within the household: "A poor little maid servant, . . . I cook, I make the beds, I clean the house. Who has bidden me? My lord and my mistress. Who has given them this power over me? God has done it. Yea, then it must be true that I serve not only them but also God in heaven and that He is pleased therewith. . . . Is it not as if I were cooking for God in heaven?"[6] God executes God's plans for the world by empowering an ecclesiastical hierarchy that might install or regulate a temporal

5. See Walzer, *Revolution of the Saints*, 160–66.

6. Sermon on Matt. 6 (1544), quoted by Karl Barth in *Church Dogmatics*, 3/4:645.

government whose leader (a monarch, say) is himself commanded by God to govern the political and economic affairs of male property owners. Those male property owners in turn as heads of households have the God-given duty to control the lives of women, children, and servants.[7]

The account of God's transcendence offered in the previous chapter is not compatible with these chain-of-being or chain-of-command justifications of human hierarchy. Instead, that account provides much the same critique of both: the charge that the radical transcendence of God is reduced.

This is most obvious for a chain-of-being justification of human hierarchy since it is predicated on the idea of degrees of being and perfection filling out a continuum between God at the one extreme and the lowest material existence on the other. According to the belief in God's transcendence with which I am working, the difference between God and created beings is more qualitative than quantitative. It is not possible to be more or less divine in nature or stature; no part of the created order can be distinguished from any other in the degree to which it approaches the character or supremacy of divinity.[8]

Both the chain-of-being and the chain-of-command strategies for justifying hierarchy conflict with my account of God's transcendence in so far as they include God as one being among others within a single, all-inclusive sphere of being or line of command. According to my account of God's transcendence, God, rather than residing within it, remains outside the whole of any created order of being or command, as what brings it to be. Indeed, in order to be the creator of all, directly and not by way of other creatures, God must be "outside" rather than within a world of nondivine beings. On a chain-of-being or chain-of-command account, God either exists or operates within the same arena as creatures, and therefore God's relation to creatures as the giver of all gifts is not equally direct or of the same quality in

7. Depending on the historical period, there are of course any number of variants of such orderings, but the basic structure of the account remains the same.

8. I am not ruling out here all talk of God as the highest or supreme being in a chain of being. This way of speaking is quite common in Christian theology especially prior to the eighteenth century, among those (e.g., Thomas Aquinas) whose theological judgment I have no interest in impugning. Theologians can use such language in ways that suggest that God infinitely surpasses or transcends even the highest of created beings and therefore in ways that level the significance of distinctions of being for God's relation with the world. Chain-of-being justifications for human hierarchy do not do so.

all cases. On a chain-of-being or chain-of-command account, God has a certain location within a single order of being or function that includes creatures, so that God's relation to them as their creator, guide, and redeemer is differentiated according to where they are placed relative to God.[9]

This indirectness of God's relation to some creatures, or its lesser degree or quality in some cases, is hard to maintain when God's gift of existence is at issue. Christian theology strongly prohibits saying that God brings to be certain creatures by way of others or creates some beings to a lesser extent or in a qualitatively different fashion than God creates others. The appropriateness of the same prohibitions is less obvious (though just as pertinent) where God's bringing to be of a salvific or providential *order* of created beings is at issue. In these cases chain-of-being or chain-of-command justifications of human hierarchy claim indirectness or a difference in quality or degree in God's relation to the world.

Laypersons might be said to become the object of God's saving grace only in so far as they maintain an appropriate relation with holders of clerical offices with a more direct line of access to God's working as savior and redeemer. At least some creatures come to obey God's will for the created order, one might say, only in so far as they obey other creatures who are more directly governed by a divine command. Intermediate created powers make one's own existence as an agent under God's will indirect. Even if a political subordinate's relation to God is not thought to go through his or her relation to a superior, one might claim for that superior a higher quality relationship with God in virtue of a direct divine commission. A higher quality relationship with God can also be ascribed to those higher in a chain of being. Thus an angel's relationship with God is not of the same quality as a human being's. It is of a higher caliber in virtue of the higher nature of angels that brings them closer to God along the scale of being. The ignorant laborer does not have the same sort of relationship with God as the cloistered contemplative. God's relation with the latter is a closer, stronger, better relation, from which the laborer

9. For more on the logical connections between the claim of God's transcendence and the claim of God's direct creation of all beings, see Kathryn Tanner, *God and Creation in Christian Theology* (Oxford: Basil Blackwell, 1988), chap. 2.

is either barred by natural deficiencies or made eligible only through a change of station.

On the account of God's nature and relation to the world that I favor, however, the relationship of God with every particular in the created world is equally immediate and invariant whatever one's created nature, personal status, or station. Differences in quality, character, or achievement may very well exist in the world God brings to be, but God creates, guides, and works to save all these different beings, without any indirection and by way of a creative relationship that is marked by no differences of degree or fundamental quality. No one is any differently or any more or less the creature of God. No one is any differently or any more or less the object of God's providential, or redeeming will, in virtue of the differences in status or constitution that might establish orders among created beings. Hierarchical orders, at least in so far as they concern God's relationship with the world, are leveled in this way. Created beings are simply not hierarchically arranged with respect to God.[10]

One can block chain-of-being and chain-of-command justifications of human hierarchy in these ways without, however, denying that the world is hierarchically arranged, that God's plans for the world are manifested by relations of superiors and subordinates, or that God's salvific will for the world includes the institution of an ecclesiastical hierarchy, even an order of the saved and the damned. God's relation to the world as its creator, providential orderer, and redeemer may not be differentiated according to hierarchical arrangements of being or status, but that does not mean that the latter do not exist within the world that God so creates, guides, and redeems.

One cannot say, for example, on my account of God's relation to the world, that God creates one being by creating another. But what God creates may still be a world of beings hierarchically arranged according to the degree of perfection of their natures. Should God's creative will extend to human hierarchy, the superiors in the hierarchy God creates are not the means God uses to bring their inferiors to be. As the creator of all, God brings into existence the whole of the hierarchy, inclusive of all its particulars, superiors and subordinates

10. This sort of leveling is commonly thought to be a contribution of Protestant Reformation theology, but I believe it to be a continuous strand of the Christian tradition from the beginning. See ibid., chaps. 2 and 3.

alike, without any created intermediaries. The whole world created in this immediate way by God is simply hierarchically arranged.[11]

According to my account, one created being also does not become part of God's providential plans for the world through the mediation of any human commanders. But this account by itself does not rule out the possibility that God's providential plans for the world include the submission of some human beings to the orders of others. God's plans for the world may include fixed relations of leaders and followers, even if God does not exercise an indirect influence over some human beings by means of others who, as the more primary agents of God's will, are supposed to order them about. On the account of God's providence I am following, every human being, ruler or subject, falls immediately under God's providential will for the whole in all its particulars. Nonetheless, the immediate way in which God's providential will extends over the whole does not stop what God wills in this way from amounting to a rigidly hierarchical distribution of human power and influence.

Finally, the spiritually adept who bring others to conversion, the religious authorities who administer sacraments, are not the means by which God's salvific will is directed to the laity or the less spiritually gifted. Each person, whatever their spiritual distinction vis-à-vis others or their place in an ecclesiastical hierarchy, stands before God's offer of salvation in Christ in an immediate and unconditioned way. God's decision to save is not mediated by or brought about through the influence of other human beings. What God decides may nevertheless involve one's religious subordination to others. God does not decide to save one because one follows the orders of the bishop and is baptized, but God's free decision to save one may amount, in any case, to the plan to bring one to a proper faith through submission to ecclesiastical authorities.

In sum, God does not require a chain of being or chain of command to create, direct, or save the lowly, but God may nevertheless

11. Short of a claim for the active intervention of superiors in the creative process, even the minimal claim that God's decision to create subordinates is conditioned by a decision to create their superiors is ruled out according to my account. Although one created being may follow another in some hierarchical arrangement, in my account God's will for the one does not follow God's will for the other. God creates the whole by way of a single, all-embracing intention and undifferentiated act. What is brought about in this way can nevertheless be a hierarchically differentiated whole.

bring about a world of hierarchically arranged beings, political powers, or religious functionaries. Hierarchical arrangements in the universe lose chain-of-being or chain-of-command justifications for their existence, but they may remain intact.[12]

Two new ways of justifying a hierarchical order in human society can fill the gap left by the loss of chain-of-being or chain-of-command justifications, and provide a positive reason for claiming that human society with such an arrangement is the sort God intends. These justifications of hierarchy are compatible with the admission that God's relation with human beings as their creator, providential orderer, and redeemer is immediate and invariant across differences of nature and status. An attempt is made simply to justify that what God so effects as creator, providential orderer, and redeemer is hierarchy. One claims that hierarchical arrangements of human beings must be what God intends for the world since they conform either (1) to the diverse natures with which God has endowed human beings or (2) to the direct mandate of God's will.[13] I consider each of these attempts at justification in turn.

HIERARCHY BASED UPON CREATED DIFFERENCES OR A DIVINE MANDATE

According to the first, God creates human beings with different natures; those natures suit human beings for distinct social functions; those functions are coordinated according to mutual need, every class of person contributing its natural capacities to remedy every other class's natural incapacities, to form an organic whole. Social roles and relations are fixed, since the created natures of persons from which they are derived are fixed. Those differences of nature are simply creations of God, and therefore the social roles to which they give rise

12. The extent to which they remain intact, especially in the religious or ecclesiastical sphere, is one of the disagreements between Protestants and Roman Catholics at the time of the Reformation. For more information on the distinction I trade on here between the character of God's active relation to world (as its creator, providential orderer and redeemer) and the nature of what God brings about thereby, see my *God and Creation*, chap. 3.

13. As the attentive reader will notice, in the next section I talk of a divine mandate in a broader way than I did in chap. 3. The meaning of the expression now encompasses, in the terminology of chap. 3, orders-of-creation, divine-mandate, and divine-commission understandings of social order as hierarchical. The bottom line is the belief that hierarchical arrangements constitute God's own will for human life.

cannot be fluid and the social relations that they produce cannot be altered. Moreover, assignment to roles is presumptive: there is no doubt about the specific roles a person is to perform—if that person has breasts and a womb, or dark complexion and kinky hair, everything is clear enough. A claim of natural differences allows one to presume rather than establish fitness for distinct social tasks by a trial. Finally, the coordination of social roles tends toward relations of superiority and submission, since some social roles entail rights and privileges that others do not, and these roles are categorically denied to certain classes of persons. For example, white men, believed to be the naturally intelligent portion of the human race, are suited to participate in affairs of state—they have the right to exercise power of that sort and reap the benefits of such a right—while white women and men and women of color, the naturally unintelligent portion, cannot. One can talk of exercising Christian virtues of mutual service within such an organic harmony of natural functions (Christians are to be each other's servants after all), but all this means is that those with power are to show care and concern for those who lack rights of self-determination, and that those without power are to submit voluntarily and surrender themselves humbly before those with the God-given qualifications to rule.

According to the second sort of justification, hierarchical arrangements in human society are not legitimated by being traced back to the natural differences among persons that God creates but are referred directly to God's plan, God's providential will, for order in human affairs. Human orders owe nothing to nature but everything to God. Different social functions do not correspond to different natural classifications of persons; they simply correspond to the different divisions of work that are required for the sort of order in human society that God wills. Since this order is believed to be one of superiors and subordinates, one can still say that one serves God by serving one's superiors.

This appeal to God's will breaks any claim that human relations of superiority and subordination are necessary in virtue of permanent features of creation that distinguish types of persons. The theologian can aver, however, that these relations are necessary in any case for the maintenance of social order—not everyone can lead, some must follow. Relations of superiority and subordination that cannot be justified in this way with reference to the need for mutual adjustment among various social tasks (e.g., is the absolute authority of a father over his household functionally necessary?) can be referred to God's inscrutable will.[14] The arbitrariness of certain privileges is no reason therefore to question their necessity when God's will replaces natural differences as the ground of human hierarchies. The absolute authority of fathers is simply what God demands, whether or not it is necessary to meet the functional requirements of society.

One might think because the second way of justifying hierarchy by appeal to God's will bypasses created differences that human hierarchy would not be rendered immune to historical change. One suspects that a motivation for basing human hierarchy on the natural characteristics of persons God creates is to block the idea that norms for human relations develop over time through a process of historical change. God as providential orderer rather than creator is associated with events in history. If human relations of superiors and subordinates are referred now to God's providential will, does that not suggest that they are alterable? Such a critical potential is only a potential, however, and can be blocked.

God's will for order in human society is often simply identified with those relations among persons that are believed to be unalterable—relations of superiority and subordination between men and women, parents and children, husbands and wives.[15] The twentieth-century Protestant theologian Emil Brunner identified God's will for order in human affairs with "existing facts of human corporate life which lie at the root of all historical life as unalterable presuppositions," facts that "are unalterable in their fundamental structure, and at the same time, relate and unite men to one another in a definite way."[16] The stability of these relations over time is a reason for attributing them to an order God wills, if one assumes, apparently, that genuine effects

14. See Ernst Troeltsch, *The Social Teaching of the Christian Churches*, trans. Olive Wyon, 2 vols. (London: George Allen and Unwin, 1931), 1:286.

15. See, for example, the writings of Paul Althaus, Emil Brunner, Dietrich Bonhoeffer, and even Karl Barth in *Church Dogmatics*, 3/4, despite his worries about natural theology.

16. Quoted by Robin Lovin, *Christian Faith and Public Choices*, 72–73. From Brunner's *Divine Imperative*, trans. Olive Wyon (Philadelphia: Westminster Press, 1947), 210.

of God's providential concern for human society can only be static. Human relations that have proven themselves to be alterable are not essential parts of the order God institutes, or such change indicates the infiltration of sinful disorder into the arrangements of human society as God ordains them. An insistence on the fixed character of hierarchical relations among persons is presumably behind the penchant in these theological circles for saying that these relations, while not based on distinctions in the created constitutions of human beings, are themselves created. Thus, they can be isolated as easily as before from the potential for providential change in history that might otherwise be suggested by talk of God's will. A social order, as created, is to be passed down through history and not altered in the course of it.

Finally, one might think that legitimations of hierarchy through an appeal to God's will would make assignment to social roles more flexible. What is important is simply the ability to do the work God requires. Questions of eligibility are not referred immediately to questions of natural classification. A presumption of fitness is not available on that basis prior to actual occupation.

Rather than favor flexibility, however, this appeal to God's will makes the question of fitness or suitability drop out altogether. One performs the job one finds oneself in, one conforms to the station that happens to be one's by birth or accident or fate, whatever one's natural qualifications or interests. The facts of historical fortune are equated with God's providence.

Furthermore, this equation of God's will with the facts of social location entails the following logical slippage. The idea that one can serve God just as well in any station or walk of life, since none is closer to God or of a grander status vis-à-vis God—an idea that follows from the rejection of a chain-of-being or chain-of-command justification of hierarchy—becomes the idea that the service God requires simply is the performance of one's given station or occupation in life. The idea that God's command finds one whatever one's social location (the implication of a rejection of a chain-of-command justification of hierarchy) becomes the idea that God's command *is* one's given status location. The idea that God's call to serve God's will (whatever that might amount to) finds one wherever one might be, however lowly one's status or prestige, becomes the idea that one's lowly status *is* the fulfillment of what God calls one to do. Thus to attempt willfully to alter one's station in life can only be a matter of arrogant presumption, contrary to God's will. One is called to serve God where one is, meaning not that one can start there to do whatever God commands and that no higher status of worldly prestige is to be envied as if God's call might find one better there, but that service to God *ends* with the loyal performance of duties appropriate to the station one already occupies.[17]

On this view, the primary reason one believes that one serves God in serving one's superiors is not because one's superiors serve God's will in asking for one's obedience (as was the case with a chain-of-command justification of hierarchy). God's call to service directly concerns the duties of one's own station, no matter how lowly. Every station deserves the respect of a sphere of God's calling. The results are the same, however: the duties that the lowly are called to perform require submission to their social betters.

On the basis of the account of God's transcendence and relation to creation that I favor, one can lodge two objections against both these attempts to justify human hierarchy. First, in the appeal to either created differences or God's will, human order is isolated in an illegitimate way from any ongoing dependence upon a free God's active will. Natural classifications of persons or the very social relations of superiors and inferiors that happen to exist are deemed finished facts to which God's will for any new thing must be subordinated. According to a created-differences justification of human hierarchy, natural differences, the results of God's *creative* will, form the basis for social relations that are immune from alteration by God's *providential* will. God's providence is bound in this way to God's work as creator as if the same free will of God were not behind both created differences and historical developments of human society. According to the divine-mandate justification, social relations as the product of God's *direct* will for order in human affairs are immune from alteration by (1) God's providential will for a further development of human society, or (2) God's redemptive will for a Christian life that exceeds the bounds of

17. I am indebted here to Barth's criticism of a Lutheran notion of calling in *Church Dogmatics*, 3/4, esp. 600–7. (Although it should be clear that I do not think his criticisms of a Lutheran notion of orders of creation in the same volume go far enough.)

prevailing social relations (whether sinful or not). God is no longer free vis-à-vis the established effects of God's own will.

According to the account of God's relation to creation with which I am working, one need not deny that differences in nature or established social station conform to God's will; it is just that God's will for human society cannot be limited to them. Because any extant human hierarchy is in an ongoing relation of dependence upon God's free will, it cannot be deemed necessary or immutable. For the same reason, role relations (e.g., what a husband owes his wife and vice versa) are potentially fluid and reversible. Finally, the social roles a person performs should be open and alterable if a person's social location depends upon what a living and free God ordains. In these ways the rigidity of social roles and relations that characterizes hierarchy is undercut.

Second, both sorts of justification of human hierarchy make the mistake of assuming that social roles, their ordering, and one's assignment to them are unalterable by human beings (not just by God) because they isolate God's doing from human doing, and therefore God's responsibility for social order from human responsibility. This exclusion of human agency would be plausible, if, as these forms of justification try to argue, hierarchical relations were themselves created or determined by created differences of nature. What God creates, human beings simply receive. Only God is involved in creating: human beings are always the results of, and therefore never the participants in, the creative action by which God brings a human form of life to be. As Edmund Burke, the famous repudiator of the French Revolution, expressed the idea: "the awful Author of our being is the Author of our place in the order of existence,—and . . . having disposed and marshalled us by a divine tactic, not according to our will, but according to His, He has in and by that disposition virtually subjected us to act the part which belongs to the place assigned us. We have obligations. . . . [that] arise from the relation of man to man, and the relation of man to God, which relations are not matters of choice."[18]

I have argued, however, that God's will for human society cannot be limited in any a priori way to what God creates. The question

18. From *An Appeal from the New to the Old Whigs*, quoted by J. C. D. Clark in *English Society 1688–1832* (Cambridge: Cambridge Univ. Press, 1985), 256.

whether God's doing excludes human doing becomes, therefore, the question whether God's providential or redeeming will for human society has to exclude human decision making. The second form of justification of hierarchy, which allows for appeals to God's providential or redemptive will, assumes just that. For example, on the question of assignment to station: if God calls one to serve in a particular station, that station is not a matter of one's own choosing.

On my account of God's providential and saving will, however, what God wills for order in human society or for the redemption of those social relations may include the choices of human beings. One cannot assume therefore that simply because a form of society is willed by God, human decision making has no contribution to make to it. Moreover, since God's will is not fixed by what has already been established, human beings in following God's will may make decisions for the alteration of social roles and the manner in which they are coordinated. Hierarchy again loses the fixity that is one of its defining characteristics. Human beings in trying to carry out God's will for human affairs may decide that fathering should take on some of the characteristics of mothering—boundaries between roles need not be sharp—or that wives should take over the traditional prerogatives of husbands—the ordering of roles need not be irreversible. They may each decide for themselves the social roles most amenable to the service to which God calls them. Finally, changing one's social location may be just as much a matter of following God's will as staying put, once God's calling is no longer identified with accidents of birth or happenstances of fortune that preclude human planning and exercise of choice. In this way the immobility of social location typical of hierarchy is broken.

THE MODEL OF GOD'S RELATION TO THE WORLD

A final manner of justifying human hierarchy models arrangements among human beings on God's relation to the world: Human superiors are to human subordinates as God is to the world. Since this justification of human hierarchy seems to avail itself of my own account of a transcendent God's relation to the world, I have to consider its various forms carefully, with the intent of dissociating myself from them or discrediting their logical merits. Otherwise I have little hope of continuing my efforts to show the politically progressive potential of the account of God's relation to the world with which I have been working. Tackling the specifics of these arguments will also give me the opportunity to explore the more general question of whether it is ever proper, according to my account of Christian beliefs about God and the world, to model human relations on the relation between the world and God. Even if human hierarchy cannot be justified by such means, might not this sort of argument be a way of addressing the need that opened this chapter—the need to develop criteria for proper human relations from my account?

First Form

The type of justification of human hierarchy that models social relations on God's relation with the world comes in two forms. The first seems worse than any justification of human hierarchy yet encountered in that it appears bent on pushing the disparity of power and privilege between superiors and subordinates as far as it can possibly go. While I have so far shown the ways in which my own account of God's relation to the world confounds theological arguments for the propriety of hierarchy, the same principles I employed—the radical transcendence of God, the immediacy of God's relation to the world, the invariance of that relation across differences of natural feature and social status—are used in this first form to justify social relations of superiority and subordination more extreme than any discussed previously in that they claim for social or political superiors absolute and unconditional rights and privileges.

Thus the following affirmations and arguments seem to be based on the three theological principles I just mentioned. First, the being, status, and power of a human ruler or authority can no more be approached by its subjects than can a radically transcendent God by its creatures. Second, just as the differences among creatures make no difference to God's relation to the world as its creator, providential orderer, and redeemer, so the differences among individuals stand as nothing before a human sovereign's right to rule. No other human jurisdictions, which might be formed with reference to those differences, exist to dispute or condition the way in which a human sovereign relates to his or her subjects. Finally, the immediacy of a human sovereign's relation to God is understood to exclude all obligations to those ruled. A human sovereign is deemed obedient to no one but God; direct obedience to God legitimates a rule that cannot be responsive to, or checked by, those subject to it. As Queen Elizabeth solemnly declared in 1585: "Kings and Princes Sovereigns, owing their homage and service only unto the Almighty God the King of all Kings, are in that respect not bound to yield account or render the reasons of their actions to any other but to God their only Sovereign Lord."[19]

In these ways, my theological principles might undercut justifications of human hierarchy and favor the leveling of social and political status differences, only to further a more simplified form of hierarchy: everyone stands without distinction under the absolute authority of a human power. For example, feudal hierarchies of inferior jurisdictions are leveled before an absolute monarchy. Women, children, slaves, and servants might lose all rights of redress before a patriarchal head of household. Indeed, in seventeenth- and eighteenth-century Europe these two logically distinct arenas of absolute rule—monarchical and familial—were often thought of together to constitute a national order justified by Christian principles. In that case a king was also considered a father with absolute rights, but his family was the whole realm.[20]

It is my contention, however, that each of these appeals to my theological principles for the purpose of justifying absolutist rule involves an inconsistency: the human authority at issue is inexplicably exempted from principles that hold for everyone else. Such appeals do not, then, properly instantiate these principles; these principles are instead misapplied and ideologically deformed.

Consider the way in which the idea that God transcends the world is used to justify absolute rule. God transcends the world in a way that does not admit of degrees—this radical transcendence of God

19. Quoted in Lawrence Stone, *The Causes of the English Revolution* (New York: Harper and Row, 1972), 94.

20. See Gordon Schochet, *Patriarchalism in Political Thought* (Oxford: Basil Blackwell, 1975). In the interest of clear types, the discussion in this section is limited to justifications of absolute monarchy: absolute rule by a monarch is obviously potentially not absolute if heads of household have their own familial sphere of dominion. The kinds of justification I am interested in here are also clearer for the case of national sovereigns.

is the grounds for claiming a difference that is also absolute between human ruler and subject. Yet such a principle of divine transcendence is violated in the very process of using it as a model for human rule: the human ruler does approach divinity. The sovereign is a "mortal god."[21] "Of all the creatures of the universe, none draweth nearer to the creator . . . so much as doth the King."[22] An absolute ruler is the very "image of God upon earth";[23] sovereigns reign "because they bear God's character, and do shine with the rays of his majesty."[24] The distinction between ruler and ruled can be absolute only if the relation between God and the world is, but in order to justify drawing the parallel at all, human rulers are exempted from inclusion in the world that God absolutely transcends. Everyone is radically other than God except the king.

Indeed, the unique standing of the ruler is needed if an appeal to God's transcendence is to justify absolute rule. If the ruler is not like God in a way that no one else is, the model of God's relation to the world might float to cover other, subordinate orders under a king, thereby implying that his rule is not absolute or unconditioned. Something about the nature of a king (or a father)—hereditary bearing, physical prowess, personal charisma, or virtue—limits the application of such a model to the king alone.

Prevented from floating free of kingship, the correspondence between God's relation to the world and a king's relation to subjects is no mere analogy that recognizes the dissimilarity between God and human rulers, as creatures like any other. The ruler is not just related to other human beings on some distant analogy with God's relation to the world that supposes all creatures, including rulers, to be infinitely distant from God's nature. No, the king has the power of God (or approaches it) because the king is divine or misses divinity by some difference of degree. Indeed, the stronger the need to justify absolute rule, the greater the tendency to raise the stakes and claim divinity for

21. Hobbes, *Leviathan*, 227, quoted by Quentin Skinner, *The Foundations of Modern Political Thought*, 2 vols. (Cambridge: Cambridge Univ. Press, 1978), 2:287.

22. J. Bede, *The Right and Prerogative of Kings*, cited by Greenleaf, *Order, Empiricism and Politics*, 53.

23. See Greenleaf, *Order, Empiricism and Politics*, 60–61, 134, citing James I, and the royalist Knolles.

24. From the anonymous author of *The Whole Duty of Man* (1744), cited by Clark, *English Society*, 127.

human rulers. Thus the notoriously uncircumspect James I of England explained to Parliament in 1609 that "[k]ings are not only God's lieutenants on earth and sit upon God's throne, but even by God Himself they are called gods."[25]

Using the principle of an invariant relationship of God to the world in order to justify absolute rule is inconsistent in a similar way. If absolute human rule is to be supported, no social distinctions or differences of human power or prestige should affect the relation of God to the world that is the model for a sovereign's relation to his people. But drawing the parallel between the two exempts the distinction between human ruler and subject from the same principle of invariance. It now makes a difference to one's relationship with God if one is a ruler. Indeed, an absolute monarch is God's "lieutenant" or the representative of God's plans for the world in a way denied to all others. The absolute monarch is the sole legislator and interpreter of God's will for social order and works to execute it with or without the consent of those affected, on the assumption that no one subject to a ruler can be a comparable agent of God's plans for the world.

If more backing for dictatorial rule is required, the sins of the people may be expounded. A human ruler provides external direction to a sinful populace just as God stands ready with an offer of aid to the whole world that lacks the resources to help itself. In this way a human ruler is exempted inexplicably from the whole world that is the object of divine help. The matter of political power distinguishes those people who are in need of God's corrective or redemptive will from those who are not. Christian justifications of absolute rule thus join a long history of identifying sin along class or power lines generally, in violation of the rule of invariance. The duchess of Buckingham, complaining about Methodist preachers in a letter to the countess of Huntingdon, expressed for the eighteenth-century English elite the sentiment of that history in a wonderfully bald fashion: "It is monstrous to be told that you have a heart as sinful as the common wretches that crawl on the earth."[26]

25. Quoted by Stone, *Causes*, 94. Oh, the difference between a capital and a small *g*!

26. Cited (without further reference) by H. Richard Niebuhr, *The Social Sources of Denominationalism* (Cleveland: Meridian Books, 1957), 61.

The notion of an immediate relation of God to the world is also employed in a peculiar way when justifying absolute human rule. As the special agent of God's will on earth, the absolute ruler can lay claim to that principle of immediacy: an absolute monarch obeys God directly. Thus a monarch's obedience to God does not require submission in any degree before a feudal hierarchy, papal legates, parliamentary sessions, common law, or popular outcry; the king does not become subject to God's will by becoming subject to any human power. The principle that held for all creatures according to my account is hereby limited, however, to absolute rulers. The king has a direct relationship with God but no one subject to the king does. The subjects of the king become followers of God simply in so far as they are loyal to the monarchy. The principle of God's direct relationship with the world is therefore turned into an exception. Only in that way can the immediacy of a relation to God buttress the unconditioned authority and absolute unaccountability of a human ruler.

Second Form

This last series of arguments has simply fended off a particularly horrid use of my account of God's relation to the world: an absolute human authority cannot be justified by an appeal to God's relation to the world without violating the fundamental theological principles of my account. This series of arguments is not sufficient, however, to prevent God's relation to the world from serving as just a general paradigm for social relations. In considering God's relation to the world as such a paradigm, one need not presume, as arguments for absolutist authority did, that the superiors in human relationships are somehow exempt from the community of creatures God transcends, or claim for them any special standing before God. These correspondences between human relations and God's relation to the world are just unpretentious parallels or analogies, in which God's relation to the world figures as the highest exemplar of order.

The supreme or highest form of relationship, God's own relationship to the world is a hierarchical relationship of superior and subordinates. The distinction between God and the world is sharp rather than fluid. God's relation to the world as creator, providential guide, and redeemer is an irreversible relation between extreme unequals. One party—the world—owes everything about itself that is good to the other—God. Why should the supreme or highest form of relationship not serve as a paradigm for, an ideal to be approximated by, every human relationship? Here is a second form of justification of human hierarchy that models social relations on God's relation to the world.

Indeed, understanding one's relations with others by modeling them on the hierarchical relation that holds between God and the world seems almost an inevitability.[27] In the wash of a culture's thoughts about order, a hierarchical understanding of God's relationship to the world will tend to bleed onto all the others. Discussing the highest form of relationship as a hierarchy is simply prone to be contagious.[28]

Someone holding my account of a transcendent God's relation to the world will begin to suspect that something is theologically amiss here once it becomes apparent that the effects of this process of modeling human relations on God's relation to the world are quite different depending upon the social status or political position of the parties involved. People with power come to understand the nature of their relations with others by modeling their status in those relations upon God's supremacy. People without power are to think of their obedience to superiors as a training ground for the obedience to God that such human relations of obedience mimic. In the case of the mighty, Christianity provides thereby an education in the nature of domination; in the case of the poor, an education in submission.

Education for such different results suggests that the respective parties do not have the same standing vis-à-vis God, and this inequality violates the theological principles I have proposed. Only the lower classes "benefit" from an education in submission. People with economic and political power or social prestige apparently do not need to be taught through their human relationships the subordination they should feel before God, despite the fact that as creatures that is the appropriate posture for them too. Indeed, one would think powerful

27. This is clearly the worry of contemporary feminist theologies that favor the rejection or severe modification of ideas of God's transcendence. See, for example, Sallie McFague, *Models of God* (Philadelphia: Fortress Press, 1987), part 1. I am about to argue that, while it may be a natural tendency, this sort of modeling of human relations on God's relation to the world is theologically inappropriate on my account of a transcendent God's relation to the world. Holding my principles consistently blocks such uses.

28. See Mary Douglas, *Natural Symbols* (New York: Pantheon Press, 1982), for the claim that the understandings of order in distinct cultural and social spheres tend to be homologous.

people would be the ones most in need of such an education. Yet, when human relations are understood on the model of God's relation to the world, habits of domination, to which superiors in human hierarchies are accustomed, are merely confirmed, not corrected.

This whole procedure of modeling relations with others on God's relation to the world is also suspect if one takes God's transcendence seriously. The radical difference between God and creatures does not by itself disqualify a similarity between God's relation to the world and a human superior's relation to subordinates. It is possible for a relation between one pair of terms to be similar to the relation between another while at least one of the terms making up the one pair is nothing like the others. But where God's relation to the world is used as a paradigm for human relations, a purportedly proper understanding of human relations is derived from what is believed about God's relation to the world. One needs positive grounds for making the parallel, and such grounds are supplied, one can only suppose, by the similarity between God and human beings in positions of power. This claim of similarity is enough to violate the principle of God's transcendence. Indeed, since hierarchical relations are irreversible, someone claiming the propriety of human hierarchy on this basis has to maintain that those holding positions of power are much more like God than those without it—so much so, that they are more like God than they are like their social inferiors. The transcendence of God, which relativizes differences among creatures so that every one of them has the same standing before God, has dropped out of sight.

It should be noted that my theological principles do not rule out altogether drawing conclusions about proper relations among persons from the nature of God's relation to the world. Such conclusions must presume, however, the radical difference between God and human beings and the solidarity of the human beings whose relations are considered as creatures of equal standing before God.

One cannot say, then, that relations between human beings are similar to God's relation to the world in virtue of the degree of likeness between God and human powers. One cannot say that because God, an absolute power, rules the world autocratically, human beings should rule their inferiors with as close to an autocratic power as their lesser capacities permit. Nor can one even say that, because God with an unflinching love and generosity cares for the world, human beings should care for those dependent upon them in a degree proportionate to their lesser love and power to help. Caring for the weak can be justified on all sorts of grounds, but this one violates the principle of God's transcendence so that the character of the human relations recommended thereby is rankly paternalistic.

One is permitted to say, however, that the same sort of relation that God has with the world holds for relations among human beings, so long as that sort of relation should hold all the more for creatures who are not God and lack what God has. For example, if God, whose supremacy is beyond compare, does not despise even the humblest among men and women, how much more then should men and women, whose value and power are as nothing compared to God's, refrain from pride before those less fortunate. The general form of the argument is: If God, who is or has *x*, does such and such, how much more should human beings, who are not or who lack *x*, do the same sort of thing.[29]

One can also say that the same sort of relation God has with the world holds for human beings in relation to one another if the parallel that is drawn trades upon the status of all parties in the human relation as creatures of God. For example, from the fact that God has a loving relation with the world one can conclude that human relations should also be loving, if the parallel is drawn by way of a recognition that all parties in the human relation are objects of God's love. One loves others out of gratitude for the love God has shown one and in solidarity with all others so loved by God.

Neither of these forms of argument permits, I think, recommendations for human relations of domination or submission. In the second form of argument, the comparable status of human beings in relation is written into the argument. In the first case, a norm of human domination cannot be based upon a radical difference between human beings and God: even if God's status justifies a relation of supremacy vis-à-vis the world, the fact that human beings lack that status counters rather than supports a claim for their own supremacy over others. A norm of human submission can be derived without violating the form

29. This is an *ad majorem* argument along the lines of the rabbinic rule *kal vechomer*. See Susan Handelman, *The Slayers of Moses* (New York: SUNY Press, 1982), 52–57, and her references; also Jouette Bassler, *Divine Impartiality* (Chico, Calif.: Scholars Press, 1979), 92–100, on Philo.

of this first sort of argument, but it will be a norm of submission to one's social inferiors. If God, whose status is absolutely supreme, humbles God's self before the least of women and men, how much more should powerful women and men, whose status is nothing compared to God, humble themselves before the lowly of this world.

So far I have raised objections in principle to the process of modeling human relations after God's relation to the world. But theologians working with my sort of traditional account of God's relation to the world have two options short of that.

In the first, the theologian seems to reject the parallel in only selected cases—for forms of divine supremacy and power that are believed to be inimitable. It might be all right to say that human beings should love one another as God loves the world in Christ, but human powers and authorities should not attempt to model themselves after God's rule: God is the only ruler of that sort; God's rule usurps purportedly analogous human roles. Thus a Puritan might oppose an English king's efforts to consolidate his rule by saying that God is the only king; kingship becomes an affront to God's majesty, as in 1 Samuel 10:19: "But today you have rejected your God, who saves you from all your calamities and your distresses; and you have said, 'No! but set a king over us.' " Or, Karl Barth might oppose Nazistic or other forms of totalitarian regimes by interpreting them as rivals to the authority and control that are God's alone.[30]

This option does nothing, however, to contest the value of relations of superiority and submission, the value of irreversible and even unconditioned privileges of power. That is the nature, after all, of God's power vis-à-vis the world. All that is important is to prevent human beings from claiming such power for themselves.

On the second option, the theologian simply contests the matter of fact, whatever his or her reservations about the general procedure of modeling human relations on God's relation to the world. Modeling human relations on a transcendent God's relation to the world might be all right; it just will not support the particular conclusion that human relations should be hierarchical. Even if it is the model for human relations, God's relation to the world will not support hierarchical

30. See David Nicholls, *Deity and Domination*, 236, who draws out the similarities between Puritans and Barthians on this score.

relations of human superiors and subordinates because it is not like a human hierarchical relation in fundamental respects.

Although I have expressed general reservations about the modeling process, my account of God's relation to the world is amenable to this second option. Hierarchical relations of human superiors and subordinates do not—cannot—correspond to at least one fundamental feature of God's relation to the world. According to my account, God's relation to the world is primarily one of giving: God bestows on the creature what it is (creation), what it does (providence), and what it is finally to become (salvation). The transcendence of God, which I have stressed so heavily for its critical potential, ensures that this giving is universally relevant and direct. God calls forth the being and active powers of the whole created order without the use of intermediaries, and does not work through certain creatures of a status or nature like itself in order to influence the being and becoming of others. The power or control that God exercises is simply a secondary concomitant of the extent of God's giving. God does not need to determine the lives of creatures by outside direction or by limiting the development of their talents and capacities, through coercion or the creatures' acquiescence before God's superior status or force. It should happen that one follows God as a matter of course, because one becomes all that one is, because one becomes oneself, as the recipient of God's empowering will. Unlike the case of human hierarchies, then, "submission" to or dependence upon God does not take away from one's own status or fulfillment. It does not make a creature less than it could be or restrict its operations. Instead, dependence upon God's will as creator, providential guide, and redeemer establishes the creature in the best that it is and can be according to its highest capacities.[31]

While this account goes some way toward countering the claim that human hierarchy, as an essentially oppressive form of relationship, is modeled on God's relation to the world, it does not prevent other aspects of human hierarchy from claiming such a provenance. My understanding of God's relation to the world still involves a quite rigid distinction between God and creatures; God and creatures do not play reversible roles; and their relationship is far from one of mutuality

31. See my *God and Creation*, chap. 3, for an extended discussion of this relationship of empowerment between God and creatures.

since God's action as the bestower of gifts must take at least some logical and causal precedence over any being or action on the part of creatures. Without a quite radical revising of the traditional sort of Christian understanding of God that I have been employing, these aspects of God's relation with the world are always available to support the propriety of human hierarchy. One can always use the simple fact that God is different from the world on that understanding to valorize, say, rigid class distinctions. Harry Overstreet, following ideas of G. H. Howison (1834–1916), captures this perception nicely in an objection to traditional theism: a democratic society "can brook no such radical *class distinction* as that between a supreme being favored with eternal and absolute perfection and the mass of beings doomed to the lower ways of imperfect struggle."[32] One could reformulate the account of God's relation to the world so as to block claims that hierarchical relations of human beings are modeled on it in any respect, but my objections in principle to modeling human relations on God's relation to the world lead away from such a strategy. (In the conclusion of the book, I argue a stronger case: that such a strategy of reformulation has certain dangers that my own avoids.)

I need to return, then, to my reservation in principle about modeling human relations on God's relation to the world, and shift my attention in the search for theological criteria to judge human relations accordingly, away from the character of God's relation to the world. I direct attention, instead, to what one can conclude about creatures on the basis of their relations with God. Is there something about the created status of human beings that would make hierarchical forms of social relation (perhaps along with other sorts) improper? This is the major question in the next chapter.

32. Cited and discussed by Nicholls, *Deity and Domination*, 149; emphasis mine.

FIVE

Christian Belief and Respect for Others

IN THE PREVIOUS chapter I attacked ways of justifying human hierarchy that appeal to the nature of God and God's relation to the world. I showed that the theological principles employed for that purpose are either incompatible with, or involve an inconsistent application of, the theological principles established in chapter 3.

With the notable exception of the third section of the previous chapter (where I considered created differences and a divine mandate as justifications for hierarchy), and some suggestive remarks in the fourth section, I countered theological justifications for hierarchy without attacking hierarchy itself. I criticized certain theological arguments supporting hierarchical relations among human beings, without making much of a theological case against hierarchy on the grounds of my own proposals about God's transcendence and universal providential agency. I need to make such a case now to show that these proposals can provide criteria for evaluating social orders.

For the most part I used my account of a transcendent God's relation to the world simply to contest the conclusion that human social relations have to be hierarchical because of God's nature and relation to the world. Although I made a number of different arguments to that effect, such a conclusion conflicts most basically with a transcendent God's freedom vis-à-vis the world: God *could* intend a world structured hierarchically, but the nature of God and God's relation to the world provides of itself no positive reason for thinking so. Thus my arguments are indirect: If, according to them, a free God might or might not intend human relations to be hierarchical, the propriety of hierarchy itself is not at issue.

In the third section of chapter 4, however, I considered additional grounds for thinking that hierarchical human relations are part of God's intention for the world, and I showed that appeals to natural differences or a divine mandate also improperly restrict a free God's continuing influence over human life where they justify immutable, rigid, irreversible, and presumptively assigned social roles. My account of a transcendent God's relation to the world did provide, therefore, some criteria for criticizing social orders: a hierarchical order with those features should fall under attack.

These conclusions are important, and I will return to them. But they are also quite limited. A reader might object that I have left what is most problematic about human hierarchy unexplored. My criteria for social criticism are not radical enough if they allow the propriety of hierarchical social relations *without* those offending features—hierarchical social relations in which, for example, people are able to change roles of radically disparate power and privilege, or in which such roles are reversible, allowing wives to lord it over their husbands now and then instead of the other way around. Nothing has fundamentally changed in a society altered to conform to my criteria if human relations are still organized around a principle of superiority and subordination, privileges and power possessed by one party but not the other. My criteria would fail to grasp that what makes things like inflexible assignment to roles, rigid role definition, or an irreversible ordering of roles objectionable is that these roles involve a disparity of prerogatives and rights. Not all persons in such roles have the same power over their lives or the same chance for human fulfillment, and those who have more of either seem to gain it at the expense of others. Hierarchical structures are oppressive, in other words.

Furthermore, the criteria for social criticism I have adduced do not seem to be based on any positive vision of proper social relations. According to these criteria, it is improper to claim that hierarchical relations are sacrosanct and immutable or to insist that roles be rigidly defined and inflexibly ordered. But that says very little about what human relations should be like.

I made a start at such a positive vision in the final section of the previous chapter, where I considered the idea of basing proper human relations on God's relation with the world and came up with two types of appropriate inferences, inferences that respect the solidarity of all human beings as creatures of God or that depend on the claim that human beings are not God. These remain, however, simply *types* of inferences about proper human relations, without actual content. Moreover, my general reservations about the whole process of modeling human relations on God's relation to the world prevent me from proceeding any further along the same lines.

A new tactic is necessary, for all these reasons—in order to avoid the indirectness of the arguments so far, to expand the focus of my criteria to more fundamental social issues, and to provide a more positive vision of proper human relations. In keeping with its importance, social oppression will be my focus. In order to avoid the indirectness of my procedure so far, I do not in this chapter (or the next) go through the various ways theologians have justified social oppression and attempt to distance my own account from them. Instead, I simply start from my own theological account and see what it implies. First, that account directly implies that certain features of oppressive social relations are improper. More specifically, my account of God and creation rules out the propriety of certain attitudes toward oneself and others that often typify social relations of oppression. But, second, I will show that at a more fundamental level social oppression is improper because of a positive vision of human social relations that my account of God and creation promotes. Both manners of attack on social oppression will be the product of the switch of attention I mentioned at the end of chapter 4. I ask in this chapter what it means to call people *creatures*, according to my understanding of a transcendent God's relation to the world.

THE DIALECTIC OF IDOLATROUS SELF-AGGRANDIZEMENT AND SELF-CONTEMPT

My first line of attack explores how attitudes toward oneself that conflict with one's status as the creature of a transcendent God are bound up with oppressive social relations. By "bound up with oppression" I mean that such attitudes are *fostered* by oppressive social relations, and themselves *promote* structures of oppression by motivating either the oppressive treatment of others or the co-optation of the oppressed. Belief in a transcendent God's creation of the world rules out these self-understandings or attitudes that help to maintain, and are in turn sustained by, oppressive social relations.

It makes sense to begin my attack on oppression with such a focus on attitude since analysis of this sort has figured so prominently in influential forms of theological ethics—for example, in the theological ethics of Reinhold Niebuhr. I do not end my critique of oppression here; but the results of this line of argument become important again when I turn to the question of activism in chapter 7.

Two sorts of self-understandings or attitudes toward oneself are opposed by my account of a transcendent creator. First, because of God's transcendence, human beings should not assume a divine perfection for themselves. They should not identify their own worth or standing with that of God. Any such identification is idolatrous. Instead, they should accept their status as creatures, limited and conditioned beings, with no pretensions to divinity. This is not to say that the perfection God represents must be irrelevant to human concerns—a possible implication of God's transcendence that I tried to block in chapter 3. But certainly the expectation of divine perfection for oneself as an achieved status is ruled out by my account of God's transcendence. Human beings must accept their status as creatures who simply are not divine.

Second, this acceptance of finitude or creaturehood should not prompt an attitude of self-deprecation. According to the doctrine of creation, the creature as the creation of God is good. Accepting oneself as the finite creature of God means accepting oneself as valuable.

The fact that, as a creature, one is not God is no reason to doubt one's own worth. Only the demand to be nothing less than God forces one's own proper creaturehood to appear worthless. The value of what is not God is denied, in that case, on the assumption that creatures *should* be God.

It is an idolatrous self-aggrandizement, therefore, that tends to veer around into vicious self-recrimination. There exists a dialectic of self-aggrandizement and self-contempt that is founded on an idolatrous disregard for God's transcendence. Either one is confident that one's own perfection rivals divinity, or evidences to the contrary plummet one into the depths of self-despair. Anything short of divine perfection simply is not good enough.

The unrealistic character of these expectations for oneself leads to self-division. An idealized image of oneself is played off against those aspects of one's actual self that fall short of perfection. One side of oneself—that side with the best chance of identification with a divine perfection (say, one's noble ideals or special talents)—goes to war against the others. The latter must be disciplined or forcibly suppressed. It is not as a unified self that one is either valuable or fallible.

These efforts at self-suppression are futile, however, given the imaginary character of one's identification with divine perfection. One cannot completely eliminate that part of the self that separates one from a divine perfection. One is left, therefore, with the alternative of self-repudiation or self-deception. Because one cannot accept oneself finally as the limited being one is, what one really is must be either finally despised or overlooked.

This idolatrous identification with divine perfection might easily fuel social relations that are oppressive. An extreme self-importance inevitably subordinates the claims of others to oneself.[1] Self-suppression becomes political repression in so far as one's social inferiors are identified with what one cannot accept about oneself. Self-hate is externalized as contempt for one's social inferiors. Besides being a natural projection of an internal conflict, such contempt plays into a strategy of self-deception. As protection against self-recrimination, one deflects fault from oneself and identifies it with the life and character of others. Moreover, the frailty of one's own claim to perfection leads one to secure it at the expense of others, to guard it against assault from without: others are a constant source of potential challenge to one's inflated self-esteem. One can wall oneself off in a narcissism that is indifferent to others, ignoring, for example, any circumstance of suffering on their part that might present a challenge to one's own moral rectitude. To excuse oneself and blunt the fury of an uneasy conscience, one might condemn others, accusing the lower classes of the faults that one imagines oneself to avoid. For example, the plight of the poor is to be attributed to their own failings and not to the immorality of one's own privilege. One can assure oneself of one's own invulnerability by a ruthless display of arrogance toward those

1. See Reinhold Niebuhr, *The Nature and Destiny of Man*, 2 vols. (New York: Charles Scribner's Sons, 1964), 1:179, 223, 236, for this connection between pride and injustice.

whom social circumstances have left in a weakened and dependent position.

Social relations between the powerful and the powerless can easily promote the dialectic of self-aggrandizement and self-contempt. One is tempted to identify one's own true self with divinity the greater the degree of privilege and power afforded by one's social position. For example, John Stuart Mill, writing about family relations in nineteenth-century England said, "Men are taught to worship their own wills as such a grand thing that it is actually the law for another rational being." He was not loath to generalize the point: "There is nothing which men so easily learn as this self-worship: all privileged persons, and all privileged classes, have it."[2] What a high social position brings—wealth, prestige, and power over others—allows one to play at an imaginary unconditional supremacy, refusing to recognize one's limitations, expecting immediate results, transforming one's needs into claims that must be respected as a matter of course by one's social inferiors. Moreover, the same privileges allow one to avoid self-recrimination by strategies of self-deception. Power gives one the final privilege of avoiding an honest confrontation with oneself.

Members of an underclass find themselves constantly accused in oppressive situations: Colonialized peoples are brutes, the poor are lazy, blacks and women of all races are intellectually inferior. Every oppressed person consequently rejects himself or herself; the image the oppressor has of one is inevitably introjected—it is at least part of oneself—even if at some later time one tries to throw it off, define oneself against it, or blind oneself to it. Thus the oppressed always live out, to some extent, the very self-recrimination from which their oppressors have dissociated themselves through self-deception.

Moreover, constant accusation produces its own demand for divine perfection. Oppressed people find that they cannot be simply fallible, corrupt, and corruptible like everyone else. They tend to aspire therefore to a perfection that would avert the hostile gaze of the oppressor.

That is what the oppressor demands. The underclasses can only prove, it seems, their worthiness for a change in treatment by their

2. *The Subjection of Women*, cited in *Women, the Family, and Freedom*, ed. Susan Bell and Karen Offen, 2 vols. (Stanford: Stanford Univ. Press, 1983), 1:396.

own perfect probity. Any deceptive dealings by a Jewish person are grounds enough for anti-Semitism; any case of child molestation by a gay man, an excuse for denying gay men and lesbians their civil rights; any case of the irresponsible use of food stamps reason enough for punitive welfare laws—while Christians retain their social privileges without regard for the honesty or dishonesty of their business dealings, straight men retain their heterosexual prerogatives despite the fact that they are in overwhelming numbers the perpetrators of sexual abuse, the rich keep the prestige that money buys whether or not it came to them by grossly irresponsible speculation.

The underclasses will often identify their true selves with a divine self, too, then; but unfortunately for them, their social position prevents them from ever deceiving themselves about achieving it. (If nothing else, those with power will always remind them of their lack of success.) They are left therefore with the self-contempt that is the converse of an aspiration to divinity. They become divided against themselves, hating at least that side of themselves that the oppressor identifies with their fault, trying to escape self-contempt by leaving behind, perhaps, the characteristics that identify them as the underclass and taking on the characteristics of the oppressor. Failing that, a member of an oppressed group might avoid at least the active self-recrimination that oppression fosters by a withdrawal of interest in herself or himself, by an alienation from self manifested in lassitude and passivity.

In short, in social structures of oppression the powerful tend to make idols of themselves while the powerless are made to idolize the powerful as the ideal to which they fall short, the ideal before which therefore they are made to feel their own degradation, an ideal they can only hope to live vicariously, under prevailing social conditions, through servility and dependence upon their social superiors.[3]

3. For this psychology of oppressor and oppressed, I have gone back to Karen Horney's social psychology, whose theological implications Reinhold Niebuhr developed so influentially in *Nature and Destiny of Man*. See her *Neurosis and Human Growth* (New York: W. W. Norton and Co., 1950). In order to supplement Horney's focus on the psychology of those with power and in order to make clear the interconnections of attitude with power structures, I have brought her work together with the psychologies of institutionalized forms of oppression found in Franz Fanon, *Wretched of the Earth* (New York: Grove Press, 1963); and Albert Memmi, *Portrait of a Jew* (New York: Orion Press, 1962); idem, *The Colonizer and the Colonized* (New York: Orion Press, 1965).

A CAVEAT

Showing the ways in which self-understandings that my theological principles rule out can be the source and consequence of social relations of oppression does not provide, however, a radical enough critique of oppression. The theologically improper attitudes I have specified may be sufficient to maintain oppressive social structures but they are not necessary.

Self-esteem that is genuinely idolatrous is not required to fuel oppressive social relations. A simple belief that one's own interests take priority over those of others will do. Nor does finding oneself in the role of an oppressor necessarily produce a sense that one's own supremacy rivals that of God. Oppressive social relations can be reproduced if they foster and are in turn confirmed by the simple self-interest of the powerful, reluctant to forgo the privileges so neatly institutionalized for them by an oppressive status quo.

Moreover, the oppressed need not feel self-contempt. (Although this is perhaps more difficult for them to avoid than idolatrous self-aggrandizement is for the oppressor.) They may be happy with their lot, taking pride in the performance of those tasks that an oppressive situation permits, and enjoying the paternalistic favor of their oppressors that they gain thereby. These attitudes will also (like self-contempt) serve to maintain or reproduce social structures of oppression.

Indeed, social structures of oppression as established structures do not have to be directly fed by any attitudes on the part of the powerful and the powerless in order to keep going. Long-standing patterns of action over generations, a whole complicated interlocking network of social causes and effects, can make individual attitudes more or less irrelevant to the continuance of social relations of systematic oppression. For example, structural forms of discrimination, in which money and class have always meant education and jobs, can be perpetuated by even the most well-meaning people in positions of privilege and power, with no conscious intent to discriminate. If anything, social structures of oppression require attitudes of omission, rather than commission: attitudes that simply stand in the way of people taking responsibility for changing them.[4]

4. I take up attitudes like these in chapter 7 when I address the question of activism.

But most fundamentally my strategy so far for attacking oppression has been inadequate because, if the oppressive treatment of others is wrong, it is wrong in itself, however it may be understood by participants, whatever its attitudinal consequences or motivations. What makes oppressive structures wrong is not so much the attitudes of its participants, although these may be repugnant and theologically objectionable. Oppressive social structures may remain in existence even when such repugnant and theologically objectionable attitudes are removed, and even in that case those structures continue to be wrong. What makes them wrong is simply the treatment of persons that characterizes them. What are the theological grounds for objecting to structures of oppression themselves?

Where social relations are oppressive, treatment of persons violates the respect due them as creatures of God. Human beings have value as creatures of God, and oppressive treatment of them conflicts with a proper recognition of that fact. My initial concern is again with an attitude, one of respect, for others as well as oneself in so far as both are creatures of God, an attitude that my account of a transcendent God's relation to the world requires, rather than rules out (as was the case with the dialectic of idolatrous self-aggrandizement and self-contempt just discussed).

RESPECT FOR OTHERS AS CREATURES OF GOD

I have already had occasion to mention in my first line of attack on social oppression that creatures are valuable according to my understanding of God's relation to the world. What a good God brings to be is by definition good. Creatures gain value therefore in virtue of their relation of dependence upon God, the relation by which they have come to be what they are and do and become.

The status that accrues to creatures generally also holds for human beings. Human beings, in virtue of their creaturehood, are valuable. To break this down further in keeping with the fact that human beings, like all other beings, are the creatures of God in all that they are and do and become, human beings are valuable in so far as their existence is the object of God's concern as creator, in so far as their activities are the object of God's concern as providential orderer, and in so far as what they are finally to become is the object of God's concern as the redeemer of the world. God exalts human beings, raises them up, first, in bringing them to be, in making them the gift of their existence and natures. God exalts human beings, second, in giving them the gift of responsible agency, in finding them worthy therefore of participating in God's plans for an historical world order. Finally, God exalts human beings in attempting to hold them to God's loving intentions, God's will for their own good, despite the failings of sin. God exalts human beings by bringing about a world in which human beings can be set anew on a path for their own good. In sum, human beings are valuable by the very fact of a good God's creating, directing, and working to redeem them.

If human beings have a value and dignity as creatures of God, then they are due a proper recognition of that fact. They are to be esteemed; they are due a positive respect as creatures of God. The nature of a respect that is due human beings simply in virtue of their creaturehood might seem a bit mysterious, however. I discuss a number of its features now, highlighting the ones relevant to a criticism of oppression. Several others are the focus of the next chapter, where my concern is for toleration and respect for difference.

First of all, this is a respect due *all* human beings. All human beings are creatures of God. That is clear from the mere fact that they exist. Therefore they are all due the respect owed to God's creatures.

This respect is not extended to all human beings because of any features or capacities that define a properly human life, features or capacities that all human beings might hold in common or share—for example, the universal reason affirmed by ancient Stoicism or the human capacities for rational self-determination that Enlightenment thinkers put forward in an attempt to break the hold of privileges and rights based on social standing or inheritance. Indeed, creaturehood is a surer, more secure grounds for respecting all persons than any such appeal to common qualities or capacities. People differ, after all, in their intellectual capacities. Some may be educated, while others remain ignorant. Not everyone has the capacity for rational self-determination (e.g., small children or those who have suffered severe brain damage). Where respect is based on common qualities, differences in those qualities must be denied (which is contrary to fact) if such respect is to be extended to everyone. Otherwise, the differences that exist supply grounds for a claim that not all persons have a right to it.[5] As Voltaire, the great defender of enlightened rational self-determination, expressed the importance of such differences to Frederick the Great: there is no point in working for the enlightenment of society "among the rabble who are not worthy of being enlightened and who are apt for every yoke; I say [one should work for it] among the well-bred, among those who wish to think."[6]

In general, if respect is based on creaturehood, no one is due that respect because of what they specifically are or can do or may become. Physical characteristics (e.g., maleness) are not the basis for this respect. Social status (e.g., nobility) is not the basis for it either. Nor is economic possession (e.g., holding property) its condition. Even moral virtue is irrelevant when determining who is or is not due it. Several conclusions can be drawn from this general fact that will further specify the character of the respect owed human beings as creatures of God.

The respect owed human beings as creatures of God is always presumptive and never a matter for proof. It makes no sense to ask whether someone is worthy of the respect owed creatures of God. No particular qualities are its basis. One cannot set out to gain it. Because nothing one does makes one God's creature or the object of God's providential and saving will, worthiness for this respect is not achieved by hard work or a virtuous life. There is just no way to earn respect owed creatures of God. This respect therefore has no eligibility requirements. If one exists, one is due respect, since it is simply as one exists that one falls under God's creative, providential, and salvific concern.

All human beings are owed the respect due God's creatures in the same degree and manner. All human beings are due an equal respect in so far as the respect at issue is owed to them as God's creatures. This is the proper inference to draw because it is the fact of one's

5. See Sanford Lakoff, *Equality in Political Philosophy* (Boston: Beacon Press, 1964), 97, on Richard Hooker's use of differences in learning to justify social inequalities. On the limitations of Stoicism for a universal regard and its differences on this score from forms of Christianity see Lakoff, "Christianity and Equality," in *Equality*, ed. J. Pennock and J. Chapman (New York: Atherton Press, 1967), 118; also Jouette Bassler, *Divine Impartiality* (Chico, Calif.: Scholars Press, 1979), 105–19; and Reinhold Niebuhr, *An Introduction to Christian Ethics* (New York: Seabury Press, 1935), 68–69 et passim. I am disagreeing here with Troeltsch, who in vol. 1 of *The Social Teaching of the Christian Churches*, trans. Olive Wyon (London: George Allen and Unwin, 1931), renders Christian belief and Stoicism indistinguishable on this question of grounds for equality.

6. Cited by Gerald R. Cragg, *The Church and the Age of Reason* (New York: Penguin Books, 1960), 227.

creaturehood that demands respect here, not what one is or does or attains as a creature. Human beings may indeed differ from one another in quality or activity or attainment, but such differences do not alter in any way the fact of creaturehood that is the basis for respect. Nothing that human beings can do to distinguish themselves—their activity, their passivity, their depravity, their efforts to be good—makes them any more or less the creatures of God, any more or less the objects of God's working as creator, providential orderer, and redeemer. No differences among creatures—no natural differences or differences in ascribed or achieved status—make a difference to a creature's creaturehood.

The respect due every human being is an unconditional and indefeasible respect for the same reason. If respect is based on creaturehood, it is not dependent on the specific characteristics and circumstances of its object, and therefore should not be affected by changes in them over time. Consequently, no one can change even for the worse in a way that might warrant a loss of respect for her or him as a creature of God. God's regard for creatures as the object of God's creative and providential and salvific will cannot be broken off by the creature's sin. Sin is never able to exempt the creature from a relation of dependence upon God, from God's creative relation to what is; therefore sin is never able to exempt the creature from the respect that is based on that relation. One is prevented from saying that someone must change before one can hold her or him in regard as a creature of God. One must respect this person as a creature of God, whatever this person has done.

Finally, if respect based on creaturehood does not require its objects to exhibit certain characteristics as opposed to others, the respect due human beings as creatures of God can be peculiarly realistic. It is a respect with no impulse to see those respected as other than what they are, a respect with no motive for substituting an imaginative construction for the real person due respect. For example, a person need not be admirable in order to deserve respect. If such a person does not appear admirable—but narrow-minded, petty, and puerile, say—one need not force oneself to overlook those facts in acknowledging this person's value as a creature of God.

Such realism keeps the unconditional and indefeasible character of respect due human beings as creatures of God from degenerating into a blanket form of regard that overlooks defects in its object or calls them good. Nothing prevents one from seeing a person's defects for what they are and working with him or her to remedy them, out of respect for the value such a person always retains as God's creature.

Notice the way in which the notion of God the creator that I have been using in the last two chapters has been at the bottom of the major conclusions I have drawn so far about the respect due human beings as creatures of God—the conclusions that it is a respect due all persons, equally and unconditionally. God is the creator of all beings within the world, including human beings: that is why human beings are owed the respect due creatures of God. God is the creator of all without any difference in manner or degree: that is why human beings are due equal respect as creatures. God never stops being the creator of someone whatever they might do: the respect due a creature of God is therefore unconditional and indefeasible.

The other major principle of that account of God the creator—a principle implicated in the others—suggests another feature of the respect due human beings as creatures of God. God can be the creator of all, in the same manner and degree, because God is the creator of every being in the world directly and not by way of any other non-divine being or beings. If that is so, then the respect due human beings as creatures of God is owed directly to each person, whatever the character of her or his relations with other people. It falls to each as an *individual*.

Respect due creatures of God does not fall to each individual, however, in an *individualistic* way. Individuality is not the basis for respect as some quality that might distinguish one creature from another, or the state of a creature at one time from its state at another. Respect due creatures of God is due them simply because of their creaturehood, not because of any of their particular characteristics or circumstances. To be due the respect of a creature of God, one does not have to be an individual eccentric or superior to the common run of humanity, one's own person set off against the crowd, striving for and achieving independence from others. No liberal theory of individualism is at work here, the product of the historical process by which individuals emerged from the confining constraints of feudal communal ties. Nor is there a Romantic appeal to the unique worth of heroes or geniuses, nor a Protestant polemic lauding individual worshipers for going their own way against ecclesiastical authority. Each person is due respect as the creature of God whatever his or her relations with others, whether or not such relations exist and whatever their character. The claim that respect falls to everyone as an individual means only that. Such a claim obviously does not require people to assert their independence from others or minimize their relations with them.

Since it is not based on a status that distinguishes anyone from anyone else, the respect that falls to an individual has an essential *social* reference. One cannot pretend to have it alone. If anyone is owed respect as an individual, then everyone else is owed that same respect too.

Indeed, the social character of the respect due creatures of God—that respect is owed to all human beings equally—is based, according to my account of God as creator, on its individual bearing. What makes it possible for all human beings to be respected equally is that each individual is owed respect as God's creature directly. God could not be the creator of all people equally, and therefore not all those people would be due the same respect as God's creatures, unless God is the creator of each one directly, not by way of the relations that a person might have with others.

INFERENCES TO TREATMENT

While I have specified some of the ways in which the respect owed creatures of God is to be extended to human beings, I have not yet said much about what such respect involves. All human beings are due it, equally and indefeasibly, but exactly what sort of respect is to be shown them? What does it mean to recognize the value of all human beings as creatures of God? How should human beings be treated if they are to be so respected?

Treatment that is compatible with respect for human beings as creatures of God must be more than a mere matter of attitude if that respect is to have any potential for criticizing institutionalized structures of oppression. It is not enough for my purposes here if the privileged recognize that the poor and powerless of their society are equal to them in worth as creatures of God while the oppressive character of their institutionalized relations with them remains unchanged.

Now it would certainly seem that there should be some content to a proper respect for the value of human beings as creatures of God. And it would certainly seem that such content should potentially have an impact on the character of one's social relations with others. How, for example, can it be proper for the interests of some people to be systematically subordinated to others in situations of structural oppression, if the equal value of all human beings as creatures of God is supposed to be respected? Oppressive social relations would seem to be incompatible with respect for human beings as creatures of God to the extent such relations presume that some persons or classes of persons are more valuable than others and so deserving of a greater consideration and respect. I will develop this line of argument later in this chapter.

Certain aspects of my account so far might suggest, however, that respect for human beings as creatures of God either can mean very little or must be restricted to matters of attitude alone. I want to deflect conclusions of this sort now: they either misunderstand my premises or draw invalid inferences from them. Implications for treatment on my account can also be blocked by certain additional theological premises, which I need to identify and from which I need to dissociate myself. Clarity about arguments of both these sorts is extremely important, since the history of Christian practice is littered with what certainly look to be cowardly and self-interested restrictions on the import of the Christian message for treatment of others. As the fate of Latin American clergy and laypeople concerned with the plight of the poor attests, a heavy price is often paid for consistency in these matters. I begin with some arguments that impede inferences to treatment by way of additional theological premises. Arguments based on problematic aspects of my own account are more difficult to defuse and therefore demand more extensive discussion.

It is not unusual in the history of Christian thought for Christians to claim that human beings are equal as creatures of God and for this claim to imply the propriety of social relations that reflect that fact. Human beings were all created equal; thus before the fall, in a prelapsarian state of nature, no human being ruled over another.[7] The import of this point for the present is blocked, however, by saying

7. See Augustine, *The City of God* 19.15, for an example of this sort of position.

that this equality and the social relations proper to it were taken away with the onset of sin.[8] Social relations that human beings enjoyed before the fall may be restored by God's grace, but implications of this restoration for the present are prohibited since such a restoration is not to be expected now. Restoration is perhaps a future state or a state after death. The association of an equality that has been restored with a graced state may indeed permit it to have some extension in the world now, but it is commonly only a limited one. Relations among Christians in the church might be expected to take that form. Or monastic organization might be modeled on it. Or respect for all as God's creatures might characterize a Christian's inner spiritual life; it might constitute a religious outlook on life in contradiction to the bare outward form of one's actions toward others that continue to conform to the world's standards.

The all-encompassing account of salvation offered in the section on sin at the end of chapter 3 opposes some of these restrictions on the relevance here and now of a claim for the equality of all persons as creatures of God. As the creator of all the world—present and future, spiritual and temporal, inner and outer—God's working as redeemer to restore that equality cannot be excluded from the whole here and now of this world. But even more fundamentally, a different claim of creaturehood underlies my derivation of a respect owed all human beings equally. Equal respect for all based on the status of human beings as created does not simply mean that such respect was the particular form of human relations that God brought forth in the beginning, before the fall. The created status that is the basis for that respect concerns a wider or broader notion of creaturehood that cannot be lost so long as one exists. According to this notion of creaturehood, it is proper to say that in sinning one remains God's creature. Indeed, in being saved (or not) one also remains God's creature. Respect for all human beings equally as creatures of God is required, consequently, whatever the state of human beings—prior to the fall, after the fall but without grace, saved or reprobate.

This account of the respect due human beings as creatures of God seems to present several problems of its own, however, for inferences to treatment. First, if human beings are owed respect simply

8. Ibid.

because they are God's creatures, this might suggest that they are not valuable in themselves and therefore due no respect for what they themselves are. These inferences would cut off all inferences about treatment of persons at their roots. Respect due persons as creatures of God simply would not translate into respectful treatment of those persons themselves.

These conclusions are not, however, the proper ones to draw from my account. The crucial inference that creatures are not valuable in and of themselves alters my premises. Arguments to that conclusion may be presuming that when creatures have value in relation to the good God who creates them, they have it as transparent pointers to a goodness not their own. But this is not my position. As nondivine beings, creatures on my account have an existence of their own; they exist with some density of being that sets them off as creatures and not God. When value is attributed to them as God's creatures, it is therefore genuinely attributed to them and not to God. Ascribing value to God's creatures is not simply another way to say that God is good.

The conclusion that creatures are not valuable in themselves could also be based on the supposition that creatures are to be considered valuable simply because God deems them valuable, whatever their natures and however unworthy in themselves they might be of such respect. But this is not my line of argument. I argue that nondivine beings have a value transferred to them as the creatures of a good God. What a good God creates is itself good. As the first chapter of Genesis affirms, God looks on God's creation and *sees* that it is good; God recognizes its own inherent value.

Finally, the conclusion that a nondivine being is not valued in itself when it is valued as a creature of God is untenable according to account, since as I understand the world's relation of dependence upon God a nondivine being becomes itself only in so far as it is created by God. All that a creature is, has been, or will be for the good, it owes to God as creator. There is nothing about the creature to be valued, then, apart from what is brought into being by God.

A second potential problem with my account is more serious. The very universal range of the respect owed would seem to evacuate it of content. Respect is not owed simply to people but to all that exists, in so far as it exists in virtue of a relation of dependence upon God. What can such respect mean if it is to be directed to plants and animals and stones as well as to people? Presumably, it cannot mean very much. Answers to this problem have to wait until answers to a third.

The unconditional character of the value ascribed to creatures in my account suggests a third problem. That claim of unconditionality can be used to construct an argument of the following general form: Since creaturehood, which is the source of value in my account, does not depend on the particular character or circumstances of the people at issue, the way people are treated does nothing to take away from or alter their value and dignity as creatures of God. (This is indeed an appropriate inference from my account.) Since people retain their value and dignity as creatures of God in any case, it does not matter how one treats them.

This general argument can come in a number of more specific forms. A first form prevents one from drawing the inference that people are due treatment necessary to rectify oppression. For example: Value before God is not in any way the effect of a creature's achievements—that is what I have said. Whether a person's self-development is hampered by institutionalized constraints should therefore be irrelevant when respect due creatures is at issue. People who respect God's creatures need not work to ensure freedoms and opportunities for them.

Another argument of this same form: Since respect is owed to creatures whatever their particular natures or circumstances, that respect is not to be translated into treatment of persons that considers their specific needs, characteristics, and desires. The particular needs and problems of the impoverished and the downtrodden are not to be a special focus of attention.

A final argument of this sort: Creatures are due an equal regard in so far as they are all creatures of God, irrespective of their actual inequalities of talent or condition or status. Remedying inequalities should have no part therefore in respect for persons as creatures of God.

A second form of the argument restricts questions of treatment to the rarified sphere of an individual's attitudes. The value of creatures holds independent of their social relations, it holds whether or not they have any and without regard for the character of those relations. It follows that respect for persons as creatures of God can be shown whatever one's social relations with them. Respect for persons as creatures of God can and should be expressed, then, in a way that leaves one's institutionalized relations with others intact. Respect for persons as creatures of God is a matter for the recesses of one's heart and mind, a matter of attitude alone.[9]

All these arguments are invalid, however, because they confuse conditions for having value in virtue of one's creaturehood with conditions for properly respecting that value. There are no conditions for having value as a creature of God; it is therefore correct to say that no matter how one is treated by other people one's value as a creature of God remains. That fact does not mean, however (as these arguments presume), that a proper respect for such value and dignity can be shown no matter how one treats people, no matter how badly one treats people. Certain forms of treatment might indeed be incompatible with a genuine respect for the value of others as creatures of God. The fact that the value of creatures is itself unconditional says nothing about whether a proper respect for that value has to conform to certain conditions.

Those conditions are set by *what* is valuable about human beings as creatures of God. What constitutes proper treatment of human beings as creatures of God is determined by what it is about human beings that must be shown esteem. In other words, limits on proper treatment are set by all those things about human beings that have value as the result of human beings' creaturehood and that are therefore to be objects of care and concern in one's actions toward others. But what is valuable about human beings as creatures of God?

When specifying what is valuable, one must remember that creatures are valued for themselves when they are valued as creatures of God. One must not suppose, because according to my account nothing about human beings forms the *basis* for valuing them as creatures of God, that nothing about human beings is to be valued. I have said that human beings have value and therefore are due respect as the creatures of God whatever they may be like, but it is what they are

9. Søren Kierkegaard seems to be making an argument like this throughout his *Works of Love*, trans. Howard and Edna Hong (New York: Harper and Row, 1962). I have generalized a type of argument from his book, and thought up new forms of it, in constructing a third potential problem for my own account.

like that is valuable and to be respected on that account. Their creaturehood, not the particular natures or capacities or achievements of human beings, supplies the *reason why* human beings are to be valued, but that does not mean that all those aspects of human life are not part of *what* has value on account of creaturehood. What is created by God has value. Human beings are God's creatures in their continuing existence and actions and achievements—as beings who remain in existence, beings who act and bring about effects within the world. All those aspects of human life are aspects of the world God brings to be. They are therefore what has value, if human beings are to be valued as creatures of God. It is the value of these aspects of human existence that must be respected, then, in treatment of human beings that takes into account their status as creatures of God.

RIGHTS POSSESSED BY CREATURES

One can sort out what God creates into classes that give rise to distinct rights to treatment possessed by creatures. According to my understanding of God as creator, God holds up into being the whole plane of the world, inclusive of the existence, nature, capacities, actions, and achievements of every being that constitutes it. All of this is what God creates. It is common in Christian theology, however, to mark a certain division among all these aspects of the world that God holds up into being, a division signaled (for instance) by Christian talk about God as both the creator and providential guide of the world. The existence and given characteristics of creatures are the objects of God's working when God is talked about as a creator in this more restrictive sense. The capacities and acts and achievements of creatures are the object of God's working when God is talked about as a providential guide. I have cautioned against understanding the distinction between God as creator and providential guide too starkly, but simply as an indication of a division among what God creates it is significant for my argument now.

The first classification of this division—the existence and natures of creatures—gives rise to a first right to treatment. In so far as the existence and natures of creatures are valuable, creatures are entitled to, they have a right to, treatment that confirms that value. They should be treated in ways that show care and concern, rather than disdain and disregard, for their continued existence as the beings are. Similarly with the second classification formed by this divisi among what God creates. In so far as the activities of creatures are valuable as a part of the world God creates, creatures have a right to self-development. The work they have been called by God to perform, the activities by which they become the beings God intends them to be, should be appreciated and supported, rather than dismissively checked or hampered.

A third right to treatment follows from the value of difference in my account. Differences among creatures are not what makes them worthy of respect as creatures of God, but such respect does concern creatures in the individual distinctiveness by which one differs from another. Respect due human beings as creatures of God falls to each person, as such, as an individual therefore, whatever her or his relations with others. One is not the object of God's concern as creator simply as a member of some universal society of creatures, but as the particular being one is. Respect for human beings as creatures of God should therefore extend to respect for each person in his or her particularity. One has a right to be oneself, a right to have one's personal integrity respected.

This right to be oneself extends to one's acts under God's providential will. The value creatures have by being included in God's providential and redemptive plans is a value that concerns the particular acts and attainments that distinguish such creatures. God does not simply call one to be, but sets one upon a path of self-affirmation through which one becomes the specific sort of person God intends one to be, by taking up the tasks one feels called to perform in one's particular situation. Respect for human beings as creatures of God is expressed therefore in respect for the special tasks that God asks of particular persons in making them a part of God's providential and redemptive plans for the world. The respect owed human beings as workers of the world God wills is not a respect that covers them simply in general and in their anonymity. If one respects them as workers of God's will, one must respect the fact that each is to live her or his own life, live it in the way in which it is specifically allotted and loaned by God.[10]

10. See Barth, *Church Dogmatics* ed. G. W. Bromiley and T. F. Torrance, trans. A. T. MacKay et al. (Edinburgh: T. & T. Clark, 1961), 3/4:385–86; and Gene Outka's discussion of the same point and its ethical implications in "Universal Love and Impartiality," in *The Love Commands*, ed. Edmund Santurri and William Werpehowski (Washington, D.C.: Georgetown Univ. Press, forthcoming).

ght to be oneself implies a right to self-determination
ılar path of one's self-development is at issue. The
e actions to which one is called by God are ultimately
wn, although they certainly need not be made in
ers. An individualistic sense of autonomy, in which
ne's own in walled-off isolation from interference from others, is not what I mean by respect for the value of the individual as a creature of God. The needs of others, the nature of the situation, and so on, can be as much a part of one's decision as one's own desires and needs, especially if one considers the fact that one's own acts are always included in God's providential and redemptive plans only along with all the rest of the world. One is not the agent of God's providential and redemptive plans without others but as part of a whole order of creatures under God's providential will. The call to develop one's talent is always at least potentially therefore a call out of isolation and self-preoccupation into relations with others.

One's decisions are not, however, to be fixed by others, according to their demands or their appeals to the limiting factors of physical characteristics or assigned social roles. Decisions on that basis are incompatible with the freedom of the God who calls one to act, as I argued with reference to natural or divine-mandate justifications for hierarchy. Indeed, although decision ends with the particular person involved, the direction of one's self-development as a creature of God should not be fixed in advance at all, even by one's own sense of self and of one's limitations. Although everyone's talents and capacities are limited, knowing one's own limitations is no more a matter of confident presumption than knowing the will of God: at a minimum, "[t]he man who is obedient to God must allow himself to be shown his capacities step by step as he exercises them, and his incapacities as he comes across them."[11]

To sum up the argument so far: Creatures have value in virtue of their simple status as creatures whatever they may be like. This basis for value implies that the existence, nature, action, and achievements of creatures, as the particular beings that they are, are what is to be valued. If those aspects of created life are valuable, creatures must be treated in ways that confirm that value: they are entitled to

11. Barth, *Church Dogmatics*, 3/4:394.

treatment that supports rather than undermines the existence, action, and forms of achievement that make them distinctively themselves. Such rights or entitlements amount to the following: (1) a right to exist and be oneself; (2) a right to self-development of capacities; (3) a right to self-determination in the process of developing what is in one. One has the right, finally, to the goods that make these three rights real possibilities: (1) a right to minimum standards of well-being; (2) a right to participation or influence in any social processes of decision that govern one's fate; (3) a right of access to what is necessary for the development of one's capacities as one sees fit.

These rights are due *all* creatures of God. They are formal rights, therefore, which hold irrespective of the character of the particular creatures concerned.[12] The character of the creatures concerned, however, gives them specificity. Here is my answer to the second problem noted previously, the charge that the universality of respect due robs it of content. The minimum standards of well-being to which one has a right will obviously vary depending upon the creature at issue. Creatures differ in the direction of their self-development, and therefore the goods to which one has a right of access for such purposes will vary accordingly. One can specify rights to participation only when one knows how decisions affecting the lives of particular creatures are actually made; some knowledge of the general forms of self-development to which a particular sort of creature is prone is also necessary to make clear what it would mean to exercise the power over the course of one's own life to which one has a right.

Some knowledge about human society and some generalizations about minimum standards of well-being and tendencies for self-development among human beings are therefore necessary to render these formal rights more concrete for the specific case at issue. Employing seemingly uncontroversial assumptions about the nature of U.S. society, the general direction of specifically human forms of self-development, and requirements for human well-being, I think it is safe to say that the formal rights I have mentioned become these more specific ones: (1) The right to housing, health care, and a decent wage.

12. I discuss the implications of this general position for ecological and environmental concerns in "Creation, Environmental Crisis, and Ecological Justice" in *Reconstructing Theology*, ed. Mark K. Taylor and Rebecca Chopp (Minneapolis: Fortress Press, forthcoming).

Those are minimum standards for human well-being, expressed in terms that make sense within a modern American context. (2) Participation in the decision-making processes that govern one's fate as a citizen, a worker, and a social being. One has a right of access to the government of those spheres of human life—political, economic, and personal—that tend to be organized around distinct institutions in modern Western societies. (3) The right to a basic education and open access to the further training necessary for pursuit of the forms of self-development to which one feels called. Self-development in human beings is mostly a matter of education and training.[13]

SOCIAL CONSEQUENCES

Although the rights I have derived set boundaries that cannot be crossed, limits to the claims that others can make on one (such limits are my focus in what follows), it is important to see that they do so within a clear commitment to a shared life together. The rights I have derived are not like rights in liberal theory that define a sphere of independence or noninterference by others on a conflictual model of human relations, thereby accentuating the distance or even absence of relation among people. The rights I have specified have an essential social dimension in that they *establish* relations among people.[14]

13. The sort of generalizations about well-being and developmental capacities that I have assumed here for human beings—generalizations about a particular class of creature—have their dangers. They can be used presumptively, in a rigid a priori fashion. Thus it might be said that a human being does not have the right to develop himself or herself in a particular direction because human beings do not properly exhibit tendencies of that sort. Generalizations about human tendencies would in this way exclude a right to develop oneself in ways that seem strange or eccentric. Once a standard for well-being has been set, one might argue one does not have the right to anything more even if one's health and happiness appear to deteriorate without it. Used presumptively, such generalizations obviously violate the creature's right to self-determination, but they also simply fail to show a proper regard for an individual's well-being and developmental inclinations. To show a proper respect for an individual's well-being, one must be attentive to his or her sufferings. To show a proper respect for an individual's developmental inclinations, one must be open to any tendencies she or he might exhibit. Generalizations about classes of people could also be used to categorically deny particular people certain concrete rights on the grounds that they are not members of the appropriate groups. The fact that the individual is the direct object of respect in my account argues against such rigid conclusions by reason of group classification.

14. For this notion of rights, see Martha Minow, *Making All the Difference* (Ithaca, N.Y.: Cornell Univ. Press, 1990), 289–311. For a philosophically sophisticated defense of communitarian rights on secular grounds, see Alan Gewirth, "Common Morality and the Community of Rights," in *Prospects for a Common Morality*, ed. Gene Outka and John Reeder (Princeton: Princeton Univ. Press, forthcoming), section 7.

More specifically, these rights establish spheres of obligation, spheres in which one has a valid claim on the attention of others. If one has such rights, other people are required to respond to the question of whether one in fact has what one is entitled to. If one does not enjoy minimum standards of well-being or the opportunity to develop one's talents freely, others are obligated to address that need.

One is obligated in turn to respond to the same claims of theirs. According to my account of the rights due human beings as creatures of God, one's claims on the attentions of others are predicated upon their equal claims on oneself. The social relations established by these rights are therefore ones of mutual and reciprocal concern. One cannot enjoy these rights by oneself since they accrue to oneself only in virtue of a status before God shared with all others. One can exercise one's own rights as a creature of God (by developing, for example, one's own capabilities) only if one also respects the same rights of all others, since in no other way would one's actions be in keeping with the fact that those rights have their ground in a relation with God shared equally by all human beings.

The relations with others that these rights establish take on a certain shape; they conform to a certain vision of community or society. Because these rights have their basis in an equal respect for all human beings, that vision is utterly egalitarian and noncompetitive at its roots: the community formed by persons with these rights is one in which all are concerned for the rights of all. The rights specifically to well-being and self-development indicate a society dedicated to human fulfillment and the enhancement of human capacities. The right to self-determination suggests a society in which democratic processes are extended to all spheres of human life.

This social vision is clearly incompatible with oppression as defined in the beginning of this chapter. It is incompatible with social relations in which not everyone has the same power over their lives, or the same chance for human fulfillment, and it is incompatible with social relations where some gain either of those things at the expense of others.

Each element of this definition brings oppressive social structures into conflict with the rights of all human beings as creatures of God.[15]

15. I am indebted in what follows to Iris Marion Young's careful discrimination of "exploitation," "domination," and "oppression" in *Justice and the Politics of Difference* (Princeton: Princeton Univ. Press, 1990).

Thus social structures that are *exploitative* are ruled out. Where society is arranged so that the efforts of some people systematically benefit others without reciprocity—where, for example, the suffering of some is the price of a high standard of living for others, where a certain class of people do the dirty work so that another class may enjoy pleasant and rewarding occupations—social structures enforce a competitive relation among persons for the rights that, according to my account, all persons should share.

Social structures in which some persons live under conditions of *domination* are also excluded. Social relations in which not every one is permitted to participate on an equal footing with others in the decisions that affect their lives violate the rights to self-determination due all human beings through institutional constraint. Thus political institutions that deny certain persons or classes of persons a say in the political process are improper. Economic institutions are improper when sharp distinctions between managers and workers take the decisions for the kind of work one does and the manner of its performance out of one's own hands as a worker.

Finally, social relations that put institutionalized checks on the achievement of fulfillment for certain classes of people are impermissible. A society in which adequate health care is denied the old or already infirm, or decent housing is denied the poor, a society in which certain classes of jobs reserved for women (e.g., home-care work) do not pay a living wage, or where jobs requiring manual labor are structured to prevent the exercise of creativity and the development of further skills, a society that fails to provide all its citizens an education sufficient to allow their genuine interests and talents to come to the surface and be pursued, falls under the censure of a social vision founded upon equal rights to well-being and self-development.

Oppressive social structures do not always deny minimum standards of well-being to those with little power in society. (That denial can indeed imperil the continuance of such structures, if oppressed members of a society perform essential social services and cannot be readily replaced.) By definition, however, oppressive social relations do take away from such classes of persons their rights to free self-development. In varying manners and degrees, oppressive structures hem in the underclasses of society restricting their activities and choices for fulfilling employment and forcing them to stay in their place.

Persons with little power in such societies may be actually coerced (as slaves). Or they may voluntarily submit to the curtailment of their activities under the simple threat of force (as colonized peoples). Without any such threat, they may simply find that they have no real option to do otherwise: they are workers too poor to own any means of production, immigrant laborers with no recourse, white women or men and women of color who, though citizens, are thought unfit to hold any responsible positions of power. Such people may even consent themselves to a narrowing of the avenues of their possible pursuits by internalizing the prejudices against them or the fixed understandings of others about the roles for which they are fit. In the more extreme cases of oppression, the oppressed may lose any sense of themselves as responsible agents, becoming the mere instruments of others' purposes. But in even the best cases, the oppressed lose the autonomy that is their right as creatures of God: what they are to be is ultimately determined for them from without.

Because equality of rights is based on respect for human beings as creatures of God, I must reject two of the most commonly used arguments for limiting the extent of those people due these rights.

First, no appeal to difference—in nature or social status or economic possession—can justify restriction of such rights to only certain classes of persons. Property ownership cannot be appropriate as a criterion for discriminating who is entitled to enfranchisement, as it was for so long in England and in early U.S. history. Appeals to natural differences in intelligence between men and women or between blacks and whites, or to differences in their degrees of dependence upon others, cannot legitimate inequalities in their right to determine the course of their own lives. Like value before God, which is their basis, rights to well-being and free self-development must hold irrespective of distinctions among persons. From this point of view, awareness of differences among people is not as likely to be the cause of inequalities in rights as it is to be their result. One should suspect, in other words, that the importance of differences has simply been *constructed* for the purpose of justifying an existing inequitable division of power.[16]

16. This argument is often made in radical feminist circles. See Catharine MacKinnon, *Feminism Unmodified* (Cambridge: Harvard Univ. Press, 1987).

In order to dispute the propriety of an unequal distribution of rights, my position on the rights due all human beings as creatures of God need not deny the existence of such differences or their pertinence to the exercise of the rights at issue. (These denials are classic strategies for extending rights to everyone on a liberal theory of rights.) There may or may not in fact be differences between women and men in innate intelligence; property ownership may or may not in fact be required for an interest in the affairs of state. Even were such differences to exist, and even were those differences to be germane to the right at issue, one must, according to my understanding of rights, continue to hold fast to the claim of equal rights for all. When certain people lack the capacity or desire for free self-determination—they do not have the ability, say, for reasoned reflection or independent thought (they are, e.g., very young children or mentally disabled adults)—that fact does not affect their *rights* to self-determination and self-development; it simply affects their capabilities to *act* upon such rights. Rights to free self-determination presuppose certain capacities and desires if they are to be exercised; but such qualities are not the reason why those rights are extended to everyone in the first place. Indeed, far from excusing efforts to take away rights from them, the fact that certain people seem to lack the capacities to exercise their rights obligates others to work to enhance their capacities.

A second general line of reasoning to deny extending rights to all is also ruled out: equality of opportunity, which follows from the right I have derived to free self-determination, cannot be used to justify denying to some people the rest of the rights I have specified. One cannot argue (as so many people in the U.S.A. do) that the lack of minimum standards for well-being on the part of some people is justified on the grounds that everyone had an equal opportunity to get into a position where adequate housing, food, and health care would have been theirs. If some people are not in that position, they were irresponsible and lazy (so this argument would run); they simply failed to make anything of themselves. If other people are in that position, that is a just reward for an appropriate expenditure of effort in life's tasks.

There are a number of things wrong with such an argument. First, it misconstrues the nature of our rights. The rights I have derived are substantive rights to enjoy certain things, such as minimum standards for well-being, and not simply the right to pursue them on an equal footing with others. Second, any attempt here to legitimate an unequal distribution of these rights to enjoyment by claiming an impartial distribution according to merit is also improper. The rights due human beings as creatures of God are simply not the sort of things that people can merit. If they are due people simply as creatures of God, they are not rewards that people may or may not earn. Finally, such arguments move too quickly to presume that people do have the same chance to arrive at the goods of human well-being, if only they were to make the effort. Such arguments tend to ignore differences in starting point (e.g., differences in capacity for self-development) or differences in social and circumstantial blocks to self-development (e.g., prejudice and disease, respectively). Or they must facilely attribute any such differences to what is within one's own control. The push to make either of these contrary-to-fact assumptions can simply have an ideological basis—such assumptions work to make unfair social relations look equitable. But it can also be impelled by the idea that equality in nature and circumstance is the grounds for giving everyone an equal chance to pursue their life's course. Rationality and economic independence from others have often been identified as the requisite common qualities. Assuming a general equality in nature and circumstance, so that appeals to equal opportunities legitimate denying some their rights to well-being, would be an easy extension of such a principle. According to my account, however, rights to free self-determination do not require any grounds in equality of nature and circumstance; no such reason exists therefore to presume them.

Because equal rights are not grounded in equalities of nature and circumstance, a society dedicated to ensuring for all people the rights I have specified need not overlook such differences when trying to determine whether all people have that to which they are entitled, when trying to determine whether all people are exercising or enjoying the rights they have. Rights to physical well-being are more difficult to satisfy given congenital health problems, or stressful life circumstances, or housing next to toxic waste dumps. Right to the basic education necessary for self-development is difficult to enjoy when one does not have enough to eat or where social conditions make efforts in that direction seem futile—for example, in the chaos and hopelessness of some inner cities. Women will have a harder time enjoying rights to free self-development in employment where traditional attitudes toward parental roles require women rather than men to take time away from their jobs. Difficulties of this sort need to be addressed by a society dedicated to the enhancement of human fulfillment.

Addressing them adequately may require inequalities of treatment. If all human beings are to enjoy the same rights that are due them as creatures of God, some of them may have to be treated differently in order to make up for an inequality of starting point. More must be done for those in need if all are to enjoy minimum standards of well-being, basic education, or the real chance to develop their capacities. More must be done for some in order to ensure an equality of result for all. The best health care where disease is liable to be rampant, the best education where apathy is liable to abound, the best leave benefits for those whose free self-development is likely to suffer most from inflexible role assignments within the home—these are not special privileges but remedies for deficits. In short, the poorest and the least powerful have the greatest claim on a society's attention; they have the cry that properly warrants the greatest social response.

Attention to the needs of such people cannot be limited, however, to differences in treatment affecting them alone. Many of the circumstances that put particular classes of people in special need are *social* circumstances. Many such circumstances are the results of oppressive structural relations among persons. For instance, stress might be produced by dead-end jobs, where one has little opening for advancement in skills and little say over the manner in which one does one's work. Allowing people in such jobs more breaks in order to help alleviate their stress, even supplying them with exercise equipment to use in that time, might be nice, but such measures obviously fall short of attention to the underlying problem: sharp distinctions between the roles of managers and workers. Structural changes in fundamental social relations are often necessary therefore to address the needs of particular classes of persons. It has indeed been the burden of argument so far in this section that my vision of a society of mutual concern for the rights of all implies the redress of certain social ills: oppression, exploitation, and domination. While value before God cannot be taken away, the rights due everyone on that basis can be taken away, by social relations that are exploitative, dominating, and oppressive for certain persons. Rights for all are to be actively pursued therefore by a commitment to social change.

WHAT THIS VISION OF SOCIETY LEAVES UNDECIDED

This vision of society gets most of its punch from what I have demonstrated so far that it excludes: social relations of oppression, domination, and exploitation. That social vision is not sufficient to single out any particular political or economic system for approbation; it is not sufficient to provide the specifics of a social form respecting the rights of all persons as creatures of God. The reasons are twofold.

First, this vision of society will not settle the question of conflict or competition among persons pursuing the enjoyment of their rights where such conflicts are generated by circumstances beyond the capacity of human beings to remedy. This vision for society does rule out exploitative social relations, social relations where competitive struggle between people for the enjoyment of the same rights is enforced against possibilities for social change, where, for example, competition for the rights due all human beings as creatures of God is maintained whatever the circumstances, not because of circumstances beyond human remedy, but according to the simple belief that certain persons are not due those rights. This vision of society calls one to work actively to create social relations in which a competition for the enjoyment of rights due creatures of God does not ensue. Such competition is likely, however, to be an inevitability in certain times and places. For example, in times of scarcity or when others approach one with hostile intent, it may not be possible in fact to show respect for all persons' rights to continued existence: it is either us or them. A simple affirmation of all persons' equal right to continued existence obviously would not be much help in such circumstances.

Even though circumstances block any simple manifestation of it, respect for the rights of all is still the presupposition for such decisions. It sets accordingly certain limits on the way those decisions should be made. Thus a decision for one party over another should not overlook the interests of the other party or systematically and callously devalue the existence and chosen pursuits of those persons vis-à-vis the existence and pursuits of others. If a notion of the differential relative values of such parties (i.e., their different values relative to certain specified ends or goods) is employed to make these decisions, one must not forget that value of this sort does not determine value pure and simple. The end or good that is used to determine such differences of relative value cannot be absolutized therefore in a way that would prevent a reassessment of the relative values of the parties under consideration for a different end or good. Finally, since all parties are still due their rights, the sacrifice of the rights of some is always to be a matter of last resort and deep regret. One is never past the effort to remedy such an eventuality by action for social change. Attention to possibilities for increased economic production, redistribution of available goods, or reallocation of priorities for funding must come before any resignation in the face of scarcity to the sacrifice of some persons rights to well-being.

The second reason this vision of society will not specify social relations more closely is this: equality in the respect and rights due everyone as creatures of God does not absolutely rule out differences in other forms of social esteem and entitlement. Over and above the bottom line of the respect due everyone as God's creature, different degrees of honor or esteem for talent, moral virtue, or physical beauty might still accrue to people. In addition, other sorts of entitlement, besides the rights due all creatures of God, might reflect differences in employment and achievement among human beings. Indeed, different social, economic, or political functions inevitably bring with them some differences in rights and responsibilities. For example, only members of Congress have the right to declare war. In the performance of any complex task that requires a division and organization of labor, different rights and obligations will follow from the nature of the separate tasks performed. Nothing I have said so far rules out differences in reward as part of such entitlements. Although everyone is due a minimum standard of well-being, some people may have the right to be paid more depending upon the jobs they perform.

The principles that underlie my derivation of respect and rights clearly do not encourage, however, such differences when, as in the cases of honor and reward, they are not strictly inevitable. If people differ in beauty or talents, my principle of value before God directly suggests a simple appreciation for differences, rather than the need to rank such persons according to the degree of honor or esteem due them. Different talents or natural gifts might be honored equally as the different ways in which creatures are and become themselves under God's creative and providential care. Moreover, the rejection of the idea that human beings merit the basic rights due them as creatures of God certainly suggests that merit may be inappropriate grounds for differentials in monetary reward. Where resources are scarce, extremely high compensation for the performance of certain jobs might be ruled out altogether as incompatible with others' enjoyment of the minimum standards for well-being due them as God's creatures. But even where this is not the case, it makes sense from my point of view to question the idea that persons performing certain jobs deserve to be paid extremely high salaries. From my point of view, it makes sense to question the reasoning behind claims to just desert.

On what grounds, for example, can one argue that differences in pay reflect differences in the value or service to society of different jobs? Do U.S. medical doctors with six-figure incomes perform a more valuable or necessary service to society than, say, garbage collectors? Might not one simply assume such differences in service or value from the fact of a difference in prestige between the two jobs? Perhaps doctoring involves a greater expenditure of effort than garbage collecting? What standards of comparison can one use to make such an argument? Does mental work require the same expenditure of effort as manual labor? Trouble in reaching firm results by comparing effort or social value—indeed, the fact that no one even bothers with the hard work of making such comparisons—suggests that appeals to differentials of effort or social value are simply ideological. Do doctors deserve to be paid so much more than garbage collectors because of the time and effort of years of prior training? Even in the case of medicine, one would be hard-pressed to prove that the educational prerequisites of the profession are necessary to the performance of its tasks. For example, how often does the surgeon apply her knowledge of organic chemistry?

High qualifications for employment should always make one question whether the qualifications demanded are required by the tasks or required to counter charges of inequity in the rewards for performing them. In general, many more people have the ability to perform the jobs that garner money and prestige in American society than are actually employed in them. Escalating the qualifications for such jobs is simply a way of disguising the inequitable manner in which their distribution is restricted—"if you didn't get the job that is because you didn't deserve to get it."[17] Indeed, most jobs require such minimal qualifications that those who hold them can hardly claim to be especially deserving of them.[18]

Finally, asserting that inequality of compensation is a matter of desert obfuscates the reality of how people get to be where they are. It assumes that differences in compensation are ultimately the result of choices for which one is personally responsible, not the result of accidents of birth, initial inequalities of wealth, opportunities for education, the erratic behavior of market conditions, or the favor of people in high places. Does anyone even attempt to make such arguments? If one tried, could one ever prove merit in any particular case?

As I said before, however, differences in esteem and entitlements are permissible over and above the equal respect and rights due all persons as creatures of God. Where such differences are admitted as part of the fabric of society, my principles work to set limits on their import. Respect and rights due all persons as creatures of God establish a framework of presuppositions within which all other forms of esteem and entitlement must be understood, a framework of presuppositions that must not be violated by these additional admissions.

Thus secondary forms of esteem should supplement the respect due all persons as creatures of God, rather than undermine an appreciation for the value, as creatures of God, of persons not so esteemed. Distinctions of honor should add to the status of some without humiliating others. In the arena of persons working to follow the call of God to self-development, those whose achievements are less grand than others should not be measured against the standard of a greater achievement and berated for what they have turned out to be. Distinctions of honor would in that way block the respect for the particular contributions of all that value before God implies. Distinctions of honor based on the job one performs and how well one does it must not stand in the way of a respect that holds across all such differences

17. See Richard Sennett and Jonathan Cobb, *The Hidden Injuries of Class* (New York: Vintage Books, 1973), 153–55.

18. See Michael Walzer, *Spheres of Justice* (New York: Basic Books, 1983), 135, 137.

according to a single standard of following God's creative will for one. There is a standard of service to God—of working to develop one's talents according to God's will for the world—that holds across all differences in achievement or relative excellence; it forms the basis of a common worthiness to be respected into which all other types of respect must be fit.

Differences in esteem or in rights and entitlements that depend upon such things as natural characteristics or work performed should also not be permitted to determine access to any of the basic rights due all persons as creatures of God. For example, differences in monetary reward for the work one does must be suspect in so far as money determines access to basic rights—that is, buys the right to adequate health care, or opens up opportunities for further employment denied to those without it, or makes it possible to avoid a military draft, or determines political influence. Such practices must be stopped. This might not require equal pay for different jobs; but where differential pay scales remain, barriers must be placed in the way of what money can buy.[19]

Finally, the inevitable differences in rights and powers that follow from the performance of different social or economic functions have to be watched carefully to guard against violations of the rights of all to free self-determination. Positions of leadership or authority should not become the exclusive prerogative of particular persons. There should be equal access to those positions themselves or to the training necessary to develop the qualifications for them. The extent to which the holders of such positions can use their authority or rights of leadership to curtail the free self-development of those over whom they exercise power should also be strictly limited. Rights over others should be restricted to what is essential for the performance of the tasks or functions at issue. For instance, one's role as a teacher gives one the right to demand from students class attendance, but not the right to have students park one's car or perform sexual favors. Privileges of a particular office—the benefits that accrue to one in virtue of its performance—should be similarly restricted, to prevent competitive social relations of gain and loss. The privileges of an office are in the performance of the functions essential to that office: for

19. Ibid., chap. 4.

example, the privilege of reading and writing for extended periods of time if one is an academic, not the privilege of a high table at meal time or preferential treatment by the police in the city where one's university is located. Privileges in this way collapse into responsibilities. Rights *to* become responsibilities *for*. In the same way, God's gifts to individuals mark out, not the privileges by which one gains in distinction from others, but the particular path of one's service, of action in keeping with those gifts under God's will for the world.[20]

20. See H. Richard Niebuhr, *Radical Monotheism and Western Culture* (New York: Harper and Row, 1970), 57–58, on the distinction between election to service and election to status.

SIX

Christian Belief and Respect for Difference

THE PREVIOUS CHAPTER filled out to some extent the general shape of social relations that conform with my account of the basic respect owed creatures of God. There is more to be said, however. The points made about the value of difference, and about the rights owed creatures of God, have social implications that I have not yet developed. In this chapter I extend discussion in this direction by asking what my account of value before God implies for questions of toleration. By toleration I mean respect for the different *qua different*. The question for social relations concerns, accordingly, the place of homogeneity or uniformity in beliefs and behaviors within a community of persons owed respect as God's creatures. Are demands for uniformity in beliefs and behaviors compatible with that notion of respect? Is a community where that sort of uniformity occurs the sort of community such respect fosters? I suggest not. The kind of community Christians holding my account of God and creation should judge appropriate for creatures of God, and the kind of community that Christians holding those beliefs should promote as members of various social bodies, is one that celebrates, rather than denigrates or devalues, differences among persons.

Christianity has an unhappy history in this regard. When Christians have held political power they have not hesitated to use it to force conformity to their own beliefs and mores. A Christian monopoly on cultural expression was often brought about by the power of the state. Moreover, when political and religious spheres were disentangled and Christian communities became voluntary associations (a process that began with the Reformation), Christians often distinguished themselves by their unmerciful condemnation of the moral failings of others and their sensitivity to the slightest doctrinal divergences among the faithful. Boundaries of inclusion in Christian communities have frequently been rigid: the different are expelled.

Boundaries with this sharpness have separated not only Christian communities from one another, but Christian from non-Christian. Christian writings often suggest that non-Christians have no access to the truth, no prospects for genuine moral rectitude or for the sort of final fulfillment that Christ promises. Assimilation to a Christian form of life is the only hope non-Christians have for such things. Believing in such sharp boundaries between those in truth and those in error, between those who are morally upright and those who are lost, Christians have been the active participants in witch burnings and pogroms; they have often favored the punitive treatment of any person who continues to resist assimilation to Christian beliefs and mores to the extent permitted them by the laws of the land and political powers. They have been at the very least pliant accomplices in the imperialist extension of Western power and the colonialist transfer to Western whites of the cultural, political, and economic decision making for non-Christian Middle Eastern, Asian, African, and North and South American populations. The lack of Christian faith of these peoples and their absolute need for it became the cover for a Western expansion that expropriated or enslaved native populations and destroyed their cultures.

It is not my intention here to tackle the complexities of any of these historical aspects of Christian practice. I am interested in them only as examples of various forms of intolerance, which I hope my account of value before God will help to counter. My primary agenda in this chapter is to determine the nature of a toleration that has respect for creatures as its basis. A number of other proposals for toleration exist, however, in the Western tradition. I refer summarily to a few of these now, for purposes of comparison and contrast, and as a general jumping off point for discussion of the toleration or respect for difference that follows from my account.[1]

1. Regarding general strategies in support of toleration, I have been influenced by Quentin Skinner, *The Foundations of Modern Political Thought*, 2 vols. (Cambridge: Cambridge Univ. Press, 1978), 2:241–54; and G. R. Cragg, *From Puritanism to the Age of Reason* (Cambridge: Cambridge Univ. Press, 1950). On specifically Christian forms of support for toleration, I have found helpful: Robert Jewett, *Christian Toleration* (Philadelphia: Fortress Press, 1982); Reinhold Niebuhr, *The Nature and Destiny of Man*, 2 vols. (New York: Charles Scribner's Sons, 1964), vol. 2, chap. 8; idem, "Zeal without Knowledge," in *Beyond Tragedy* (New York: Charles Scribner's Sons, 1937), 227–47.

FORMS OF TOLERATION AND A CHRISTIAN RESPECT FOR DIFFERENCE

One form of toleration discussed in the Western tradition presupposes a position of moral, intellectual, and political superiority: a toleration of largesse, in which one permits people different from oneself to proceed without interference although nothing about them qualifies them for such respect. This toleration of concession marks a temporary relaxation in otherwise strict standards for action and belief, a toleration of condescension from a standpoint of one's own presumed rightness that continues unchallenged. Toleration is something that people who are morally, intellectually, and socially superior have the right to give or take away. It is the sort of toleration that Thomas Paine impugned in *The Rights of Man* (1791).

When respect for human beings as creatures of God supplies grounds for toleration, objections to this toleration of largesse will be similar to those expressed by Paine. The right to develop one's own judgments about proper belief and action, free from coercion and constraint, and without fear of reprisals, is a right due each individual as such. It is not an alienable right or a right that is the product of anyone else's liberality of giving. The indefeasibility of a right to one's own judgment follows from the unconditionality of *any* right due creatures as creatures. As the previous chapter showed, rights of free self-determination, like all rights owed creatures of God, are due each individual as such.

The toleration that replaces a toleration of largesse is thus one based upon liberty of conscience. This claim is common in the Western tradition, but it is backed up here by a distinctive line of argument. This line of argument appeals to rights of free self-development owed each individual as such—a line of argument one can find, for example, in John Stuart Mill—but the reasoning in support of such rights is nevertheless distinctive. The backing provided for them involves no appeals to utility—for example, no claim that society would be enriched were rights of free self-development granted to individuals and conformity not compelled. Nor is there any argument here from the requirements of human nature—there is no argument that the specific nature of human beings requires that individuals be given rights of free self-development in order to be fulfilled.

According to my account, forcing or compelling conformity to one's own judgments about proper belief and action is wrong because it violates the respect owed creatures of God by standing in the way of what they are called to believe and do as the particular individuals they are in their own distinctive circumstances. Behind the proper respect for the individual integrity of human beings that such practices violate stands the particularity of God's working. God's working covers everyone but it covers each person as the particular person he or she is, in the particular place, class, and cultural tradition where he or she is situated. God's working calls forth therefore a particular response of action and belief consonant with such person-specific features of an individual's existence. Impelling others to comply with the standards one has determined for oneself, or risk persecution, one disregards the fact that the calling of those others is to be their own. One attempts to make such decisions for them. Or one attempts at least to ensure that the conclusions such persons reach for themselves are the same as those one would draw oneself.

By insisting that others conform to one's own opinions, one interjects oneself between these people and their God. In other words, by forcing other people to comply with one's own standards, one usurps the place of God in relations with them. For these people to become themselves under God they must accommodate themselves to the judgments of others about appropriate belief and action. These people are to hear only the din of demands for conformity to one's own judgments when listening for God's call.

The liberty of conscience based upon respect for human beings as creatures of God does not, however, foster an "anything goes" toleration, without limits. The toleration produced is not of a purely formal or procedural sort that equalizes the rights of all persons to express and act upon what they believe to be true or proper, whatever the content of those judgments. It is instead a substantive toleration: toleration itself is what is being valued. Intolerance, therefore, is not to be tolerated. Beliefs and actions that would undermine the conditions that make toleration possible—for example, espousal of a neo-Nazi state in which deviants from WASP America would suffer persecution—are not to be tolerated.[2]

2. See Glen Tinder, *The Political Meaning of Christianity* (San Francisco: HarperCollins, 1990), 132–33.

The toleration that I recommend does not, moreover, represent any absolute value. It is not of value for its own sake. Toleration is valued instead because of what it is at stake: a proper respect for human beings as creatures of God. That respect and the rights it implies also present therefore limits on toleration. A toleration that is derived from respect for human beings as creatures of God naturally will not tolerate beliefs or actions that fail to show such respect by violating the rights due human beings as God's creatures. The toleration I recommend does not tolerate words or actions that promote injustice.[3]

These two limits on toleration do not, however, open up the possibility of a flagrant disregard for the value and rights of those whose beliefs and actions promote intolerance and injustice. Respect for all human beings as creatures of God sets the terms for what intolerance of words and deeds that promote injustice and intolerance might amount to. A commitment to the value and rights of all creatures must underlie the form that intolerance of such words and deeds takes, if those who are acting to further toleration are not to be as unjust as those they oppose. For example, if one murders white people who propose to lynch blacks, one's values become indistinguishable in character, if not in specific effect, from those one opposes. In working to counter intolerance and injustice one should therefore violate the rights of the people promoting them (for example, their rights to free self-development or well-being) only to the extent necessary to block the deleterious effects of their beliefs and actions upon others.

What that means specifically depends on the particular circumstances. Where neo-Nazi sloganeering presents no real dangers for others, people might be free to be identify themselves as neo-Nazis and organize along such ideological lines. Public expression of neo-Nazism in words or deeds will need to be curtailed where such expression endangers the basic rights of, say, Jewish people or people of color. In general, opposition in the form of rational argument and persuasion is preferable to forcible suppression of beliefs and actions conducive to violation of the basic rights of others. But the possible insufficiency of such measures is always to be seriously considered.

3. I am helped here by Ronald Dworkin's reservations about a general right to liberty understood as the absence of constraint, in his *Taking Rights Seriously* (Cambridge: Harvard Univ. Press, 1977), chap. 12; see also Robert Jewett, *Christian Tolerance*, 98–99.

Again, toleration is not an unconditional value; it is derived from a concern to respect the value of persons as creatures of God and thus must remain subservient to such an end.

This second limit on toleration makes especially clear that the toleration I recommend is not toleration in the form of indifference. Being tolerated as a creature of God does not mean that others simply put up with one's beliefs and behaviors; it means that one's distinctive efforts to be oneself are welcomed and prized by them. Some forms of toleration manifest a blithe unconcern about what other people think and do, individualistic forms of toleration in which one cannot be bothered about other persons, "each to his own" or "do your own thing" sorts of toleration. These forms of toleration obviate any need to bring others into active relationship with oneself. Toleration based upon a positive respect for the value of others as creatures of God rules out such forms of toleration. The inherent social dimension of that respect, which I have discussed in chapter 5, makes the toleration I recommend more a matter of mutual nurture and concern than a matter of simply agreeing to leave others alone.

Forms of toleration for which one can give only pragmatic defenses also cannot be identified with the sort of toleration I recommend. Because toleration is a positive value in itself, simple expediency, for example, cannot be the main motive for it, as seems to have been the case so often in post-Reformation Europe. The futility in principle of attempts to compel assent—at most one achieves outward conformity—or difficulties in achieving compliance from people with the wherewithal to resist, can also not be appropriate grounds for the toleration I recommend. A halfhearted toleration in the face of obstacles to an ideal of conformity is not what I have in mind.[4]

A worry about the untoward consequences of attempts to compel unity of belief or action—for example, the fact that intolerance as a social policy leads so often to civil strife—is not a good reason for toleration, either. Toleration based upon the value of creatures before God is not a toleration subservient in that way to an ideal of peace or harmony.[5] Because the basic value of creatures that demands toleration

4. See, for example, G. R. Cragg, *From Puritanism to the Age of Reason*, chap. 12, for a discussion of pragmatic reasoning of this sort in favor of toleration during the latter half of the seventeenth century in England.

5. See Skinner, *Foundations of Modern Political Thought*, 2:241–54, for the European development of this sort of pragmatic form of toleration in the interest of national unity.

also demands justice, the simple fact that toleration would serve the interest of, say, national unity is no adequate reason in favor of it. In situations where the convictions of certain parties threaten to undermine respect for the value of God's creatures and the rights that give such respect its substance, political or social harmony cannot be of paramount value.

The tolerance I propose is similar to other recommendations of toleration in the West in that it is designed to counter an intolerance bred of dogmatism or fanaticism. The tolerance I propose counters a form of intolerance in which overweaning conviction and an inflated sense of the probity or rectitude of one's own judgments exempt one's opinions from the possibility of error while discounting any element of truth in the positions with which one disagrees. A simple distinction separates truth from error in that case. The simple truth of one's own position is matched by the simple falsity of positions one opposes. At best, absolute distinctions like this promote patronizing dismissals of opposing opinions. At worst, they prompt demands for conformity from the holders of such opinions, whatever their reservations of conscience, and ugly reprisals for any failure on their part to do so.

The antidote I propose to an intolerance based on dogmatic or fanatical adherence to one's own convictions is also shared with other proposals of toleration: an honest recognition of human finitude and therefore of human fallibility. Recognizing the limitations that beset one's all-too-human nature—limitations of scope of vision or perspective, of historical situatedness and vested interests—one cannot presume that one's own espousal of the truth is the absolute truth. Like everyone else's convictions about proper belief and action, one's own are susceptible to correction and criticism. Toleration follows upon the recognition that human opinions are always fallible.

The reasons I give for this recognition of finitude and fallibility differ from other proposals. For example, a straightforward humanism can prompt the recognition of limitations upon human claims to know what is true or right. Such limitations become apparent to any outlook attuned to the finite and thereby humanized by being turned away from preoccupation with God—in the manner of Renaissance humanists who find this world of sufficient interest in itself, or British empiricists for whom questions of God drop off precipitously into obscurity, or atheists like Albert Camus who lack any belief in God with which to be concerned. One acknowledges the limitations of the human because there is no motivation for (in the case of Renaissance humanists), or point to discussing (in the case of British empiricists), or real basis for (in the case of atheistic existentialists) any alternative to them that God might represent. According to my account of Christian belief, however, a similar admission of human finitude is compelled by directing attention to a divine standard that human beings, because of God's transcendence, cannot claim to achieve. The arrogance of fanaticism or dogmatism that fuels intolerance falls away for the reasons I mentioned in chapter 2. Claims for the final truth of any human understanding are undermined where ultimate truth is located with a transcendent God. The absolute certainty about the truth of one's own opinions, which underlies an intolerant rejection of opposing views, is condemned as a form of pretension to a divine status.[6]

The tolerance that replaces dogmatic or fanatical hubris, according to my account, is not based on a lack of conviction or a lack of concern for the truth. Although radically skeptical arguments have been used to undercut dogmatism in the history of Western thought, the simple loss of the inflated confidence that fuels persecuting zeal need not leave behind a total absence of certainty that would make commitment to any particular position impossible. The suspension of judgment favored by classical skeptics is not the only alternative to dogmatism. When undermined by a sense of one's own fallibility, dogmatism is not replaced by indecision but by a willingness to allow the opinions one has to be challenged and enlarged. That sort of openness is not a barrier to conviction; rather it is the only solid basis for it. If one has been and continues to be so open, one is justified in maintaining one's position, knowing that it is the best that one's reason allows at the present time. Nothing is wrong with conviction, therefore, so long as it does not involve one in arrogantly privileging one's own beliefs and effectively immunizing them against criticism. There is a great difference between believing one's opinion to be true because nothing so far has decisively counted against it, and assuming it to be true with the effect of discounting all possible objections to it.[7] My

6. See the references to Reinhold Niebuhr in n. 1 for further discussion of the connection between dogmatism and intolerance.

7. See John Stuart Mill, *On Liberty* (London: Penguin Books, 1974), 79. I have been following quite closely here Mill's analysis of what follows from fallibility.

position precludes the latter as a presumption that is an affront to God, but comfortably admits the former.

Moreover, far from being a product of a lack of conviction, the toleration I recommend against a dogmatic or fanatical zeal is itself based upon certain Christian convictions—about God and God's relation to the world and the value of creatures. Those convictions may themselves be matters of dispute. If what I have said about forms of legitimate conviction holds, toleration in such a case does not mean one has to give up those beliefs; it merely means that one cannot hold on to them dogmatically. Christian beliefs must be defended against objections that are taken seriously enough at least to warrant being addressed. I have not engaged in defense of that sort in this book, but have simply presumed such beliefs for the purpose of figuring out their implications for action and attitude. One implication is the demand for reasoned defenses of Christian belief. Even were one simply to presume Christian beliefs without argument, such beliefs will themselves demand public discussion of their merits.[8]

In general, the toleration I recommend does not presume indifference about matters on which people disagree or the unimportance of decisions concerning them. Christians, as believers in God, and therefore believers in a truth about proper behavior and belief beyond the relativities and contingencies of human life, are zealous for the truth. A prohibition on dogmatism based on God's transcendence simply prevents them from being zealous for their own understanding of that truth. Following a notion of toleration based on my account of God and creation, one can insist upon the importance of the truth for which people search without feeling compelled to require assent to any one party's formulation or depiction of it. The beliefs at issue may be of great importance, but even on matters of the greatest concern one cannot afford to ignore the fallibility of one's conclusions as a

8. This demand for openness to criticism sets an additional limit on the intolerance that can be shown beliefs that promote intolerance and injustice. One must tolerate such beliefs enough to address them in one's own rational reflection. People holding them may even have the right to present arguments for them in forums dedicated to reasoned discussion among people with opposing viewpoints. Indeed, showing up the hatefulness and ignorance that underlie even the best arguments for them by their exponents might do more to damage them than simply silencing the people who hold them. To offset the danger to others of such publicity, someone holding my position must assume, however, the actual existence of forums where participants and audience are genuinely dedicated to the truth without hindrance—a tall order indeed.

finite creature. Arguments are serious—truth is at stake—but if one is genuinely zealous for the truth, the convictions that carry the day simply cannot be sheltered from new or continuing sources of dissent. Immunizing them from criticism, by refusing to hear or discounting opposing viewpoints out of a sense of the rightness of one's own position, is the easiest way to lose the truth rather than maintain it. One presumes the truth without allowing for the only means available for legitimately claiming it: successful argument against opposing viewpoints.[9]

The toleration I recommend goes beyond a mere suspicion of dogmatically held certainties. It goes beyond the mere recognition that one might be wrong and the views one opposes right, beyond the proposal that one should therefore attend to them, if one is genuinely interested in the truth, in case they are. As I have already suggested, the toleration I advocate has a positive basis in an active respect for the decisions of others. The decisions that other people make according to their own best lights are positively valuable in and of themselves. The Christian grounds for finding such positive value in the decisions of others are not the same, however, as the usual ones in the Western philosophical tradition: some underlying commonality of beliefs or norms that bind one's own judgments and those of others.

According to the usual grounds for a positive respect of others' opinions, the decisions of others are due respect only in so far as they conform to a specified standard for belief and comportment. In order to be worthy of respect, their beliefs, values, or forms of action must meet the standard. A demand of this sort leads to toleration only if *all* the parties at issue do so. The beliefs, values, or norms that constitute the standard are therefore very basic ones—beliefs, values, or norms that all parties can accept, whatever their other disagreements.

Toleration is based upon agreement, then, on a link of identity: most often, in actual beliefs or norms; sometimes simply in the ultimate referent of beliefs or norms. For example, the value of every religion is to be respected in so far as each affirms some locus of ultimate concern and the importance of upright behavior. Or every religion might be due respect as a filling out in beliefs and norms of an encounter

9. I come back to these issues of nonfanatical commitment in the next chapter, where the discussion turns to prerequisites for activism in Christian thought.

with that object of ultimate concern from a particular standpoint. In both cases, toleration is based on what all parties share or hold in common.

If intolerance is not to flare up with respect to beliefs and norms that are not shared, the significance of these differences has to be undercut. They are perhaps matters of indifference, *adiaphora*, inessential features of the positions under consideration that could just as well be dropped. Or the significance of such differences can be relativized by viewing them as alternative accounts of the same thing. The differences might be important in the latter case as essential discriminating features of the positions under discussion, but the possibility that such differences could become matters of contention is ruled out a priori by the claim, for example, that the same referent is being described from different points of view. In sum: Different outlooks are either only apparently different (according to the first sort of argument), since they agree on fundamentals. Or they are really different (according to the second), but those differences are simply alternative ways of developing the same agreement on fundamentals in accord with the particularities of place and time.[10]

The odd thing about this way of grounding toleration in claims of commonality is how closely it parallels grounds for *intolerance*. Where some underlying commonality of beliefs or norms is a requirement for respect, difference is not valuable as such—difference is not valuable without a reference to something that is the same. The unrepentantly different, difference that cannot be reduced to the inessential or that cannot be inescapably tied to commonly held beliefs or a common referent, is suspect. Others are not *rejected* for being different. The value of their positions can be accepted, but only in so far as difference is not the last word.

Grounds of this sort for respect have an obvious potential, however, for intolerance, for disparagement of what is different simply

10. The first version of justifying toleration by an appeal to underlying commonalties is typical of Renaissance and Enlightenment thinkers who lack a more modern sensitivity to historical difference—for example, Pico della Mirandola, Guillaume Postel, John Locke. See Skinner, *Foundations of Modern Political Thought*, 2:244–49 for France, and the discussion of the Latitudinarians by, for example, G. R. Cragg in any of his books on seventeenth- and eighteenth-century England. I am implying here that the main thing that distinguishes the work of, for example, John Hick from some of the oldest arguments for liberty of religious conscience is attention to the significance of historical variation.

because it *is* different. Should certain parties not conform to the standards specified, this nonconformity can only indicate some defect on their part. Difference that stands in the way of such conformity is understood as deviation from a universal norm of validity that such standards represent.

A toleration based on common or shared belief cannot tear up these grounds for devaluation of the different at their roots. As long as shared standards are a requirement for respect, devaluation of the different is always a possibility. Toleration of this sort can only hope to contain this ever-present possibility by formulating standards that are never able to rule out respect for any position. A proponent of this form of toleration can specify standards of belief so extraordinarily vapid that dissent is next to impossible, or simply insist that all parties really presuppose the beliefs in question (whatever the extent of their apparent disagreements), since they must finally be talking about the same thing. (In the latter case, one's generosity of spirit goes so far as to render the putative universality of those standards immune from empirical disconfirmation.) In these ways a claim for universal standards loses the prescriptiveness necessary to promote intolerance, and becomes instead a claim for the universality of these standards in fact. A claim for universality no longer functions as a norm specifying what *should* be. The commonality of those standards is not something to be achieved. To the contrary, it always already exists in the form of a set of beliefs or a subject matter actually held in common.

Christian grounds for a toleration of positive respect can counter in a more radical way the potential for intolerance that lodges with commonalities of beliefs or norms as conditions for respect. My position is not forced to make the best of those grounds for respect. Instead, it directly attacks and displaces the various elements of those grounds with the potential to fuel intolerance.

The elements for attack are three. Taken together they constitute a general scaffolding or scheme for reasoning to the conclusion that people different from oneself are unworthy of respect.[11] First, the claim

11. I have been influenced in my formulation of the three elements of this scaffolding by theorists who attack colonialist or sexist forms of discourse. For the former, see Edward Said, *Orientalism* (New York: Vintage Books, 1979); and Tzvetan Todorov, *The Conquest of America* (New York: Harper and Row, 1984). For the latter, see Elizabeth Minnich, *Transforming Knowledge* (Philadelphia: Temple Univ. Press, 1990); Martha Minow, *Making All the Difference* (Ithaca, N.Y.: Cornell Univ. Press, 1990); and Elizabeth Spelman, *Inessential Woman* (Boston: Beacon Press, 1988).

to specify a standard or norm for all is suspect on my account. My account of God's transcendence insists upon the particularities of creatures and my account of the value of creatures celebrates them in ways that are incompatible with this first appeal to a single standard for all. Second, sameness or identity with such a norm is not the basis for respect. My account of the value of creatures celebrates diversity in a way that conflicts with such a requirement. This second aspect of the grounds for respecting others that I oppose suggests a third one, which figured in the discussion of forms of intolerance based on dogmatism: absolute distinctions between self and others. This third element is also ruled out by my account. Existence before God, as I understand it, relativizes differences among creatures so as to exclude claims of absolute differences among them.

I expand on the arguments against each of these elements in turn before closing this chapter with a look at what my proposal for toleration suggests about proper social relations.

UNIVERSAL STANDARDS AND THE VALUE OF PARTICULARITY

The first element of a general scheme supporting intolerance, the claim to have determined standards of respect for the beliefs and behaviors of all other people, is to be suspected of hubris according to my principle of divine transcendence. A universal standard does exist, a standard for truth and goodness that holds for all. This standard is located, however, with a transcendent God. Knowledge of that fact should make the particularities of one's own judgment stand out and act as a counsel against their elevation to a standard to which all others must conform in order to be worthy of respect. Using a standard one has arrived at oneself as a benchmark for respecting the beliefs and actions of all others, one forgets one's own particularity, the circumscribed character of one's existence that narrows one's focus to a particular time and place and to the interests and pleasures specific to oneself, the very particularity that a standard for all that resides with God should highlight. What one believes and does becomes a standard that all others must meet in order to be worthy of one's respect, as if one's beliefs and actions were somehow exempt from the particularities of interest and historical circumstance that affect all creatures. The particular becomes the universal in this way and usurps the prerogatives of God alone.

One must be careful to specify precisely the meaning of this charge that particulars are illegitimately elevated to universals when used as general standards of respect. First, the charge cannot be limited to obvious cases of parochiality—"the food is bad if it is not meat and potatoes" kind of obvious parochiality. Even where a standard for respect is set after attempts to broaden one's horizons and admit the value of the beliefs and practices of other people, the very process of setting it is lodged inextricably in one's own particularities. Any standard for respect that results from such efforts is inevitably one that one sets oneself from one's own particular standpoint. Making it a standard for respecting all others one forgets the particularity of the standpoint occupied in the very process of constructing it.

Second, according to my account of a transcendent God, there is nothing wrong with doing one's best to figure out what is true or right. Moreover, one's conclusions at any particular time will obviously stand as a criterion for assessing the truth or propriety of others' beliefs and actions. There is nothing wrong with that, either, so long as one remains open to the revision and critique of such criteria. What I object to is the use of these conclusions as criteria for the very respect for others that is necessary for such openness to criticism by them. Those who disagree with one's own understanding of truth or goodness are never in the position to challenge that understanding if their disagreement is grounds for not respecting their opinions to begin with. What I have ruled out, in sum, is not conclusions about truth and goodness per se but their use as general criteria for determining who is worthy of respectful attention. Used in that way, judgments about what is true and right disparage and marginalize the people with whom one disagrees. They render such people unworthy of a hearing, and consequently condemn them before they have had the chance to speak on their own behalf.

Someone might try to argue, against what I have said, that one can retain universal standards for respect while countering such uses. These standards must be only provisional ones, open to revision by those with whom one disagrees. I would argue in response that in that case the standards are no longer of the sort at issue. They no longer function as preconditions for respect if they are open to revision by those not agreeing with them.

The particularity of proposed standards for respect can be disguised by the way in which they reject the particularities of all those beliefs, norms, and values that do not conform to them. Such a rejection of particularity might give the impression of universality; it might suggest that the standard proposed is not itself particular. What it really proves, however, is that a certain form of particularity is held onto exclusively. Thus the middle class or bourgeoisie of Europe effectively suppressed the cultural life of the lower classes (e.g., carnivals), on the assumption, apparently, that everything characteristic of lower-class life is dirty, low, despicable, or dangerous, if it is not what the middle class are prone to do. This repudiation of the particularities of the life of others did not make the values of the middle class somehow universally valid, as middle class thinkers were prone to assume. It simply showed them to be intolerant.[12]

The particularity of a standard will uncover itself by way of a peculiar lack of reciprocity in its application. In order to conform to a purported standard for all, some classes of people need to renounce their particularity while others do not. Thus, white middle-class women meet the standard for business behavior in so far as they do not act like women—for example, they demonstrate an aggressively competitive nature. Gay white middle-class men meet the standards of public propriety in so far they do not act gay. Men and women of color meet standards for civility in so far as they do not act like people of color—for example, they speak "proper English." But straight white middle-class men are always just right the way they are. White women, gay men, and men and women of color conform to these standards for respect to the extent one can say of them that underneath all that apparently distinguishes them as the particular people they are there beats the heart of a straight white middle-class man. The same bifurcation of surface appearance and essential reality, of external particulars and inner essence, is unnecessary, however, for straight white middle-class men. They can be wholly themselves. No one will ever suggest to them that they have the potential to conform to universal standards

12. This is one of the arguments made by Peter Stallybrass and Allon White in *The Politics and Poetics of Transgression* (Ithaca, N.Y.: Cornell Univ. Press, 1986).

because underneath that straight white middle-class exterior they are really black, or feminine, or lower class, or gay.[13]

From the standpoint of my position on the respect owed human beings as creatures of God, the problem that this lack of reciprocity points out is not a problem with particularity per se. If a purportedly universal standard for respect were applied so that everyone had to renounce what makes their particular lives distinctive, that would be no reason for commending it. The problem with the fact that straight white middle-class men do not have to renounce their particularity like everyone else in order to gain respect is not that they too should have to renounce their particularity. The problem is that *anyone* needs to. If human beings are valued as creatures of God, it is the very particularity of their existence, the very distinctiveness of each of their lives, that is to be valued.

The claim that human beings are due respect as creatures of God is a standard for respect for all but it is not a standard that requires anyone to renounce her or his particularity by conforming to it. It is not a standard for respect that points to itself as some selfsame set of values or beliefs that everyone must espouse. Other people are not required to believe in the value of human beings as creatures of God, and act with such a belief in mind, in order for their beliefs and actions to be respected. (Although if they believed and acted in that way, they would be believing and acting properly, in my opinion.) Their beliefs and actions are worthy of respect not because they conform to anyone else's but simply as the manifestations of their own particularity, simply as the results of their own efforts to be themselves. My standard for respect points away from itself, therefore, to distribute a worthiness for respect to the distinctive particularities of others. Conforming to my standard of respect for all does not demand the repetitive instantiation of the same material beliefs and norms. To the contrary, it requires that everyone actively formulate what it is that makes them the particular beings they are.

IDENTITY AND DIFFERENCE AND RESPECT FOR OTHERS AS GOD'S CREATURES

When a partial standard becomes a universal norm, conforming to it requires the renunciation of one's particularity because identity or sameness is what is meant by such conformity. This is the second

13. See Spelman, *Inessential Woman*; and Catharine MacKinnon, *Feminism Unmodified* (Cambridge: Harvard Univ. Press, 1987).

element of the scheme of reasoning that supports intolerance. A particular standard can be passed off as a standard for all only if those others can be squeezed into some sort of identity with it, or devalued in so far as they are different. Both strategies can pertain, indeed, to the same parties. Thus women are valuable in so far as they can be classified in the same terms as men; those aspects of their nature by which they differ from men (i.e., those aspects that make them specifically women), however, are at best worthless, trivial, unworthy of notice or respect.

In general, then, when the partial standard elevated to universality is one's own, others become worthy of respectful treatment only in so far as they are like oneself. Others are worthy of membership in the community of those persons owed the same basic rights as oneself, in so far as their speech, dress, actions, or feelings are the same as one's own. Any difference from one's own attitudes and behaviors devalues them. If others are like oneself, they are respectable. To the extent they are no longer like oneself, they are no longer respectable.

Sameness is in this way the condition for equality of respect. Difference is immediately translated into terms of superior or inferior value. If others are not like oneself, there is something wrong with them. As something different from oneself, the other is pathologized. Thus to the extent other people's beliefs about truth and goodness are not in agreement with one's own, such beliefs are irrational. The disagreement is a product of some defect on their part; their decision making has been corrupted by political interests or a vision narrowed to the needs of a specific historical circumstance.

Even if the other is like oneself, the other qua other is devalued. Someone other than oneself can never perfectly reproduce one's own opinions or behaviors. In even the best case, therefore, others tend to be viewed as impostors, like what one knows but still strangely and disquietingly unlike it. For example, when viewed through Orientalist spectacles, Muhammed is familiar and therefore a potential candidate for respect in that he seems to be like the Jesus Christians know; finally however, he is alien and therefore a fraud, because although similar to Jesus in some respects he is after all not like him in others.[14] In even

14. See Said, *Orientalism*, 72.

the best case, others are defective versions of the positions one has achieved oneself—still on the way to becoming them or falling away from them through some unhappy process of devolution.[15]

Thus a mere likeness is ultimately not good enough. Others can never be too much like oneself. A strict identity between their beliefs and actions and one's own is required in order for others to be worthy of respect. Any perceived dissimilarity becomes the excuse therefore for promulgating an absolute difference in value between oneself and others. Their opinions are simply wrong; one's own are simply right. One's own behaviors are rational, just, generous; the others are merciless, fanatical, barbaric. Whatever infects their decision-making processes so as to corrupt their conclusions is simply absent from one's own.

An asymmetrical application of principles of evaluation is therefore appropriate. For example, a hermeneutics of suspicion should only be turned against opinions different from one's own. There is no need to turn it against one's own because they, of course, are objective.[16]

Any difference at all between peoples can become grounds for a claim that others simply lack cultural acquisitions of value. Witness Christopher Columbus's tragicomical difficulties in communicating with the peoples of the Americas. They must be speaking his own language; if not, they must not be speaking any language at all.[17] Their religion does not seem to be like his; therefore they have no religion. Their norms for the treatment of others do not seem to be his; therefore they have no morals.

Differences in beliefs, attitudes, or norms are naturally heavily emphasized in order to justify such claims of an absolute difference in value between one's own group and others. Differences between one's group and others should, indeed, themselves be absolute. If they are to seem so, differences that actually distinguish only some members of one's camp from some members of the other must be overgeneralized, and the differences that hold within each of the opposing camps

15. For a discussion of such processes of devaluation with regard to "the East," see again Said, *Orientalism*.

16. See Barbara Herrnstein Smith, *Contingencies of Value* (Cambridge: Harvard Univ. Press, 1988), esp. chap. 3, for a general critique of appeals to objectivity on similar grounds.

17. Recounted by Tzvetan Todorov, *Conquest of America*, 30, who draws the same conclusion as I do here.

must be underemphasized. For example, that some poor people spend on impulse and some rich people save their money becomes the overgeneralization "the poor spend on impulse and the rich save their money." That some poor people watch every dime and some rich people buy even the most expensive items on a whim is consequently overlooked. The classifications that result from procedures like this form two closed, perfectly homogeneous, and self-consistent monoliths. The others and those like oneself, each side becomes a general object, a type that no differences among individuals can disconfirm. One seems justified in claiming, therefore, that all the others are alike in their depravity, and all of one's own people are alike in their nobility.[18]

The peculiar dialectic of identity and difference we have just been discussing has clear social consequences. Whether one considers others to be absolutely different or just the same as oneself, either way they are assimilated to the self's own projects. If others are absolutely different from one, they become mere fodder for the development of one's own concerns. They do not have the standing to require consideration in the course of one's own self-interested pursuits. One has the right to bend them to the instrumentality of one's will without attention to their own wishes or interests—one has the right to kill them, to enslave them, to expropriate what they own or produce. The indigenous peoples of the Americas were treated this way by the conquering Spanish: their resources in body and land exploited by those who believed them to be so different from themselves. If others are like one, the projects of one's own group will serve the ends of those others as a matter of course; if they are really like oneself there is no need to ask them whether their wills conform to one's own. One may not kill them, enslave them, or take away their property as one's interests direct—one would not, after all, treat the members of one's own camp in that fashion—but one still takes hurried steps to make them over in one's own image—changing their customs, religion, and forms of exchange, by force if necessary, to match one's own. Thus

18. See once again Said's *Orientalism*. The overlooking of differences among women in favor of a claim of a general female essence is a common object of derision among some feminists. See, for example, Sandra Harding, *The Science Question in Feminism* (Ithaca, N.Y.: Cornell Univ. Press, 1986), 175–76.

even the most well-intentioned among the Spanish, for example, Bartholomè de Las Casas, were complicitous in practices that ran roughshod over Indian rights to self-determination.[19]

I have said enough at this point about the way these last two elements—a demand for identity and presumptions of absolute difference—form a peculiar dialectic of identity and difference, and about the way in which respect is distributed according to this dialectic, to begin now a critique from the standpoint of my own account of the respect due human beings as creatures of God.

First, it should be clear from everything said so far about respect for human beings as creatures of God that identity or sameness is not a condition of it. The human beings owed respect as creatures of God might well be very different from one another. Indeed, they might have nothing in common: they might exhibit no similarities in beliefs or form of life. That would do nothing to alter the respect due all of them equally. On my account of respect, differences among creatures can be recognized as real differences, even irreducible differences, while each one of them is nevertheless celebrated as a gift of God. Identity in fundamental beliefs or ultimate reference is no precondition for respecting the different belief systems of various peoples. Sameness is not in general the ground upon which equality of respect is claimed.

Second, when differences between oneself and others are recognized there is no need to construe them as absolute differences, as differences that constitute fixed binary oppositions. No motive like the one discussed previously exists for such a construal, since degree of sameness or difference does nothing to affect the conditions for respect in my account. The positive value granted to differences among creatures by my account means, moreover, that one can easily attend to such differences—differences among those people who form either one's own or another group. There is no reason on an account like this, where the value of differences is highlighted, to essentialize either one group or the other, to view either as a homogeneous type. If neither party is essentialized, differences between the two become accordingly a relative matter: difference everywhere confounds binary oppositions.

19. See Todorov, *Conquest of America*, for the sort of analysis I have offered here of the actions of the Spanish in the Americas.

Drawing absolute distinctions of value, however—absolute distinctions of fault or approbation—is simply improper on my account of basic respect. In drawing such distinctions one exempts oneself from the created status that should hold for all, and breaks solidarity with others as creatures like oneself. According to my account there is no way to exclude oneself from the fault that one finds in others. Even if the particular failings of others are not one's own, the fallibility of the creature that such failings represent must be accepted as one's own. Just as one cannot attribute fault to others while denying that it also pertains to oneself, so one cannot claim for oneself an essential worthiness to be respected that one categorically denies to others. God has already accepted those others, along with oneself, into an all-encompassing community of creatures owed respect. If God recognizes their value in this way and welcomes them to participate in a community under God, how much more so should a human being affirm their value and welcome them into community. God accepts each human being on the same terms. One should therefore accept others as one has been accepted.[20]

As I have already suggested in the previous chapter when considering oppression, distinctions of value can only be relative, not absolute, when they are used to differentiate the value of some persons from others. One person may be a good citizen, and another not, but the lack of praise for the latter on that score cannot take away completely from her or his value. A difference in value on such grounds cannot be used therefore to justify any absolute difference in value between the two. The latter remains valuable as God's creature no matter what good or collection of goods his or her actions fail to manifest or achieve. Moreover, since one's value vis-à-vis a certain good does not determine one's value absolutely, it is always possible that one's value might be differently assessed vis-à-vis some other good. The poor citizen might be a good friend. Just as likely, the good citizen might be a poor parent. Distinctions of right and wrong, of purity and impurity become relative matters in this way: no hard-and-fast differences distinguish one party from another.

20. The reader should recognize here the two ways of drawing conclusions about relations with others from the character of one's relation with God that I permitted near the end of the discussion of hierarchy in chap. 4. See above, pp. 152–54.

To sum up: According to my account of God and creation, what one would like to attribute exclusively to others (e.g., faults, failings, falsity) one must see also in oneself. What one would like to attribute exclusively to oneself (e.g., truth, goodness, light) one must come to see also in others. The two poles of self and other—which are absolutely opposed in the peculiar dialectic of identity and difference I discussed above—are only relatively distinct in my account, not simply because each pole is heterogeneous, but because the heterogeneity of either one may include characteristics of the other.

The first point—that the failings one attributes to others belong to oneself—is ironically confirmed by the way one gains value for oneself when respect is based on the dialectic of identity and difference that I oppose. In order to maintain one's value according to that dialectic, one has to deny the value of those different from oneself. If the opinions and behaviors of others are valuable and genuinely different from one's own, that is a challenge to one's value, a challenge to the propriety of the conditions for respect that one meets in virtue of being the particular sort of person one is. Constructing a characterization of others that denies value to them is therefore necessary in order to convince oneself of one's own value. Such a characterization is designed to be a counterpoint to the goodness that only people like oneself exhibit; it should therefore keep others as alien to oneself as possible—here the tools of over- and undergeneralization that I mentioned previously prove useful. The ironic result is that those claiming all goodness actually possess of themselves the failings they attribute to others, because those others in their absolute difference from oneself are one's own imaginary construction, produced in the very process of trying to sustain a claim of goodness for oneself. The supposedly absolute distinction between self and others is ironically included within, is bridged by, the self whose project it is to valorize itself by those means. To put the point another way: The other one constructs to demonstrate one's own goodness is not really an other, but an other-than-self, a mirror image of one's own purported goodness. The other is the self's *own*. The other is one's own *alter ego*. The valorized self or valorized group must include therefore both itself *and* its other. An identity gained by excluding the failings of others from oneself produces a subconscious heterogeneity, a subconscious identity formed by a struggle between the self one wants to affirm and the self one wants to deny. "I am not those others" is the struggle that constitutes the valorized self. There is no simplicity to this self because there is no simplicity to its self-affirmation; this self's identity is constituted by the other it denies.[21]

This failure to let others be genuinely other is a general consequence of the way respect is distributed according to the dialectic of identity and difference I oppose. If the other is the same as the self, it is immediately assimilated to the self. But even if others are recognized as different, an opposition between self and others is included within an overarching project of the self's own attempt to convince itself of its own value. The other lacks any real exteriority. It is not outside the self, but the self's own other, a moment in a totality of the self's own construction—even when, ironically, the difference between self and other is proposed as absolute.

The social consequences of a failure to let others be other confirm the ones mentioned previously. The projects of the self on this basis can be characterized only by a boundless self-expansion: no others have the exteriority to self that is necessary to prevent those projects from progressing according to simple self-interest. Others are straitjacketed into a position of presumed passivity and nonobstruction, with the results discussed previously: others are either so like oneself that their opposition to one's projects is unimaginable, or so unlike oneself that they have no independent rights to be taken into account when furthering one's plans.

My account of God and creatures lodges a strong criticism against the propriety of all these assimilations to self. Indeed, one virtue of my account is that it lets others be other—genuinely distinct beings from oneself and potential blocks to one's own projects. My account of God's transcendence and of the value of creatures before God combine to reveal the possibility of respectful relations with others who are not assimilable to the self and its projects. God and other human beings, on my account, are genuinely other than oneself in ways that need not confirm the self's own goodness or further its projects. God and other human beings are always potentially breaks, counters, loci of contestation and disorientation, vis-à-vis the self's need to affirm

21. See Stallybrass and White, *Politics and Poetics of Transgression*, 194, for an argument like this concerning bourgeois values.

itself and achieve its ends. Others are not then matters for comfortable presumption but for potentially disconcerting discovery.

This letting others be other is true of the relation between human beings and God. God is other than human beings in my account: the fundamental relation that grounds the self is a relation with divinity whose transcendence prohibits any mixing or confusion with the creature. One's relation with God the creator, a relation that brings to be all one's other relations, is a relation of difference or plurality in which the other must be recognized *as other*: God is not like oneself.

God is not, however, the simple other-of-the-self: the self's own other or alter ego. The traditional theological claim of God's aseity, literally, God's "in-itselfness," the claim that God has God's being in God's self, points to the fact that what makes God God, what makes God different, is not God's relation with the creature. God is not the simple opposite of what the creature is, as if God and creation formed a binary opposition within some overarching ontology, God and creatures oriented around the same set of qualities that they respectively possess or lack. Rather, the otherness of God is that otherness that gives rise to all discriminations of absence and presence, like and unlike. It cannot be incorporated among them.[22]

Moreover, the self does not form the totality within which God might be distinguished from the self as its other. In so far as God's creative working is behind the whole of the created order, God's otherness is logically anterior to all such discriminations of self from others. On my account of a transcendent God's relation to creatures, God's otherness cannot be considered the creature's own, a construction of, and means of furthering, the self's own interests, because the creature is always already constituted *by* that other. The self is first constituted by its relation with God; God cannot therefore be a moment in any creature's self-constituting subjectivity.

A consequence of this logical anteriority of God's working is that God is not an other under the creature's control: God's working

22. In the interest of simplicity, the formula for the *ad majorem* argument I gave at the end of chap. 4 on hierarchy did not fully reflect this complexity. Creatures cannot claim the supremacy that is God's; this was the import of "creatures who are not God or who lack what God has" in the formula. But the radical difference between God and creatures that my account of God's transcendence tries to capture does not imply that creatures are not important or significant in their own right. Their standing is not simply determined by the fact that they lack the supremacy that is God's (and vice versa); they are not simply what God is not.

as creator logically precedes all actions by which the creature might exercise an influence on God. The otherness of God therefore has a supremacy in virtue of this anteriority that prevents it from ever being finally put to rest, presumed to conform to the self's wishes or interests, overlooked or overridden in the self's efforts to realize them. Although the military or economic might of the self may enable it effectively to ignore the claims of others upon it when those others are creatures, the power of the self as a creature is never sufficient to ignore safely the claims of God.

According to my account of God's transcendence, then, one respects God in so far as one recognizes God as other: the most fundamental relation of the self, which brings it to be as the creature it is, is a relation in which the other cannot be assimilated to oneself or one's own projects.

My account of the respect owed God's creatures also shows that the same sort of respectful relation with others, in which the other is recognized as such, is appropriate for relations among human beings. People are worthy of respect, insofar as they are other than oneself, and they are understood to have an exteriority to self with the potential to break the self's own projects.

Indeed, checks on projects of boundless self-expansion are simply written into my account of the rights due all human beings. The possession of rights by those other than oneself is a check upon the way in which one exercises one's own. Claims for oneself cannot categorically override the claims of others. The weakness of others, which permits their own claims to be overlooked, which allows their interests to be assimilated to one's own, is something that one is called to rectify. My account of rights owed human beings as creatures of God implies a social commitment to the exercise of those rights by others. In meeting that obligation one contests the oppressive and disempowering conditions that would make it possible for the rights of others to be ignored when furthering one's own interests.

But on a more fundamental level my account of the respect owed human beings as creatures of God blocks motivations for assimilating others to oneself by imagining them either in one's own image or as one's alter ego. If human beings are owed respect as creatures of God, they do not have to be like oneself to be worthy of it. If one wishes to respect them, one can still see them as the distinct beings they are.

This is part of the realism of respect owed human beings as God's creatures that I discussed when developing this notion.

Furthermore, one need not fear that the simple value of those other than oneself will take away from one's own value. This fear is the motivation discussed previously for thinking of others in the form of an alter ego to one's own goodness, but it is also a motivation for assuming others to be like oneself. If others are valuable and genuinely other than oneself, then the qualities one exhibits must not be the standard to be met by those worthy of respect. To avoid this result, one must either not think of them as other than oneself or think of them as one's opposite. According to my account, if the other is genuinely other she or he will have the ability to contest or block one's own evaluation of self or one's own projects. If the other has a genuine independence of self how could that be avoided? But the other, on my account, is not necessarily by the mere fact of its otherness an affront to the value of the self or its projects. Contrary to a dynamic that assumes so, the respect owed human beings is of a noncompetitive sort when it is based on creaturehood, for a number of reasons.

First, if the respect due one as God's creature cannot be earned, one cannot lose one's worthiness for it, and therefore one need not jealously guard one's right to be respected. One need not be self-protective about one's own ability to command a respect of this sort. Second, the essential basis of this respect in solidarity with others means that when another person is due respect this is no refutation of the respect owed to oneself but a proof of it. If another is due respect simply as God's creature, this is a confirmation rather than a challenge to one's own worthiness also to be so respected. Third, because respect is owed to one as an individual, regardless of one's relations with others, one can affirm one's own worth directly and with an innocence one does not find when one's respectability is assessed vis-à-vis others, when one's own respectability is a matter of being better, one hopes, than someone else. One can take a short route, as Søren Kierkegaard affirmed, to valuing oneself, rather than the circuitous one that depends on what my value is relative to others.[23] One is simply valuable as

23. Søren Kierkegaard, *Christian Discourses* (London: Oxford Univ. Press, 1939), 40–50. Jean-Jacques Rousseau was also an advocate of such a short route, although on fundamentally secular grounds; see Nicholas Dent, "Rousseau and Respect for Others," in *Justifying Toleration*, ed. Susan Mendus (Cambridge: Cambridge Univ. Press, 1988), 115–35.

oneself in so far as one is valuable as the creature of God. As the creature of God, one should find an immediate joy simply in being the particular person one is. One need not therefore take the long route of denying value to others in order to gain value oneself. One need not think to oneself, "I am not them, they are not good, therefore I am valuable."[24] One need not denigrate the value of God's nature in order to value oneself as a creature. The value of a divinity who cannot be identified with the creature is no affront to the creature's value. The creature is valuable in itself, in its standing as a creature who is not God. Furthermore, one need not deny the value of other creatures in order to affirm oneself: the valorized self does not first need to be constituted by denying value to these others.

SOCIAL CONSEQUENCES

I have come to the end of my discussion of Christian grounds for toleration. It is time to draw some general conclusions about the shape that social relations would take if such toleration were to reign. On the basis of the claims I have made about toleration, we can say that a community founded upon the value of creatures before God would be a pluralistic and radically inclusive community characterized by interpersonal relations of mutual respect. Christians holding such beliefs should work for that kind of society. Christians should use this idea of society to criticize social relations as they presently exist.

A society constructed according to my ideas about toleration is not a community that demands identity, a community requiring a social cement of mutual recognition in which each is to see her or his own beliefs, values, or attitudes mirrored in those of all others. It is not a community that must have the like-minded for members.

Instead, it is a community of solidarity among those who are permitted genuinely to differ from one another in their concrete particularity. In such a community, one need not fear being different, one need not be apprehensive about one's own specific indissoluble particularity, because the cohesiveness of the group is not brought about

24. I am influenced in this description of the "long route" to self-affirmation by Friedrich Nietzsche's analysis of slave morality in *Beyond Good and Evil* and *The Genealogy of Morals*, and by the analysis of those two works by Gilles Deleuze in *Nietzsche and Philosophy* (New York: Columbia Univ. Press, 1983). Nietzsche, of course, viewed this long route as a defining characteristic of Christianity—something that I am disputing here.

through an insistence upon homogeneity. Instead, the cohesiveness of the group is a matter of what one might call nonunifying love, a joyful affirmation of difference and of the particular contributions to the group that each person makes in becoming himself or herself.[25] In such a community human beings are not "cramped and dwarfed," as John Stuart Mill feared they would be, by demands for conformity to social norms; people are helped, instead, to cultivate and unfold the capacities God gave them, helped to be what they can be, in delight at their differences.[26] This is the social task that makes a community out of people who remain quite different.

Used as an ideal to criticize present social relations, this notion of a community celebrating and cultivating difference does not rule out associations of those in similar circumstances—associations of women, blacks, Christians, the politically concerned—when these associations are formed for the purpose of making a wider society more genuinely pluralistic, more respectful of the different people within it.

Consciousness-raising groups are a case in point. Like binds with like and a sharp distinction is posed between members of one's own group and outsiders, in order to make clear what differentiates the people who come together in this group from others. The purpose of such associations is to counter the lack of regard for such differences, in situations where identity is a requirement of respect, and where the particular needs and interests of the people who come together in these groups have been assimilated to those of more politically or economically powerful classes of persons. The principle of identity that binds such groups is not intended to override the value of difference for the wider society; it is to make those differences clearer, the wider society more genuinely pluralistic, and to serve as a platform for a demand that such differences be given their due of respect and rights.

The ideal of social relations that celebrate difference does suggest, however, that when calling the wider society to task, these groups should not overlook differences and their value within their own ranks. The tendency to ignore differences within one's own group when drawing sharp distinctions between one's own group and others is an

25. The expression "non-unifying love" is Todorov's in *Conquest of America*, 249.

26. See Mill, *On Liberty*, 126–27. The theological arguments Mill makes here are, of course, not characteristic of his thought.

essentializing tendency that should be resisted. The highlighting of what all people in the group share should not be overemphasized: it is a provisional tactic, limited in significance to its service for the ends just mentioned. When campaigning for women's rights, one should not presume that women are all the same and one should not identify what they have in common with the circumstances of white middle-class women. The differences among women who come together for purposes of political change—differences that are the product of such things as race or economic class—should be recognized; all these different women should have their own voice. Associations among those who are alike in circumstance should always be recognized therefore as coalitions among the different.

If the community based on my ideas about toleration is one that celebrates differences among its members, it is also radically inclusive. Differences among people will not keep some people out. The community of human beings owed the rights due creatures of God is a community that includes all people.

As an ideal for criticizing present societies, this idea of inclusiveness means at the least that a society should have no clear boundaries for membership based on differences between people. No partial standard should be permitted to restrict admission to full privileges and rights of membership. For example, white men should not set the standard for full membership; white women and women and men of color should determine the standard as much as white men do.[27] All the different people within a society, all the different people that enter into it, should be included, with full attention to their differences in determining who is to count as a full member. If they are so included, eligibility requirements are always tentatively drawn and subject to expansion. It is not even possible finally to exclude those defined as outsiders within a society (e.g., resident aliens), or those with whom one regularly has to do (e.g., for purposes of trade) beyond a society's commonly marked geographical borders.

Respect for the rights of others to self-determination, which is part of what I have meant by toleration, implies social relations of mutual respect, social relations that should be characterized, if at all

27. For a philosophy of law compatible with this rejection of partial standards, see Catharine MacKinnon's treatment of the legal rights of women and Native Americans in *Feminism Unmodified*.

possible, by noncoercive forms of interaction, for example, relations of cooperation and dialogue, in which influence over others is achieved through rational argumentation and persuasion. In a community that celebrates difference, there is no reason to think the goal of such interactions is consensus or an ultimate identity of ends. If such interactions are genuinely based upon mutual respect, they should put a priority upon mutual or common understanding: one owes others the respect of listening to what they have to say and of understanding what they say and do on their own terms. Understanding is a two-way exchange. Others are not to be the passive objects of one's own representation and judgment: they are to speak for themselves.

As an ideal to criticize society, this idea of mutually respectful interactions means that where structural oppression limits access to means of self-expression according to political or economic influence or racial and ethnic background, the least powerful have the greatest rights to be heard. If the poor and the oppressed are to represent their own viewpoints and be heard, they must claim attention in a way that the privileged do not. If communication media are owned by big businesses run almost exclusively by white men, one must conclude that white women, the poor, and people of color have the greater right to representation in those media. The same ideal of mutual understanding supplies a reason simply for structural change of oppressive institutions in the direction of equalizing enjoyment of rights to self-expression.

To continue the discussion of interactions of mutual respect: What others say and do in these interactions may not be to one's liking. This follows from the fact that the other remains a genuine other in the course of such interactions. Mutual respect implies mutual self-recognition in the sense that one is to see the other as a second self—as someone with a right, like oneself, to self-determination. But it does not imply that one is to see the other as oneself. True diversity must be permitted to exist among those who show one another mutual respect.

Where such diversity exists, it may outrun one's expectations or plans. It may disturb one's self-understanding, particularly the perception of one's own truth or rectitude that is presumed when one is intolerant. In respecting others enough to understand them, one may not return to a comfortable self-identity, as Hegelians might have it, in which others are reconciled to oneself.[28] The other need not provide the material for a self-understanding that continues along the same lines; the other may not present a stage on the way within a continuous project of self-understanding or self-realization, in which breaks and interruptions represent mere occasions for incremental corrections. The other has the potential to stop one cold, to turn one's self-understanding and one's projects upside down, by revealing, for example, a fundamental moral fault one has hidden from oneself, or the truth of praise, of which one would otherwise have believed oneself unworthy. In a community of others owed basic respect, one respects the other as a second self even if it is a respect without prospect of a return, without obvious service to one's own self-perception or interests. In a community of those owed basic respect, one leaves oneself open to the unanticipatable influences of genuine others. One's relations with these others are not defensive, as if truth and goodness were already one's own possession and one had simply to guard them against others. Nothing rules out a truth or goodness that may come to one from without. The culture of self-criticism, with which the previous chapter ended, becomes a culture that opens itself to potentially radical criticism from without.

These are the shapes that a society should take if it is founded on my ideas about toleration. They thus join the social vision of a nonoppressive society discussed previously. The obvious next question to ask is, Does the account of God and creation I have developed have the potential to support efforts to realize the kind of social relations I have commended? What sort of activism might that be? I turn to questions like these in the next chapter.

28. On Hegel's dialectic as a complacent return to self-identify, see Emmanuel Levinas, *Totality and Infinity* (Pittsburgh: Duquesne Univ. Press, 1969); and Gilles Deleuze, *Nietzsche and Philosophy*, 8–10.

SEVEN
Christian Belief and Activism

IN THIS CHAPTER I return to a question raised at the end of chapter 3—the question of an activist posture to remedy social ills. In that chapter I discussed the Christian beliefs that make an activist posture meaningful, beliefs that suggest present social conditions can and should be changed and that such a process of change can be furthered by human working. I have now specified a rather full-bodied point or goal for action: giving all persons their due as creatures of God, working for social relations in which the basic dignity and rights I have talked about are guaranteed to all persons, a society where differences are respected therefore and not made the focus of oppressive or exploitative relations among persons. In this way I head off, as I could not fully do in chapter 3, the suspicion that my emphasis on God's transcendence merely makes for an undirected, purely critical stance, a stance whose lack of direction permits nothing more than a continual demand for change for change's sake or a stance so undirected that action in any particular direction is simply precluded. One can now see a direction for action on my account: the direction is toward justice.

This goal or direction for action is a formal rather than a material one: in whatever one feels called to do, one should try to serve the cause of justice as one goes about it. Only as a formal end will the cause of justice be compatible with the emphasis on diversity in the previous chapter. Not everyone is called to make agitating for justice the explicit focus of their life's work, for example, by becoming a community organizer or political lobbyist for minority rights. One can do all manner of things with one's life, but in the process one should be attentive to furthering a respect for the basic value and rights of all persons as creatures of God.

The end of justice cuts across in this way all particular callings under God's providential or salvific will. It is not the only end for which God summons one to act—who can prejudge what a free God will ask of one? Who knows how far beyond social relations of justice the salvific will of God ranges? But as the most basic or fundamental implication of the simple claim of living lives under God, a concern for justice should be part of all those ends to which human beings are called. The salvation in which we are to participate may amount to something more than social relations of justice; but it can amount to nothing less than them.

Suspicions may remain, however, about my account. One might worry whether it is compatible with commitment to a particular course of action or compatible with the decision-making processes necessary in order to form conclusions about what such a course of action should be. Indeed, grounds for suspicion might center specifically around the kind of totalistic or universalizing judgments I employed in chapters 5 and 6. I said, positively, that all persons are called by God to be God's agents by becoming themselves; I claimed, negatively, that all persons are finite and fallible, that no person can be exempted from sin. These sorts of judgments were made in showing that differences among persons are irrelevant to the determination of basic respect and rights, and in countering the absolute distinctions of good and bad that fuel intolerance. Might not such universalistic claims preempt meaningful judgments about the differences between persons that lead one to side with one camp or another and commit oneself to action on its behalf?

I will have much more to say about this, but it should be clear simply from the previous chapter that differences among persons are far from dropping out of the picture of the respect and rights due human beings as creatures of God. Differences are the very things to which one must attend when working to ensure that social relations reflect the basic dignity and rights of all persons. Distinctions of right and wrong are relativized, but that hardly means that they are insignificant or eviscerated of practical force. Everything true and good is not to be attributed to one camp while everything false and morally repugnant is attributed to another, but nothing prohibits determinations of greater or lesser fault, relative to the specific matters at hand. The impropriety of such absolute distinctions does not keep one from establishing that the agendas of certain classes of persons are most responsible for enforcing oppressive social relations of a certain sort, and from taking action, accordingly, to counter them. My rejection of absolute difference highlights the importance for practical purposes of difficult contextual and historically specific judgments about the mechanisms of social oppression.

Ironically, the very extent of attention to difference in the previous chapter might present additional grounds for suspicion about the compatibility of my account with activism. Won't a tolerant respect for differences get in the way of a committed decision for a social agenda that not everyone shares? What sort of commitment is compatible with openness to correction by those with whom one differs?

Again, I indicated in the previous chapter the general direction that answers to such questions will take. In this chapter I address more fully this and the other grounds for suspicion I have mentioned, in the course of a treatment of attitudes conducive to activism. In chapter 3 I asked whether Christian beliefs can make sense of an activist project. Now I ask whether they can produce the dispositions necessary for activism, the self-understanding and attitudes that foster activist engagement. It is one thing to know that unjust social relations can be altered by one's own actions; it is another thing to be inclined to take up the challenge, to have the sort of attitudes toward oneself and others that make it one's own business to do so. Are the attitudes that I derived from beliefs about God and the world in the previous chapter (e.g., the attitude of respect for all human beings as creatures of God) of the proper sort? I argue here that they do in fact represent the general sort of psychological dispositions necessary for an activist stance. Because the self-understanding that informs activist engagement has specifically Christian grounds, the activism that results has a distinctive shape, however: Christian activism is neither cocksure of success nor desperate; it is firmly committed yet humble, uncompromising about the goal of greater justice yet flexible and free to maneuver with respect to the means to that end.

NONIDOLATROUS SELF-ESTEEM AS GROUNDS FOR ACTIVISM

I need to review the attitudes fostered by belief in God and creation before making an argument about their connections with an activist stance. Combining what I said in chapter 6 about proper and improper attitudes—what I ruled out in the discussion of the dialectic of self-aggrandizement and self-contempt, and what I developed in the treatment of respect owed creatures of God—I call the primary attitude toward self and others that accords with my account of God and creatures a nonidolatrous esteem. It is a complex attitude with two parts—one negative, one positive.

On the negative side, one must have the humility to accept oneself as not God. One must honestly acknowledge oneself as a finite creature, limited by circumstances and inherent capacities, unable to stave off moral and intellectual failings in all respects or in any respect indefinitely, conditioned ultimately by God who gives all and provisionally by each creature that acts under God's will for the world.

On the positive side, one must esteem what one is, as the finite creature of God, encompassed by God's providential and salvific intentions for the world. My account blocks the overidentification with a divine perfection that leads one to deny any relative worth to the being and action of creatures. Humility should not turn therefore into humiliation or shame. There is no shame in not being God, there is no shame in being fallible, there is no shame in being conditioned by relations with others. All this is just what being a creature *means*; and the creature in itself is valuable.

According to my account of the respect due creatures, one should consider valuable the particularities of one's own being and doing, all those things about one's own nature and inclinations that distinguish one as the particular being one is, that make one a distinct individual before God and other human beings. Moreover, one should consider oneself valuable as someone called specifically to determine one's own life, called to make one's life one's own. One should see oneself therefore as a responsible agent, empowered to become something by one's own decision and initiative. Finally, self-esteem of these sorts should give one a sense of entitlement to treatment that accords with a proper respect for one's status as a creature of God.

The two general attitudes of humility and self-affirmation that I have discussed should be mirrored in one's attitudes toward others. No one else is due an idolatrous esteem. All others should be respected as one respects oneself, in so far as they too are creatures of God, called to become themselves. Indeed, part of one's calling as a responsible agent is to demonstrate such respect in the actions one takes in becoming the particular person one is.

In what ways might these attitudes toward self and others be conducive to action for social change? I start with attitudes of self-worth and move from there to consider humble acknowledgments of finitude.

The sense of oneself as a distinct person before God and other human beings counters any absorption of oneself by the state, or by the particular persons with whom one is in relation. Conversely, respect for the distinctness of others discourages any attempt on one's own part to violate the boundaries of others by assimilating them to one's own projects and interests. One has a sense of self, whatever demands others may make on one, and one acts so as to give others the space and encouragement to be themselves.[1] Thus this sense of persons' distinct identities as God's creatures constructs a platform for disobedience to the social order, for dissent in the face of injustice on behalf of oneself or on behalf of others whose distinct voices and concerns one hears. Self-sacrificing obligation to others under situations of oppression or domination or exploitation cannot take away one's sense of self, cannot erase one's proper concern for oneself as God's creature, or make one less a proper focus for the concern of others.

Moreover, a sense for the positive value one has as a person before God disinclines one from equating one's value with one's present social status or with any role to which one could aspire under prevailing socioeconomic conditions. One has value as the person one is because one is the creature of God, however other people or one's institutionalized relations with others distribute esteem and its material rewards. The conservative, or at best reformist, effects of identifying one's value with the status positions of a particular society are in this way blocked.

1. See Mary Potter Engel, "Evil, Sin and Violation of the Vulnerable," in *Lift Every Voice*, ed. Susan Thistlethwaite and Mary Potter Engel (San Francisco: Harper and Row, 1990), 160, on sin as a distortion of boundaries.

One can identify one's value with the status one has as a creature of God rather than, for example, with the lowly social esteem granted those in one's social location. Human beings may treat one with disdain and disrespect because one's work is unskilled or undignified or poorly paid, but one knows that as a creature of God one's dignity and worth are far greater than they recognize. The legitimacy of such treatment is thereby undermined, since according to my account a sense of entitlement should properly follow a sense of one's value as God's creature. However lowly one's present status according to the usual social standards (e.g., money, property, education), one's dignity as a creature of God gives one the right to expect—indeed, the right to demand—treatment that respects that dignity.

This sense of oneself as possessing a value independent of a demeaning social status permits one at least a psychological freedom from oppressive conditions. It takes away the anxious preoccupation of comparison with those socially esteemed, the worry that one is perhaps not worthy of consideration because of one's lowly social position. It keeps one from being humiliated. It helps one to bear up under oppressive circumstances, to do what one is forced to do, through lack of opportunity or covert or overt threat of force, without the servility or abject submissiveness that break a person's spirit.

It helps the oppressed to continue, in other words, and therefore it can help to maintain the institutional structures under which they are oppressed. But the psychological freedom that knowledge of one's value before God brings never occurs, on my account of it, apart from a demand for better treatment. Psychological freedom cannot spell contentment. One's standing before God does not permit one to dissociate oneself completely from a standing before others in which one suffers ill-treatment. A sense of one's value as God's creature is instead always grounds for a sense that one is entitled to some other life.

The standing one has in virtue of a relation to God the creator may indeed far outweigh in importance one's standing before human beings. It does not make that social standing unimportant, however, since certain forms of respect and treatment by others are an implication of one's standing before God. For these reasons one is never a "happy slave," without concern for a change in one's circumstance, knowing of one's value before God whatever others may think about or do to one.[2] One's spirit is never broken under oppression in the sense that one never accepts the propriety of what is thought about or done to one. One remains resistant, at least in spirit, and if in spirit then always also in anticipation, waiting for the opportunity when one's demands for respectful treatment might come to something more. At least in spirit, but never merely in spirit when the opportunity for resistance in fact appears. It is clearly improper on my account to appeal to a value before God that holds independently of one's social standing, in order to downplay efforts to realize better treatment where those efforts have a chance for success.

A sense of one's value before God does not lead therefore to quietism. Dignity as a creature of God does compensate for indignities suffered at the hands of human beings, but it is no opiate, inuring one to mistreatment. Present treatment cannot take away one's dignity before God, but that treatment is hardly a matter of indifference consequently, a matter one should bear passively. The sense of one's own dignity, which the disrespectful treatment of others cannot take away, is a constant reminder that such treatment is unjustified.

Moreover, value in virtue of one's relation to God blocks the co-optation of the lower classes whereby they identify themselves with the values of an upper-class life. When one recognizes one's value before God one has no need to escape the demeaning character of present circumstance by aspiring to the status of a higher class. Gaining the status qualities of the upper classes is not the only alternative when searching for a sense of value for one's life that is missing in one's present social location. Because one is not maintaining a sense of one's own worth by identifying with the upper classes, one need not repudiate associations with classes of persons beneath one, associations that are necessary for mobilizing forces for change; and the change one anticipates out of a sense of being entitled to a better life need not be a change in status or position that leaves the overall structure of society the same.

According to my account, moreover, the right to ask for changes in a society's procedures does not depend on first establishing one's

2. I owe the expression "happy slaves" to a book on consent theory by Don Herzog, which begins with statements like this one from George Fitzhugh in 1857: "negro slaves of the South . . . are the happiest people in the world." See Don Herzog, *Happy Slaves* (Chicago: Univ. of Chicago Press, 1989), ix.

value on society's terms. The changes requested also need not be steered by that requirement in the direction of superficial reform. The dignity that gives one the right to question how society treats people is not an achieved status. No matter how low one's social status, one already possesses that dignity; it is one's own simply as a creature of God. One does not need to gain anyone else's esteem in order to legitimate such complaints. Insecurity about one's own social standing need not hamper therefore an uncompromising criticism of the norms according to which a particular society shows its respect for people.

A sense of personal worth as God's creature also blocks the conservative effect of identifying one's value with the high social standing one already possesses. What holds for oppressed persons holds also for privileged ones: dignity before God is not the same thing as one's social status. One has the same value as God's creature no matter how high (or how low) one's social standing. The consequences of recognizing that fact are different, however, for the privileged than they are for the oppressed, in keeping with their different situations. This situational or audience-specific unpacking of the practical import of Christian claims is an important feature of the analysis in this chapter.

The dignity before God that psychologically empowers the poor and oppressed to *claim* their rights psychologically empowers the privileged to *forgo* what they possess at another's expense. If one has a value before God irrespective of one's social standing, the privileged need not fear the loss of the social esteem that is their privilege; they need not grasp after it and work to protect it against forces acting to bring about a circumstance of greater justice for all. Just as identifying one's value with one's value before God corrects the self-denigrating tendency of the oppressed to take their social standing to heart, it corrects the self-congratulatory inclination of the privileged to identify their value with their social prestige. Like those of little social esteem, the privileged should stand at a remove from their social roles, ready to criticize the social mechanisms that brought them to be where they are. The sense of their own worth under God should give them the courage to respect the claims of others without fear of the threat to their own social position. Indeed, becoming the persons they are called to be under God may lead those of high social esteem to take the place of those who have little esteem in the eyes of the world. That renunciation of a place of social esteem may be the only way to respect the value of others as creatures of God.

Of more direct consequence for one's inclinations to work for social change is the fact that as the creature of God one should feel empowered to act, empowered to take responsibility for oneself. One's dignity before God, particularly the dignity that comes to one as a participant in God's providential and salvific plans for the world, should give all parties an indelible sense of themselves as responsible agents. In the case of the oppressed this means that, although things like rigid social roles and the prejudiced perception of others about one's capacities can prevent one from being a responsible agent in fact, they cannot destroy one's sense of oneself as an actor on the stage of one's own life. A sense of one's dignity as a creature of God should work against the demoralizing, deadening effects of oppression that keep people from a sense of their own capacity to resist.

If one belongs to a socially privileged class rather than to an oppressed group, the same indelible sense of oneself as a responsible agent counters any tendency to shirk personal accountability for one's participation in a system that seems too large for one's own actions to affect. Whatever the impersonal complexities of present-day monopoly capitalism, for instance, one is called to take action oneself and to take responsibility for the life one lives. As a member of a privileged class, one has the power to be heard and to have one's demands met, the power to decide for oneself the shape of one's own life in a way denied others and to exercise control over the lives of others in keeping with such decisions. One's sense of oneself before God, one's sense of oneself as a responsible agent, keeps one from forgetting those facts of power in an attempt to avoid accountability for one's own actions.

One is called to act but one should not see oneself called to act alone. The failure of others to act does not exempt one from the obligation to take action oneself, but in taking action one should expect aid from others. Given my account of a society formed by relations of mutual respect, one should see oneself as a responsible agent in solidarity with other people who also respect themselves as they respect others.

It is probably true that one's actions as an individual are ineffectual when it comes to resisting one's oppression or one's complicity in oppressive institutions. Because one has a sense of oneself in solidarity with others, one need not settle for individualistic efforts at reform (e.g., efforts of psychological resistance or self-transformation). As I made clear in the last two chapters' discussions of what stands in the way of the enjoyment by all of the rights due them as creatures, there are social causes of situations in which self-development proceeds competitively, causes having to do with the way people habitually relate to one another. Social problems require social solutions. Because it has an essential social component, respect for oneself as God's creature inclines one toward the cooperative ventures necessary for such solutions.

A sense of human finitude—the other side of nonidolatrous esteem—should not keep one from holding onto the social goals I have specified (i.e., the goal of social relations in which the basic rights of all as creatures of God are respected). Such goals may not seem realistic in relation to present social conditions, but one is not freed thereby from the obligation to work for them. Such goals may not be realistic, for example, if realism is measured by the possibility of an ameliorative strategy for achieving them, if realism is measured, by the possibility of working within the present system and the options for social action it legitimates. One must work for such ends anyway, by revolutionary means if necessary. Indeed, the distance from social roles that I have just mentioned should favor a highly imaginative construal of those means. Options for action cannot be limited to presently approved social roles (e.g., the roles of politician, good citizen, lobbyist).

A humble recognition of one's own finitude does, however, make *action* for such goals realistic in a certain sense. An understanding of one's finitude leads to a realistic appraisal of what it is one can do. It leads away from expectations of an immediate realization of one's ends. Action for such ends may very well require hard step-by-step work, and intense and patient efforts; it may very well involve compromise and merely partial successes fraught with reversals and setbacks. If one accepts oneself as a limited, fallible agent and makes no psychological identification with God, one will not waste effort longing for a fantastic or easy way out. Instead, one will be prone to tackle realistically one's situation and the possibilities open to one; one will be prone to assess realistically one's own strengths and weaknesses and the missteps or successful strategies that one has taken so far.

The difficulties and partial results of one's efforts present no reason therefore for despair, for demoralization that leads to the renunciation of further efforts. Difficulties, small steps, and partial results are just what is to be expected from an agent who is not God. The fact that hindrances and incomplete achievement of one's goals are to be expected does not make compromise laudable in itself or transform it from a provisional means to a greater goal into a final end of action. It simply means that compromise is not viewed as some insurmountable obstacle to the ends one is called to further.

The fact that one is a finite agent *under God* is also an antidote to despair and renunciation of effort in the face of partial results and setbacks. Indeed, the knowledge that one is a finite agent under God is probably the only antidote when difficulties and setbacks might realistically be appraised as overwhelming. In the face of military force, police surveillance, and social disempowerment, one can retain a courage to act that comes from knowing that as a finite, fallible agent one works under God's will for the world.

That recognition does nothing to lessen the finite, fallible, and effort-filled character of one's own acts. It presents no escape from an honest admission that one's acts will always be of that character. Even as one acts under God, one does so, one knows, as a finite agent. The knowledge that one acts under God does mean, however, that a realistic self-appraisal can be joined with the hope that one's actions will make a difference, the end of justice furthered in some way thereby, whatever the odds against that happening. One can hope, indeed, that with the help of God even the most partial results at the end of all one's struggles will be enough to further justice.

Because it is found together with the knowledge that one acts as a finite agent, hope in God's help does not involve a blind optimism, an optimism incapable of fathoming the difficulties one must face in working for greater justice. Hope in God when joined with a knowledge of one's own finitude is a counterintuitive hope that presumes instead a full recognition of those difficulties. It does not help one to overlook them, it helps one to cope with them, by countering an action-paralyzing anxiety that might otherwise arise should such difficulties recur or appear insurmountable.

As such a counter to despair and renunciation of effort, hope in God's help is not a prescription for apathy. A sense of one's own responsibility to act remains indelible. As a feature of one's standing as a creature of God, one is called to act in any case, to try as best one can to further justice in the world, however inhospitable the circumstances, in whatever way circumstances may allow. Hope in God is not a substitute for one's own action therefore; it can never mean, on my account, that one need not take action oneself. For the same reasons, an assurance that things will work out fine in the end if God has anything to do with it does not supplant the need for one's own efforts in continuing the struggle. Hope in God's help doesn't mean one does not have to try as hard. Whether hope in God's help gives you the assurance that something or everything will be gained, it represents no facile escape from the obligation to act as a creature under God's providential and salvific will.

Rather than work to preempt the need for one's own action, rather than rule out the point of it, hope in God's help prompts such action in cases where one's own efforts appear futile from the start, and sustains such action, assuming one has already begun to act, against feelings of impotence and ineffectuality. If and when circumstances limit the possibility of action, so be it. Belief in God's help does not prejudge the point where that limit is reached, thereby undermining one's efforts ahead of time. It simply heads off despair over the apparently insignificant effects of one's own best efforts in adverse circumstances and gives one the courage to go on. In absolutely dire circumstances, where all possibility for action to further justice is ruled out, one may be left with only one's hope in God. That hope should not exist alone, however, in any circumstance short of such an absolutely dire one. Even where it exists alone by the force of circumstances, however, belief in God's help does not encourage resignation. Instead, it opens up at least the psychological space for a continued expression of rage at present conditions and the continued expectation of a society organized along different lines. Anger and dissatisfaction are channeled or disciplined by hope, away from outbursts of counterproductive and self-destructive rage, so that one is readied to make effective use of any opportunities for action the future might bring.

NONIDOLATROUS SELF-ESTEEM AND INCLINATIONS TO SELF-DEVELOPMENT

The nonidolatrous self-respect I have been discussing is conducive to the kind of action required by my account of the value of all creatures; it does not promote just any kind of action but the particular sort that constituted the vision for society set forth in chapters 5 and 6. Nonidolatrous self-respect promotes self-development, according to one's own best judgment of what it is one is called to become, in which the same basic rights of all others are respected. One's sense of one's own value as a creature makes one feel worthy of development as the distinct person one is and worthy of being respected by others in the course of one's attempts to do so. One's sense of one's own finitude and fallibility keeps that sense of one's value within limits, one's sense of entitlement within proper perspective. One's own value does not overshadow that of others; it does not give one the right to deny basic rights to others or to benefit at their expense.

All persons do not start from the same place, however, with respect to this nonidolatrous form of self-respect that inclines one to responsible self-development. Here is another place where my analysis is differentiated by audience.[3] The oppressed may not believe themselves worthy to develop their capacities at all or may not have the self-confidence to do so in ways that are contrary to what is socially prescribed. The privileged have the self-esteem to develop their talents. Their problem tends to be an inflated sense of self that serves to justify a partial and inequitable distribution to others of the basic rights they enjoy themselves. They may simply believe themselves worthier than those others to enjoy such basic rights. The privileged in that case tend to be self-conscious oppressors. At the very least, however, the privileged often have an unjustified sense of self-satisfaction that keeps them from acknowledging any impropriety in the way they exercise their rights to self-development along the lines laid down by society. This is another kind of inflated self-esteem which allows the privileged to maintain passive support for oppressive institutional structures.

The lack of self-esteem among the oppressed and the inflated self-esteem of the privileged converge for the same effect: no one questions a status quo of injustice. Neither party is open to a call of God beyond anything that might conform to established social roles

3. In what follows I have been heavily influenced by feminist analysis of the different meanings of sin and salvation for men and women. See Judith Plaskow, *Sex, Sin, and Grace* (Washington, D.C.: Univ. Press of America, 1980); Valery Saiving, "The Human Situation: A Feminine View," *Journal of Religion* 90 (1960): 100–12; and Susan Dunfee, "The Sin of Hiding," *Soundings* 65 (1982): 316–27.

and relations. Individuals of neither group are able to see themselves as agents, as I have described them, under a free God's providential and salvific will for the world. Each party ends up breaking thereby its relation with God. Moreover, neither party is open specifically to a development of self in which self and others are considered of equal value as creatures of God: both parties act as if the oppressed lack the worthiness for self-development that the privileged possess. The self-understandings of both parties block action therefore that accords with the value of all creatures under God. Neither party is in a position to accept a call to act in ways that respect the equal value of the privileged and the oppressed.

In sum, both parties are to be convicted of sloth, of a complacent inaction in which one shuts one's eyes and ears to the possibility of action to counter present injustice. Neither party recognizes a potential to do otherwise as agents of God; they both isolate themselves from the call of God and refuse to acknowledge the value and rights of all persons that call out for action in repudiation of social relations in which such value and rights fail to be respected. The oppressed, because they lack self-respect, refuse to try to leave the burdensome yet secure place in which oppressive social relations have put them, in order to take up the challenge of becoming themselves as agents under God. Their sloth is expressed in a failure to resist, in complicity in their own oppression whereby they take what they can get under present social conditions, accept the view their oppressors hold of them, and abdicate responsibility for their own lives. The privileged, because they have too much self-esteem, continue along in the roles and activities that exploit others, with the complacent security that what they are doing is right, with the complacent confidence that everything is all right as it is. The privileged believe themselves too perfect to be implicated in courses of action that cry out to be changed; the oppressed consider themselves too worthless to merit any action for change on their own behalf.

The self-understandings of both the privileged and the oppressed need to be altered therefore to bring about the same result for both: a noninflated sense of self-worth that opens one to hear the call of a free God and to serve justice in doing so. The means of achieving that correction of self-understanding are quite different, however, in the two cases. Where attitudes toward self and others work to sustain a status quo of injustice, the oppressed and the privileged act in accordance with the belief that the lives of the privileged are worth more than those of the oppressed. But this equivalence of belief translates into very different self-understandings: the oppressed fail to see in themselves the worth they are willing to attribute to others; the privileged see their own worth but not that of the oppressed. The oppressed do not think highly enough of themselves; the privileged think too highly of themselves in so far as they continue to participate in social relations that fail to treat others with the same basic respect that they enjoy. Correcting such different self-understandings requires a comparable diversity of means: the oppressed must be exalted, convinced that they have a worth as creatures of God equal to that of their oppressors; the privileged must be brought low, by pointing out to them their finitude and fallibility and their solidarity as finite creatures with all other creatures of God. One side of my account of the attitudes appropriate for creatures under God—the self-esteem side—becomes a corrective therefore to the oppressed person's sloth of nonresistance. The other side of my account—an honest recognition of finitude and fallibility—becomes a corrective to the self-righteous confidence whereby the privileged, with no apparent pangs of conscience, continue to exercise the powers and responsibilities society grants them in the exploitation of others. Bringing the privileged to recognize their finitude and fallibility helps to correct the sloth characteristic of the exploiter.

When the privileged are convinced of their own finitude and fallibility, they are brought to see the likelihood of their own fault in the social relations in which they participate and are opened thereby to the call to work for greater justice. In responding to such a call, they repent of what they have done to others in developing themselves and exercise self-restraint accordingly. They renounce the rights that have been bought for them at the price of unjust relations with others, and redirect their action elsewhere in a use of God's gifts that respects those of others.

When the oppressed are convinced of their own value, they heed the call to work for greater justice by attempting to become themselves in the way they now see fit. They regret what they have not done because of rigid role expectations, social hindrances, and lack of self-confidence, and work to be the sort of persons they feel called to be, work to claim what they have hitherto been denied.

As the history of the use of Christian beliefs makes clear, however, it is possible to bring the two different sides of the attitudes appropriate for creatures of God to bear against the wrong parties. In that case, one rubs the face of the oppressed in a proclamation of the creature's limited, fallible, and conditioned existence and strokes the egos of the privileged with talk of the esteem they are due as creatures of God and their distinction as agents of God's providential and salvific will. In this way one confirms rather than corrects the attitudes of those parties that support a status quo of injustice.

The impropriety of such a procedure becomes clear in its effects: Neither the oppressed nor the privileged are brought to a healthy self-respect. Rather than bring about a healthy self-esteem among the oppressed, such a procedure encourages them to overlook their own worth as the distinct individuals they are, to feel humiliated and impotent. It teaches them to resign themselves accordingly to the limitations on their existence posed by the actions of their oppressors and to sacrifice themselves in an abject submission to the interests of others.

It is wrong for Christians to busy themselves pointing out the finitude and fallibility of the oppressed not because such charges of finitude and fallibility are untrue, but because the oppressed already know those things too well. The oppressors, for one, are in the business of pointing these failings out to them. (Indeed, their oppressors and these Christians are often one and the same.) Welfare fraud, drug running in poor neighborhoods, black-against-black aggression, are constant themes of the mainstream, white-dominated press. The poor and the oppressed, with few options for employment or education, dying young from disease and the violence desperation breeds, are the last ones, in any case, who need to be reminded of the limits that hedge their existence all around. Christians who point out the finitude and fallibility of the poor and the oppressed inform the poor and the oppressed of what they are never in danger of forgetting. They tell them what they do not need to hear.

In doing so, they give the oppressed the wrong impression about the significance of the limitations and failings of will and spirit they experience. Limitations, for example, are an inevitable feature of the lives of creatures, to be accepted as such; but in making this point to those who are oppressed, one gives the impression that any and every limitation on one's action is to be passively borne, whatever its character. Without any justification, a point about a general feature of created existence is made to hold for the specific limitations that the oppressed face. Certainly, at some point everyone will find themselves confronted with a limit that they cannot surpass by their own efforts (e.g., death) or limits that one feels one is not called to breach as an agent under God, but that is not sufficient of itself to justify the assumption that the limits the oppressed face are of those sorts. The oppressed are encouraged to see the actions of others upon them as the actions of God, as if they were to respond to such actions in a merely reactive way and were not also to see themselves as agents under God and active participants in the direction of their own lives, as if some of these limits upon their own action could not be the grotesque results of sin on the part of their oppressors, as if the mere fact or apparent intransigence of present social obstacles were good a priori grounds to be resigned in the face of them. All these interpretations of the actions of others are ones that I have ruled out in previous chapters.[4]

The oppressed are encouraged to understand the respect owed to others as necessitating their own self-sacrifice, a sacrifice appropriate to their own comparative worthlessness. Such sacrifice conflicts with my account of the respect owed human beings as creatures of God, in which one respects others for the same reasons one respects oneself. On my account, one acts in service of others in recognition of one's own powers and gifts, out of self-respect and the recognition that this is how one is called to be the distinct person one is. In order to show a proper respect for others, self-sacrifice should (like sacrifice of others for one's own sake) be a matter of only last resort in cases of conflict in basic rights. Self-repudiation is appropriate only if, and in the extent to which, one has developed oneself at the expense of others.

Finally, because of such a simple conflation of self-sacrifice with a proper respect for others, the oppressed are encouraged in the mistaken belief that any act of rebellious self-assertion on their part is the

4. The choice of language here that brings to mind the statements of H. Richard Niebuhr and James Gustafson is not accidental on my part. Although neither of them would be happy about the implications I mentioned, to my mind they come dangerously close to suggesting such things in so far as they fail to specify the audience for their remarks. For a criticism of Niebuhr and Gustafson on this score, see Kathryn Tanner, "A Theological Case for Human Responsibility in Moral Decision Making," in *Journal of Religion*, Special Issue on Realism and Responsibility in Ethics (forthcoming).

result of pride or inflated self-esteem. It is as if they must believe themselves better than others to demand what is their due as creatures of God, as if the inflated self-esteem of the privileged were not itself incorporated in the social relations of injustice they would be contesting by such acts.

When Christians focus primarily on the value and dignity of the privileged, the same sort of thing happens: the privileged are confirmed in the self-understanding they already possess, they are told what they do not need to hear, they are confirmed in their privilege by such an address rather than questioned regarding its propriety. They can take away with them a sense for the propriety of an isolated autonomy in which one develops oneself without regard for others. They can take away from such an address the idea of self-development as if one were not a finite agent in a situation of being constrained by, and exercising influence over, others. Such an address does nothing to stop selfish kinds of self-promotion on the part of the privileged without care for who might be hurt by their actions.

It is true that the privileged should have a sense for their own dignity as creatures of God, but they take away from such an address to them the wrong impression of what that dignity means: respect for their own worth without obligation to show the same respect to others. This is self-respect without the kind of equal regard that is implied by my account of the respect due human beings as creatures of God.

RELATIVE JUDGMENTS AND PARTICULAR COMMITMENTS

The attention I have been giving to the different situations of privileged and oppressed is, as I pointed out in the previous chapter, what my account of respect for human beings as creatures of God fosters. In virtue of that attention to difference, the universal judgments that are also part of that account—all people are valuable, all people are finite and fallible as creatures of God—are kept from being the kind of abstract generalizations that prevent one from making relative discriminations among persons. Thus all persons, whether they are privileged or oppressed, should be esteemed as creatures of God, but that does not mean (as I showed in chapters 5 and 6), that all their attitudes and behaviors, without distinction, are proper and just. All of creation, as H. Richard Niebuhr was fond of pointing out, may be *good* but that does not mean the relations among those creatures are always *right*.[5]

What sort of discriminations can one make within the general claim of human finitude? All human beings are prone to moral failure; they may all in fact fail. Crucial for my purposes, however, is that they do not all do so in the same way, with the same effects, or from the same starting points. As already mentioned, the oppressed denigrate themselves and consequently fail to do justice to themselves. The privileged denigrate or fail to do justice to others, and benefit thereby. Fault on both sides does not form a generalizing haze with which to excuse the privileged. Although both parties may be at fault, only one side benefits at the expense of others. Moreover, the fault of the privileged is not excused by the fault of those they oppress, because both parties are not at fault for the same thing. There is no fault in being placed in an oppressive situation, in being denied opportunity, in being beaten or abused, in having one's sense of self as a worthwhile person and responsible agent taken away by such treatment; the fault comes in not doing what one can to resist such treatment, in not acting on the psychological and political capacities that remain to one in an attempt to alter such a state of affairs. The fault that oppression represents—inflated self-esteem and a disrespect for the value of others as creatures of God—remains therefore the oppressor's. The oppressor is guilty of the injustice, not the oppressed.

It is true that oppressed people may become accomplices in their oppression through their own fault of complacency, by failing to resist to the extent that they can. This failure can be compounded, for example, by violence against others that is borne of frustration and hurt, by the use of one's own sacrifice of self to justify control of others that is inattentive to their needs ("you say that to me after all I've done for you !?"), by a failure to give of oneself to those who are also oppressed because one feels there is not enough of oneself to give. Such an eventuality does not, however, equalize the faults of the privileged and the oppressed. These faults of the oppressed are reactions, secondary formations, to those of their oppressors. They are

5. See H. Richard Niebuhr, *Radical Monotheism* (New York: Harper and Row, 1970), 38.

responses (flawed ones) to the effect of the oppressors' fault upon them. The inordinate self-esteem of the privileged promotes and sustains the unjust treatment of others; the oppressed repudiate themselves as a result of such treatment and manifest that self-understanding in flawed relations with others. The prior fault (logically and causally if not temporally) is that of the privileged. The privileged have the greater responsibility therefore, and the greater guilt. Moreover, the failings of the oppressed cannot lessen the fault of their oppressors. Those failings do not make the fault of oppression any more justifiable. Their moral purity is not what makes oppressed people worthy of respect.

Finally, one could claim with some truth that the oppressed who are accomplices in their own oppression always exhibit the same traits as their oppressors—despising those below them, or at least holding jealously onto their own limited privileges as "good wives" or "good Negroes" at the expense of solidarity with people who suffer even more than themselves under the same system of oppression. The fact that the oppressed are oppressors should not disguise, however, the fault of *their* oppressors. The fact that those one oppresses in turn oppress others does nothing to lessen or excuse one's own fault. It simply means that those one oppresses are to be faulted for the same thing too. The greater fault will indeed always lie with the more privileged oppressor: the more privileged oppressor bears the greater blame for the same sort of fault. The more power one has in circumstances of oppression, the more one's guilt if one fails to use that power to contest such circumstances.

Because one can make these relative discriminations of fault—fault in different respects or degrees—the universal claims of value and finitude that I make do not stand in the way of a commitment to particular courses of action, for the direct benefit of particular groups of people. Everybody is at fault, nobody is at fault. How is one to know what to do to remedy the situation? Both the oppressed and the oppressors may be at fault, but because they are not so in the same respect or degree judgment about what to do is not incapacitated. The oppressed who oppress may stand in need of the same sort of correction as their oppressors, but it makes sense to target the more privileged oppressors for direct action given the more fundamental or primary character of their fault. It is appropriate to be committed to a policy aimed at getting the privileged to renounce what they enjoy at the expense of others. Because of the privileged standing of oppressors in a system of oppression, change of behavior by that class brings the whole system down. Such a policy, it is true, will directly benefit the oppressed and not the privileged. In that sense one sides with the oppressed against their oppressors. It is not a policy, however, that thereby overlooks the fact that the privileged have value and dignity too. On the contrary, it presumes the truth of a universal right to respect.

Finally, relative distinctions, which my account of the respect due creatures fosters by its attention to difference, help block those appeals to the universality of sin that maintain the status quo by promoting a pessimistic or defeatist attitude toward change. What is to prevent change from simply instituting new forms of oppression? If fallibility and fault are inevitable features of human existence, they are sure to infect future social relations whatever moves have been made to counter present forms of injustice. What is the point then of those efforts?

My account of human finitude gives one no a priori reason to presume that change will be for the better. Unanticipated side effects of even the best-intentioned human action for social change cannot be ruled out. One cannot exclude the possibility that new social relations will turn out to be equally bad or even worse than at present. When one sort of oppressive relations is corrected, some other sort may take its place. As Reinhold Niebuhr warned, the more one advances on one score, the greater the dangers on some other.[6] (Witness, for example, all the dangers that technological advance brings—pollution, which disrespects the rights of the planet and of its life forms, and new weaponry, which has the capacity for the quick and brutal annihilation of whole populations.)

My account does not allow one to presume, however, that *no* progress will be made. First, it is certainly appropriate for finite agents to hope for partial advances that lay the groundwork for others, and on that basis for others in turn. Second, an a priori insistence upon a failure to advance will conflict with belief in a free God's sovereignty. People who rush to pronounce all efforts for change futile are therefore suspect of an interest simply in maintaining the status quo.

6. See, for example, Reinhold Niebuhr, *The Nature and Destiny of Man*, 2 vols. (New York: Charles Scribner's Sons, 1964), 2:315–18, et passim.

Prior certainty about progress or the inevitability of advance is not needed to justify action to rectify a wrong. The mere possibility of advance is enough to make such action at least a serious consideration. That possibility is not ruled out by the fact that new dangers replace old ones. Although novel forms of fault or the redistribution of old ones will certainly accompany any advance if human beings are the agents of it, those eventualities need not nullify the fact that some progress has been made. For example, American white women could use newly gained rights of political expression to hamper the extension of the same civil rights to African American men and women. That would not nullify the fact that the extension of the franchise to white women marked an advance on previous forms of social relations in the United States.

No advance is likely, however, if those working for change do not have a humble recognition of their own finitude, a sense of their own limits of vision and moral impurity. A simple reversal of oppressed and oppressors without any fundamental alteration of the character of social relations is liable to result. Activists convinced of their own purity are likely to turn on the privileged the same treatment the privileged were accustomed to show the oppressed. In that case one is no closer to egalitarian relations of mutual respect.

ACTIVISM AND THE RECOGNITION OF FINITUDE

Talk of the finitude and fallibility of human beings is therefore appropriate not only for correcting the complacency of the privileged. It should also have its place in forming the attitudes of those who actively contest the oppression of themselves and others. Activists are creatures too: they are finite and fallible; if others sin, so do they. What does this acknowledgment of limitation mean, if it is not to hamper efforts at resistance?

It means that one does not demonize one's opponents. All fault and fallibility do not lie with them, leaving those who work for change free from the possibility of criticism. Because my account of the respect owed creatures disallows absolute distinctions, struggles for justice cannot be considered holy wars, opposing factions allied for all intents and purposes with Satan and one's own with God.

Those people one opposes retain their dignity and worth as creatures of God. In working to bring about the respectful treatment of the oppressed, one should be mindful therefore of the dignity and value of their oppressors. In opposing them one should try as best one can to treat them with the respect due them as creatures, avoiding vengefulness, cruelty, and vindictiveness in the struggle for justice. The end for which one acts, after all, is a world in which social relations confirm the dignity of *all*. In seeking to redress a particular wrong, one must have in mind to respect the rights of all others. The intent in seeking redress is not to elevate the downtrodden and the poor at the expense of the respect due their oppressors as creatures of God, but to ensure to all what is their due in virtue of such a standing.

Aware of one's own faults and fallibility, one should be ready to forgive those one opposes. The activist is in solidarity with those she or he opposes in so far as they are both sinners needing the forgiveness of God. One's enemy is not beyond redemption; the privileged may reform. If God offers forgiveness to the oppressor, how much more should the activist, who is a sinner, be willing to forgive her or him. That forgiveness does not, however, mean forbearance, passive acquiescence in the fault of the oppressor. Forgiveness in recognition of one's own faults must be kept in the context of one's dignity as a creature of God. Forgiveness of others cannot mean that one overlooks one's own value. According to that value or dignity before God, this oppression remains unacceptable. Forgiveness means, instead, a psychological liberation from the emotional chains of oppression. Activism is focused not on hatred of the oppressor but on the principle of justice that one wishes to serve.

Even as the oppressor opposes action to give others their due, he or she remains (like oneself) an agent under God's providential and salvific will for the world. In so far as the oppressor opposes the just treatment of others, the oppressor's will can obviously not be identified with God's will. Because the oppressor acts nonetheless under the sway of God's power, one cannot, however, rule out the possibility that other actions of the oppressor or the unintended consequences of the oppressor's resistance to the struggle for justice will in some way amount to a salutary reproof of activist proceedings. It is possible that activists have something to learn from their opponents about their own failings.

They might learn, for example, that their own activism is predicated, like the oppressive actions of their opponents, upon a sense of their own moral superiority. My account of human finitude prohibits, however, any identification of the will of the activist with God's will. The activism it favors is therefore not an activism of titanic presumption, of idolatrous hubris. It is not an activism of fanatics, secure in the sense of their own righteousness. Indeed, it is not an activism based in any way upon a comparative assessment of moral virtue. Siding with the oppressed against one's oppressors, or standing up for one's own rights as an oppressed person, has nothing to do with whether the oppressed are better persons than their oppressors. The value of all persons as creatures of God is the basis for resistance to oppression, and that value exists independently of any relative moral standing. One resists oppression because it is wrong in principle to deprive anyone of their basic rights, without focusing therefore on what such resistance suggests about one's own moral character. Proving one's moral probity is not the motivation for or point of activism. The energy and passion of commitment proceed from a recognition of an offense against the value of human beings as creatures of God and from a sense of one's own obligations as a responsible agent, not from moral self-righteousness and the desire to prove that one acts on a higher moral plane than one's opponents.

In addition to blocking the demonization of one's enemies, recognition of one's own limitations involves humility in adhering to any particular activist agenda. The possibility of error should not stand in the way of what remains an obligation to act to further social relations that respect the dignity of all people under God. Because it is an inevitability of human existence there is no point in trying to avoid error by hovering above the fray in some presumed stance of neutrality. The possibility of error does mean, however, that one should be open to criticism, willing to revise one's plans in order to address effectively problems that arise and redress the evil consequences of actions one has taken so far. Instead of being complacently confident in one's own judgments, one must remain attentive to the possibility of error, responsive to the words and actions of others that bring a criticism against one. Given the inevitability of fault, this is an activism of constant repentance, always asking for forgiveness for the harm one was not able to avoid committing, always reassessing strategy accordingly, attempting to rectify past faults and go on. The activist's answer to the imperfection of human action is to set to work anew.[7]

Thus one must commit oneself to courses of action without any final certitude about the correctness of one's judgments. One must commit oneself, take a stand in accordance with one's own best lights, even though one knows no amount of careful weighing of alternatives precludes a mistake. Zeal is appropriate when struggling for justice but it should be a zeal that accepts the limitations of its own viewpoint.

One need not worry here whether conviction and the acceptance of limitation can go together. Acceptance of limitation rules out only some forms of conviction. The simple fallibility of one's judgments does not mean one is not warranted in standing by them prior to learning of evidence that contradicts them; it simply means one holds them with a willingness to give them up in the future should such evidence appear. Knowledge of one's finitude does not amount to any reservations about commitment therefore; it simply prevents conviction from becoming arrogant and complacent, self-righteous about its own rectitude. It stops commitment from lapsing into an unthinking dogmatism.

Judgments about what one must do to further justice thus take on a provisional character. None of these judgments is absolute or final. They can be changed should circumstances, or new evidence, or the voices of friend or foe warrant their reassessment. Knowledge of one's finitude gives one therefore the freedom and maneuverability with respect to such judgments that is necessary to address the shifting realities of life.

Judgments about what one must do to further justice are consequently flexible and situation specific. No blanket judgments about fault hold independently of specific circumstance. One person or class of persons may be more guilty of a fault than another at a particular time and place, but such judgments are relative to that time and that place; they do not hold irrespective of circumstance. Faults are multiple and shifting. There is no simple solution to them, then, as if one could pin down and fix a single party for approbation. The mechanisms of

7. See Helmut Gollwitzer, "The Kingdom of God in Socialism," in *Karl Barth and Radical Politics*, ed. and trans. George Hunsinger (Philadelphia: Westminster Press, 1976), 91, citing Barth.

oppression may be systematically linked but they are also complex: what keeps black women with abusive black men is perhaps not what keeps black men and women under the political and economic thumb of whites. One sides with the oppressed at all times—that is the constant—but the oppressed in one situation may not be the oppressed in another. For example, white women may be oppressed in their dealings with white men but not with men of color. The oppressed at one time may not be the oppressed at another. Especially when one's efforts in the struggle for justice effect some change, one must be open to alliances with new or different groups of weak and dispossessed persons. Indeed, one should not let a myth about one's own purity blind one to one's own potential as an oppressor in circumstances where successful agitation for the rights of one's own class gives one the power to make such a potential a reality.

CONCLUSION

There is a political importance to how one interprets social reality and one's place in it. One's reactions to material deprivations that are institutionally enforced will vary, for example, depending on whether one sees the social world in which one lives as an unchangeable order and the roles one plays as fixed in the nature of things. Interpretations of social reality lie behind the acceptance of such social relations as proper. They also lie behind the minimal requirement for maintaining social relations as they are—passive compliance on pragmatic grounds. One may not like how things are run, but if one believes the status quo is inescapable in any case, why not make the best of it?

The elemental claims making up any such account of social reality are not, however, the property of a conservative social agenda, for the following reasons. First, the claims themselves are too various to be locked into a single political or social program: a rearrangement or change of emphasis can alter the practical force of a standard account. Second, the meaning of those elements is not fixed but varies with shifting discursive contexts, with the other claims with which they are logically allied. Finally, the social context in which they are employed helps in great part to determine their practical force. Nothing stops one from unhinging claims from a particular social setting and deploying them elsewhere.

In this book I have used all three of these strategies. First, I have highlighted an account of God's transcendence and brought it into close connection with an account of God's relation to creation, while, second, specifying the sense of both sorts of Christian belief. I have delineated the force of universalistic claims about the value and fault of creatures that follow from these beliefs about God's nature and relation to the world and determined the way in which such claims should be used, in the third place, to address different audiences. I have pursued these strategies in order to show that traditional Christian claims about God and the world present resources for a relentlessly progressive social agenda with potentially radical or revolutionary effects.

In the process I have not been blind to uses of Christian doctrines that encourage social conformity and servility, a self-satisfied "all's right with the world" air on the part of the privileged and an almost masochistic submission to the status quo on the part of people who stand to benefit least by doing so. I am not blind to the way in which Christian perfectionism can devalue the small, messy steps necessary to further political change, or eviscerate commitment to justice with a demand for nothing less than moral purity on the part of those who take it upon themselves to struggle for it. I am not overlooking the potential for a Christian fanaticism unresponsive to the claims of others, or for overconfident appeals to God's will that either undercut the need for one's own efforts altogether or channel action in the direction of the laughably naive or the grotesquely fantastic.

My point has been to show with what right one can subvert, from within, such uses of Christian doctrines. The Christian beliefs that this book has focused on remain dangerous. One must be constantly on guard against uses like the ones just mentioned. But such beliefs are not unredeemable.

The power of this strategy of internal critique is that it piggybacks on an already valorized tradition. The Christian doctrines that I have shown to have a politically progressive force are as uncontroversial as any used for politically conservative purposes. Indeed, a number of the arguments I have made show my own use of a traditional account of God's transcendence and relation to the world for politically progressive purposes to be a more consistent extension and application of fundamental Christian claims than an interpretation and use of much the same claims for politically reactionary purposes. I do not believe it is easy, therefore, to charge my own account with heresy or "paganism" or faithlessness to Christian tradition.

The downside of this strategy is closely connected to its strengths: much the same claims that I show can be used for politically progressive purposes have a long history of contrary uses. In the light of that history is it enough simply to tinker with such claims? Are the associations and implications of such claims that I wish to dispute shirked so easily? Does not a history of contrary uses demonstrate conclusively that these traditional claims are too dangerous to retain and that a more radically revisionist strategy is consequently called for?

These worries cannot be dismissed. Indeed, I cannot hope to prove finally that such worries do not warrant rejecting a strategy of internal critique like mine. I can only hope to put before readers the pros and the cons and let each person weigh them.

I have attempted to make such a history of contrary uses an asset rather than a hindrance, to turn it to my advantage. A history of contrary uses at least allows one to pin down the characteristic ways in which traditional Christian claims have been used for conservative effect. Armed with this knowledge one has a fighting chance to block those uses, recognizing all the while, however, that the effort to parry them will be a constant occupation. One can never let down one's guard; one can never rest secure, certain that one has finally fought oneself clear of danger.

It may be that a strategy of internal critique should exist as a supplement to others. If the kind of mainstream account of God and creation that I have been exploring here is itself made up of various elements in tension, it is also the case that it has no clear boundaries. The belief that Christian doctrines have fixed boundaries that are not subject to constant dispute is as much a myth about culture as the idea that organic connections among doctrines and between doctrines and Christian practice form some take-it-or-leave-it monolithic block. Historically marginalized forms of Christian discourse remain in circulation, waiting to be appropriated for sociopolitical purposes. Some newly minted version of Hegel's account of the truth of Christian talk about God and the world perhaps deserves to be pushed to the center of Christian thought.[8] Or some other notion of God's embodiment

8. I am thinking here of Peter Hodgson's intriguing proposals in *God and History* (Nashville: Abingdon Press, 1989).

in the world, disparaged in theological traditions that take God's incorporeality in a too literal and dualistic fashion, might be worth pursuing.[9] The historically marginalized voices of Christian women are certainly long overdue for a hearing on an equal basis with men. In these historically marginalized places one may very well discover resources for Christian teachings about God and the world that help avoid the politically oppressive or escapist effects of traditional theism. Traditional theological models and images of God and God's relation to the world do not have a monopoly after all on the interpretive unpacking of Christian belief.

When reconstructing Christian teaching along historically marginalized lines, it still seems salutary to me, however, to avoid totalizing critiques of mainstream Christian theology, all-or-nothing refusals of traditional Christian talk about God and the world. Demonizing traditional Christian theology is perhaps not as bad as overlooking its faults but it has its dangers nonetheless. One does not successfully avoid politically oppressive or reactionary uses of one's own theological constructions simply by assigning all possible dangers of that sort to the traditional Christian theology one repudiates. If, as I have argued, there is no simple connection between belief and practice, revisionary constructions of God and God's relation to the world are not immune from interpretations and applications that radically alter the practical force that the authors of such constructions intend them to have. Demonizing traditional Christian theology, one can be easily misled into thinking one need not be vigilant or on one's guard about the employment of one's own theological position the way those engaged in an internal critique should be. Such an assumption would be a mistake. Objections to traditional Christian theology should not seduce one into a belief in one's own inviolable innocence.

Sounding such a cautionary note should not lead one, however, to prejudge the capacities of new theological constructions to avoid the problems of traditional Christian theology. The claim that radically revisionary theologies are not immune to problems gives one no call to assume that the problems of those theologies and of traditional

9. See Grace Jantzen, *God's World, God's Body* (Philadelphia: Westminster Press, 1984); and Sallie McFague, *Models of God* (Philadelphia: Fortress Press, 1987), for creative constructions of a notion of God's embodiment in the world.

Christian theism will somehow balance out in fact. Revisionary theologies are often expressly designed to avoid the politically reactionary consequences of traditional theism by radically rethinking traditional theological claims for our own time and place. It is not unusual for the liberating potential of Christian beliefs to be the overriding criterion for theological revision and reconstruction. No matter how well entrenched, the claims of traditional Christian theology are rejected outright if they are shown to be implicated in a disempowering politics. Such a critique is wielded therefore with a freedom that I have eschewed in my attempt to retain traditional theological claims. It is highly likely then that these revisionary theologies will be able to avoid the dangers of traditional Christian theology with an ease and efficacy that my own proposals cannot match.

New dangers may arise for these theologies, or old dangers in new guises. For example, such theologies tend to stress divine immanence in a way that could suggest a lack of respect for difference, for distinct, irreducible personal centers. Talk of God as an empowering ground of mutually supportive relations (e.g., in the work of Carter Heyward, and the Jewish theologian, Judith Plaskow[10]), or even talk of God as such a nexus of relations (e.g., in the work of Sharon Welch and the recent writings of Gordon Kaufman[11]), might lead one to downplay the importance of uncooperative individual agents of dissent, to valorize consensus and harmony at the expense of a right to maintain ethnic or racial or political diversity. Such talk might be susceptible of development in the direction of a totalitarian holism, social needs overruling individual needs, which are viewed as selfish and purely personal preferences.

None of that is clear, however, before the fact. These theologies have not been in a position of theological prominence long enough to confirm whether these inklings of danger are serious. Or, if they

10. See Carter Heyward, *The Redemption of God: A Theology of Mutual Relation* (Washington, D.C.: University Press of America, 1982); Judith Plaskow, *Standing Again at Sinai* (San Francisco: Harper & Row, 1990), 154-69.

11. See Sharon Welch, *A Feminist Ethic of Risk* (Minneapolis: Fortress Press, 1990), 172–80; Gordon Kaufman, *Theology for a Nuclear Age* (Philadelphia: Westminster, 1985), 56: "God . . . [is] the unifying symbol of those powers and dimensions of the ecological and historical feedback network which create and sustain and work to further enhance all life."

are serious, whether and how one might effectively block their development.[12]

Unless revisionary theologies are willing simply to drop their claims about God and the world that demonstrate a potential for a disempowering politics, however, they will find themselves in the same boat with me: carefully qualifying the sense of divine immanence, making clear the logical relations among their distinct theological claims, and specifying the way such claims should be employed in particular social contexts. When revisionary theologies have their own history of uses and misuses perhaps one can put internal critiques of traditional theism, like my own, on a scale with revisionary theologies and see how they balance out.

Moreover, the likelihood of present success in avoiding the politically reactionary consequences of traditional Christian theism is bought by revisionary theologies at the price of an extremely close connection between their theological accounts and a particular political agenda. The theological description and the social agenda may simply mirror each other: God is the sort of friend or parent or lover that one should be; a trinitarian account of God as a society of equals in mutual relation is what human relations should also be like. Ludwig Feuerbach summed it up: divinity encapsulates those qualities that human beings (should) hold most dear.[13] The parallel drawn between human beings and God may indeed be more than simply a strong analogy: God is somehow in the world or the world is somehow in God and therefore human beings should follow God's lead in their social relations, loving themselves and those with whom they are in relation as God shows a care and concern for the world that is God's body, bringing forth those relations of mutual nurture in which God is present, the relations in which the divine is realized. In either case—whether a strong analogy holds between human relations and God's, or where God and human beings are included within a single metaphysical description of proper relations—theological account and social

12. See Sallie McFague, *Models of God*, 69-87, for a nice discussion of some possible problems and her attempts to counter them. See David Nicholls, *Deity and Domination* (London: Routledge, 1989), 242–43, 123–24, 187, et passim, for unflattering treatments of divine immanence and what he calls the "welfare God" of modern theology.

13. See Welch, *A Feminist Ethic of Risk* 176–77; and McFague, *Models of God*, 134: "we image God according to what we find most desirable in ourselves."

agenda seem to be convertible. They differ very little: the theological account seems to be just a redescription of a social agenda to include another personal agent, God, or to encompass a cosmic dimension.

This close connection may indeed help to prevent the theological account of God and God's relation to the world from being unhooked from a progressive social agenda and deployed for other, more conservative purposes. It has its own downsides, however. First, it seems at times that belief in God is doing very little work besides valorizing a prior commitment to social change. Talk of God is just a way of dressing up what one already believes. On my account, however, Christian belief does not confirm one's self-understanding; it radically alters it for one's correction, for example, elevating the poor in spirit, bringing low the proud. The self-corrective potential of cultures with a belief in God's transcendence has indeed been an ongoing theme of this book. If, to the contrary, talk about God merely reflects what one already believes, how can it show up the limitations of those beliefs?

This may seem an ironic charge, since the political program that revisionist theologies often valorize is not clearly distinguishable from my own.[14] The traditional beliefs about God to which I appealed in forming such conclusions also suggested, however, that these conclusions should be left open to criticism, that they should be held with an ear to dissenting voices, with an ear to a new word. This openness to criticism is not a similarly necessary feature of the political program of revisionist theologies. So close a connection between theological and political accounts can easily discourage such self-criticism.

This is the second downside of the close connection between theological account and political program in revisionist theologies, which makes internal critique an appealing option in comparison. Openness to criticism makes my own derivation of a progressive political program more susceptible to a politically conservative turn than the political programs of revisionist theologians, but it avoids the dangers of a self-righteous adherence to them. It counters the possibility of an uncritical insistence on keeping to a particular plan of sociopolitical change whatever the circumstances.

14. My conclusions about the sort of social relations and activism compatible with basic dignity are, for example, very close to the proposals of Sharon Welch in *A Feminist Ethic of Risk*.

Revisionist theologians of course do not have to fall into a dogmatically inclined conviction about the rectitude of their own political programs just as they are. Everything depends upon the particular political program they espouse: political programs can include their own demands for ongoing critical reevaluation. My point is simply that their theological beliefs are not the crucial contributing factor to such a demand for self-criticism, over and above what can be concluded from their politics alone.

The third danger of so closely connecting theological accounts with political recommendations is that theological analysis may come to replace a sociopolitical one. In my account there is no expectation that theological claims will do the work of a concrete analysis of what is wrong with a particular society and what should be done specifically to correct it. The assumption of revisionist theologians—that social relations should find their correlate in a theological account of God and God's relation to the world—may lead them to expect from theology what it cannot deliver. If one does not supplement a theological account with sociopolitical analysis geared to specific contexts, one will be left with only vague recommendations. What exactly does it mean, for example, to further "right relations" in a late twentieth-century U.S. context? Theological redescriptions of human relations can only go so far in the directions required for the practical, detailed work of social change.

In keeping with the respect for difference discussed in chapter 6, I see no need to insist on the overriding virtues of either an internal critique like mine or the more totalistic critique of traditional Christian theism presumed by radically revisionary reconstructions of Christian beliefs. There is no need to chide revisionary theologians for a "theoretical Manicheanism"—"traditional Christian theism is bad pure and simple; theology revised from the bottom up is good"—only to fall into the same thing oneself—"revisionary theologies are simply wrongheaded; internal critique of traditional theism is the only proper solution to the ignominious history of Christian political practices."[15] Respect for difference favors a politics of solidarity; it favors coalition building. Both internal and totalistic critiques are in the business of cultural revolution, to the end of social change, in the service of greater justice. Power is to be gained, then, in cooperation.

15. For this sense of "Manichean," see Abdul JanMohamed, "The Economy of Manichean Allegory," in *Race, Writing, and Difference*, ed. Henry Louis Gates, Jr. (Chicago: Univ. of Chicago Press, 1985), 78–106.

Index

Printed in the United States
41574LVS00004B/1-75